BREAKFA

Alan Winnington in Korea
during the war

BREAKFAST WITH MAO

MEMOIRS OF A FOREIGN CORRESPONDENT

ALAN WINNINGTON

LAWRENCE AND WISHART
LONDON

Lawrence and Wishart Limited
39 Museum Street
London WC1A 1LQ

First published 1986

© Ursula Winnington, 1986

This book is sold subject to the condition that it shall not, by way of trade or otherwise, be lent, re-sold, hired out or otherwise circulated without the publisher's prior consent in any form of binding or cover other than that in which it is published and without a similar condition, including this condition, being imposed on the subsequent purchaser.

Photoset in North Wales by
Derek Doyle & Associates, Mold, Clwyd.
Printed in Great Britain by
Oxford University Press.

Contents

	Frontispiece	2
	Publisher's Note	7
	Foreword by Neal Ascherson	9
1	Studious Purgatory	17
2	The Threepenny Manifesto	31
3	Banners in Piccadilly	38
4	Professional Communist	53
5	En Route to China	64
6	Arriving at Nothing	71
7	With the Chinese Red Army	82
8	Beijing Changes Hands	100
9	War and Massacre in Korea	108
10	Chinese Strategy and American Fire-power	118
11	The Inn With the Wooden Door	134
12	Germ Warfare	149
13	The British Prisoners	159
14	Ideological Reform and Old Beijing	172
15	One Hundred Flowers	185
16	The Great Leap Forward	202
17	Nuclear Bombs and Paper Tigers	218
18	Back to Tibet	227
19	Comrade Ah Lan Becomes a Non-Person	241
	Name Index	252

Publications by Alan Winnington

I Saw the Truth in Korea (pamphlet), 1950
Koje Unscreened (with Wilfred Burchett), 1952
Plain Perfidy (with Wilfred Burchett), 1954
Tibet, 1957
Slaves of the Cool Mountains, 1959

Children's Books
Silberhuf (in German), 1969
Silberhuf zieht in din Krieg (in German), 1972

Novels
Himmel muss Warten (in German), 1963
Duel in Tschungking (in German), 1977
Kopsjeger (in German), 1965

Crime Novels
Catseyes, 1967
Berlin Halt, 1970
The Fairfax Millions, 1974
Der Doppel Agent (in German), 1981
Anglers Alibi (in German), 1980
Ridley and Son (in German), 1981

Publisher's Note

Alan Winnington suffered a stroke while at the final stage of completing his memoirs; he never recovered and died on 26 November 1983. The publishers are grateful to Ursula, his widow, and to Ted Brake for their assistance in finalising the text.

Foreword

One foggy morning in Bethnal Green, as I was making the family breakfast, I glanced out of the window and saw an apparition. Three figures were floating towards me across the garden, wading through a mist which hid their legs completely and left only grey silhouettes of their heads and shoulders. One outline was tall, another was short and round. A battering on the door: I opened it, and found myself confronting Alan Winnington, Wilf Burchett and Andy Condron, the ex-Marine who stayed in China after the Korean War. God knows where they had been all night, but they felt like breakfast. They strode in, pulling off coats wet with dew, and the house was suddenly full of noise and laughter.

That was a romantic method of appearance, almost the last time I saw Alan, and – looking back on his life and his character – it's right to see him as a romantic of a very English variety. By that I mean that he combined passionate commitment to a vision, to a Communist future, with an earthy, debunking common sense. He was a great reporter, one of those adventurers who takes off on his own and vanishes into the mountains to return, months later, with notebooks full of truths which officialdom in this place or that would intensely prefer not to hear. He was, all his life, the nightmare of bureaucrats; he had a searing contempt for desk-bound functionaries and – as this book demonstrates – a habitual suspicion of that breed of intellectual which gets drunk and incapable of judgement on a thimbleful of distilled ideology. Alan, a famous celebrator and host, could hold his liquor in every sense. He might not have liked the comparison, but he came out of the same mould as George Orwell. Both men had powerful, underlying beliefs which were not really up for debate; both violently refused to inhabit the world of middle-class achievement and privilege for which their education had prepared them; both applied a pitiless and sometimes coarse mockery to those who seemed to them to ignore the obvious needs of ordinary people or the patent realities of a situation. Winnington and Orwell, both refugees from foundering middle-class families determined to keep the aspidistra flying, detested outworn puritan values and insisted that life was for living and enjoying – a doctrine which Alan practised more successfully than Orwell. Both were fearfully obstinate men and, in a corner, cantankerous.

Alan Winnington was a witness to some of the moments of history which have determined the shape of the century; in a few of them he was the only European witness. He was with the Chinese Communist leadership before and during the capture of Beijing as the revolution triumphed; he lived through what he calls the 'golden years' in China that followed, and then watched the nation slew off course into the madness of the 'Great Leap Forward'. As the *Daily Worker* correspondent, he went into Korea with the North Korean and Chinese armies in 1950, following them down into South Korea, back again to the Yalu river and then down once more to the 38th parallel. It was then that he became internationally famous – and notorious. As he records here, in a passage of unforgettable horror, he was taken in the wake of the North Korean advance to see the mass grave at Rangwul, near Taejon, where perhaps 18,000 political prisoners had been massacred by the South Koreans in the presence – so Alan claims – of American observers. A *Daily Worker* pamphlet about Rangwul, published in London, brought the first mutterings about 'treason'. But worse was to follow. As the ceasefire talks got under way at Kaesong and Panmunjom, Alan and Wilf Burchett settled in as accredited correspondents on the Northern side; over the interminable months that followed, they maddened the American briefing officers by constantly undermining the version of the talks they gave to the 'United Nations' journalists and, frequently, by proving them liars on the basis of documents Alan and Wilf were able to obtain from the conference room. In 1952, Alan Winnington began to report the allegations – never satisfactorily disproved – that the

Foreword

Americans were using bacteriological warfare against North Korea, the occasion of one of the most embittered propaganda conflicts of the Cold War. But it was the accusation that Alan had taken part in the interrogation and 'brainwashing' of British prisoners of war in Korea that brought down on him the full fury of the Establishment at home. He was called a traitor, threatened with prosecution for treason if he set foot in his own country, and – after his return to China – deprived of his British passport. There followed almost twenty years of exile until, in the late sixties, the British authorities were persuaded to reconsider the case and issue a new passport to him in Berlin.

Alan always used to dismiss the 'interrogation' charge with contempt. He had regularly visited the British prisoners, taken mail for them, talked and drunk and smoked with them, arranged marriages by proxy, spoken at discussion meetings ... but nothing more. I believed him when he talked to me about it, fifteen years later, and reading his account of the business here, I believe him still. For all the vengeful bluster about him from both Labour and Tory politicians, nobody has ever come forward from the ex-prisoners to substantiate that charge, and many have stoutly denied it. Alan, on balance, liked the prisoners a great deal more than the 'owlish' Chinese cadres appointed to indoctrinate them. He liked their toughness, good humour and resourcefulness, and the way they co-operated to survive, and he contrasted them with the American prisoners who in comparison cracked up so easily: 'beweaponed delinquents, and at the same time the most pampered soldiers in history'. Alan never liked or understood Americans, and his view of them, like his explanation that they displayed no solidarity because they came from a free-enterprise society, was in fact just the sort of *a priori* verdict on ideological grounds which he attacked in others.

His own opinion was that the British sanctions against him had in reality nothing to do with his activities in the camps but everything to do with American pressure to do something about that 'Commie newsman' who had sabotaged their version of the ceasefire talks. His reaction to the 'treason' charge was a sardonic narrowing of the eyes and a snort of laughter. And yet it hurt him, more than he showed. Alan loved England very deeply; like his mentor Harry Pollitt, whom Alan regarded as the greatest man he had ever met, he 'regarded revolution as a very English thing'. As a young man, he and his brother Dick (later to become the first great film critic in Britain) tramped the English countryside, living off the sketches which they sold in pubs. And he loved London, especially that maze of alleys and pubs around Fleet Street where he cut his teeth as a journalist and a Communist. He was a wild rover, but not a man who had ever contemplated the life of a political exile, and it might have gone very hard for him indeed, especially after he had been forced to quit an increasingly hostile Maoist China and settle in the German Democratic Republic. But he was lucky in his second marriage; in Berlin, Ursel and her two children made him the secure home he had never had before. Because of them, he was able to remain 'an Englishman abroad' and never sank into the self-pity and paranoia which are the occupational diseases of exiles. He lived in Berlin, cooking wonderful Chinese meals for his friends, writing for his paper, producing a series of detective stories and thrillers very much in the English 'murder in the vicarage' tradition, until his death in 1983.

He visited England occasionally, after the return of his passport. One had the impression that it didn't entirely live up to his memories. A lot, certainly, had changed. London life had become more hectic and less intimate. Pubs had vanished, or been ruined with carpets and muzak. People had less time to drink and laugh and, perhaps, more money than was good for them; they seemed less fun. The warm-hearted, heroic old London of the thirties and the Blitz had vanished, and the working class itself was changing, losing its ancient solidarity and impertinence, its contempt for ambition and its political certainties. And his party, too, was growing away from him.

If Alan thought something was wrong, he said so – loudly, scornfully and often with a force that scalded people less tough in spirit than he was. His political outlook was, essentially, a simple one: there was a world struggle to the death going on between socialism and capitalism, and those who lost their nerve and tried to find refuge between the two fronts simply failed to understand the world they lived in. The Soviet Union, warts and all, was on the right side in this struggle; a

Foreword

Communist party which failed to show solidarity with the Soviet Union in times of stress and crisis was giving aid and comfort to the enemy. All international problems, in Alan's view, could be reduced to this question of power. After the Warsaw Pact intervention in Czechoslovakia in 1968, Alan was among those who found themselves at loggerheads with their own party leadership when it deplored the intervention. Characteristically he spoke his mind; he lost some friends and acquired some enemies. A 'Stalinist'? Whatever that overworked word means, it does not fit a man of such truculent independence as Alan Winnington. His opinion of Stalin, which emerges with stark clarity in this book, is that, for all his crimes and ruthlessness, such a man and such a policy were the only combination which could have beaten Hitler and kept Marxist socialism alive in the world. He supported the Ribbentrop-Molotov Pact and, when the Comintern declared the war a mere conflict of imperialisms, he supported that too, even against his beloved Harry Pollitt. Some of his arguments in these pages, like his defence of the 1939 partition of Poland, seem to me indefensible. But it's interesting to see how often these arguments were conducted in terms not of ideologies but of personalities: the argument of authority, certainly, but conducted by reference to people supposed to be infallible. There is a fascinating passage in this book, its scene inimitably set by Alan in Henekey's with Dave Springhall and a bunch of comrades 'leaning on the cast-iron stove enjoying a pony of the tenpenny Amontillado'. Somebody suggested that Stalin had really taken the 'imperialist war' decision himself, and used the Comintern as a mere rubber stamp.

> Springie screwed up his knowing eyes and said, 'Well, I'm a bit of a mug and easily bamboozled, but I suppose you know who the General Secretary of the Communist International is?' Without pausing for a reply, he went on, 'It's Georgi Dimitrov. Do you suppose that Stalin or anyone else – God included – could put one over like that on Dimitrov? And if Stalin, Dimitrov and all the rest, right through to Dutt, think the same ...

It's a period piece, a style of argument that's utterly gone. Alan, being the sort of man he was, tended to put his trust in individual human beings rather than programmes. Not all of them turned out to deserve it, and as he grew older, Alan became more sceptical of political leaders and more impressed by those they led. The underlying theme of his account of China in this book is his deep affection for the Chinese people and his growing suspicion of the *ganbu* – the time-serving hordes of bureaucrats and petty officials who would serve any regime and carry out any psychological contortion.

The self-tormenting, self-denying fanaticism of the *ganbu* was increasingly offended by Alan's own robust life-style in Beijing. He gave parties, he offered his guests plenty to drink, he played rock and roll, he hobnobbed with bourgeois journalists and foreign diplomats and he laughed too much. Confronted at the news agency with stories alleging that Mao's thought had enabled a pig and a cow to be crossed, or a bicycle to be driven by a wind-turned propeller on the handlebars, he not only laughed but suggested that such stories should not be put out to the world. He refused to join in the campaign to kill all the birds in Beijing, and even made a refuge for persecuted sparrows in his yard. He was not impressed when the New China News Agency joined the campaign to produce its own steel: 'out of all the expenditure of electric power, coal, scrap-metal and idle chatter crept or was dragged a sluggish mess looking like asphalt ...' Still less did Alan respect the agency's special contribution to progress, the 'Great Leap Forward Extended Water Closet Flush Chain', to be pulled by the foot.

It's tempting to quote. Alan was one of those rare men as funny on paper as round a table with a drink. But the absurdities that he found in China are only marginal to his profound love and understanding for the country. Alan Winnington took on where Edgar Snow left off – and Alan was the better writer. He knew the old Beijing, the world's most marvellous city, still imperial behind its great walls but swarming with ancient street life, 'bright with the genius by which the Chinese can make the simplest everyday things attractive'. And he saw the beginning of its destruction: first the street vendors and stalls swept away, then the brilliant clothes and the multifarious petty social customs stamped out, then the little streets bulldozed and finally the mighty walls

Foreword

themselves toppled – the most awful and unnecessary urban crime in modern history, today bitterly and vainly regretted by the Chinese themselves. He knew the extremities of the Han domain, the regions where few Chinese, let alone Europeans, had ever ventured: *The Slaves of the Cool Mountains*, the book he wrote about the slave-owning Norsu tribal society, which he found a week's hard marching 'north of the great bend in the Golden Sands River', is one of the classics of modern English travel writing. He went to Tibet just after the Chinese occupation and again four years later, recording with horror the vandalism, insensitivity and arrogance inflicted on this unique nation by 'Great Han chauvinism' at its worst. Alan firmly believed that the Chinese entry in 1955 was justified ('Tibet had to change'), but he had taken seriously the initial Chinese assurances that change would be a matter of gradual reforms, respecting Tibetan institutions and beliefs.

His time was nearly up. The 'golden years' were ending, and China was sliding away into the years of madness, nearly twenty of them, which began with the Great Leap and ended with the Gang of Four. Alan knew all the leaders, their strong points and their weaknesses (he's oddly reticent and ambivalent about Zhou Enlai, though), but he had to leave as the Sino-Soviet rift opened up and made his job finally impossible. Some of the foreign community strove to surf on the muddy torrent, and became 'holier than Mao', denouncing their colleagues and themselves for thoughtcrime with equal abandon. Alan found all this disgusting, worse than anything that had happened in Russia, 'the cult with bells on', as he puts it. So he left, and watched the turmoil from the remoteness of Berlin.

At the end of his life, as the insanity drained off China at last, Alan went back for a last visit and they welcomed him like a hero. That was good, and yet his departure marked an irretrievable waste. He knew more about China than any non-Chinese journalist in the world, and yet there was little he could do with his knowledge, unable to report from Beijing and forbidden – through the loss of his passport – to live and write in Britain. His voice should have been heard, and it was not.

Or not until now. This book, published nearly thirty years

after the events it describes, will remain one of the essential foreign first-hand sources for the history of Eastern Asia in the decade after the Chinese revolution. But that is too stiff a salute. It is a brilliantly readable book about events which changed human history (and nearly, perhaps, ended it prematurely), an account which is witty, personal, passionate and disconcerting in turn. This last of Alan's many books seems to have meant most to him, to contain more of himself than the others. And, for his friends, that is the best recommendation of all.

Neal Ascherson
London, 1986

1
Studious Purgatory

It did not seem so remarkable then when he told me, as it does now with hindsight, that my grandfather saw the last man publicly hanged in London. Much else that he told me about the Victorians I only appreciated later.

I was too young to visualise hanging or the millions killing and being killed in the war in France under the same blue sky.

He used to take me in his gig through the leafy gravelled lanes to Epping market for home-brewed beer and chitterlings and other bygone delicacies, and he let me jump down to hold the horse's head when one of those rare motor cars came in view. Those trips had to stop when I was old enough for school. We were friends and it saddened me when he died.

My elementary school headmaster, Mr Hants, was one of those schoolmasters Dickens described as ignorant, sordid and brutal. He had a narrow concave brow, stooping posture, bandy legs, large hairy hands and sharp little eyes. He and the other masters believed in knocking boys' native evil out of them to make space for knocking knowledge in.

But the headmaster reserved for himself the privilege of ceremonially beating boys on the buttocks and was possibly the last living exponent of a degrading style of flogging known as the 'tightbreech'. This was performed before the whole school and the date fixed well in advance so that the quaking victim and his fellows could savour the coming event.

At the appointed time and before the assembled school the culprit was dragged in to kneel facing the headmaster who gripped the boy's neck between his knees – the cause, I thought, of his bandiness. Grasping the top of the boy's breeches he pulled the cloth tight and lashed the clamped and screaming child with a cane whose tip was bound with a cobbler's waxed end.

Otherwise it was a hand-caning school and on most days boys came back from the front of the class in tears with their hands under their armpits to ease the pain. But still, this brutal torture of this most beautiful part of the human body was probably less psychologically harmful than the other.

Most feared of all the masters was Mr Moss – Mossy – who did not use a cane at all. He was, unfortunately for me, my form master, a drinker with a fierce red face, invisible lips and long pinkish hairs in his nose and ears. He would poke this flaming visage forward, stinking of stale alcohol, and shout, 'Eh? Eh? Why don't you know? Eh? Eh? Why? Why?' With each query his hard thick hands, glinting with pale bristles, took the cringing child on each side of his head – left, right, left. 'Eh? Eh? Why bother to come here?' Smack. Smack.

By being born when I was I had apparently missed a period known as the Good Old Days which it was asserted would return now that Jerry had been dealt with and there would be ample chances to Get On. It was an article of my father's faith that people Got On according to their Application, a view based on solid empirical ground.

Having left a similar school at fourteen years he got himself a job as office boy at a few shillings a week, caught cheap workmen's trains, studied shorthand and accountancy sitting in parks and waiting-rooms and pulled himself up the civil-service ladder.

He planned to launch his children from the higher level that he had achieved. We would go to 'good' schools. The boys would apply themselves to getting on in a middle-class way and the girls would become office secretaries while waiting for Mr Right.

Birth control not being what it is now, his plan foundered when I arrived ahead of schedule. The money would not stretch and I must continue on the thin gruel of state education at Mossy's hands or compete for a free scholarship place in a 'good' school against hundreds of studious boys from all over the district. A terrible prospect for a boy of eight or nine.

Not for him the smell of grass, the shouts of evening summer play. He must cram – working out about those two

Studious Purgatory

trains passing each other going from A to B.

In my world of council school boys, those at posh schools – the Smith minors and Jones majors, wearing ties, school caps and long trousers – were natural enemies from the upper class world of Greyfriars. Joining them I would at once become an enemy of my old friends and have to go around in absurd clothes to. I had no intention of really trying until my father promised me a bicycle if I won.

Corrupted, I became a convert to learning, the boy who was called on to explain gravity and long division. My friends grudgingly agreed that the chance to get a bicycle made a difference. But those months of studious purgatory marked me for life – robbing me of the guiltless enjoyment of being simply idle. So I won a free place at Chigwell School, opposite the King's Head, made famous by Dickens as the Marpole Inn in *Barnaby Rudge*, said to have been built in the reign of Henry VIII and slept in by Elizabeth I.

Chigwell was a public school and proud of it. Small though it was – 300 pupils – it had been founded in Shakespeare's day and urchins who called themselves Chigwellians were no less toffee-nosed than rich boys who carved their names on the desks at Eton. It was expensive, its masters wore gowns, it taught the classics, it had an Officers' Training Corps and a chapel and both masters and senior boys were entitled to flog younger pupils. Taking Evelyn Waugh's grades of school: Leading School, First Rate School, Good School and School, mine was a Good School.

Along with others of its kind, Chigwell was concerned with producing members of the ruling-class-to-be – the old-boy network – and in this process beating played its part. Whenever a flogging was in the air, boys gathered to watch if possible, at least to listen to the cracking blows, perhaps cries of pain. Commonly the beaten would vanish privately to display their bruised buttocks to voluptuously excited intimates. It was a freemasonry, the basis of what is often called the English vice – the English public-school vice, flagellation.

For all kinds of reasons scholarship boys met hostility. Pupils whose parents had paid for their education felt cheated by these pushing paupers with their common talk and shoddy clothes – brainy types, too, liable to get to the top of the form and dominate the prize-giving. Masters also failed to hide their feeling that such rough diamonds depreciated their own status as teachers at a school for the sons of gentlemen.

Our headmaster – a great flogger – had each scholarship boy on the carpet on arrival to tell him that he was a guest and implied that as such he had diminished rights. For one, he should 'choose' to take both Latin and Greek. By the time the boy discovered that his rights differed in no way from the other pupils', it was too late.

Our headmaster was lying, with all the authority of his heavy eagle's nose and great eyebrows, to quaking little boys in order to inflate the figure of classical pupils – this rightly being his idea of what the governors wanted. So we endured years of dead languages for twelve periods a week, Latin and Greek taught like army drill. That people used to communicate in them seemed as absurd as that a pterodactyl could have flown.

Educationally I was a Mock Turtle, at school in an anachronism, a unit of the British public school system specifically designed to create and nurture a master social stratum. From any point of view the notion of free places for the poor was absurd: no doubt a sop to some guilt feeling but in fact like putting a stray dog to train with a pack of foxhounds; it was unlikely to become one but was almost certain to become muddled.

I had to lead a double life. My friends remained for the most part elementary school boys. Near home I removed my school cap with the bishop's mitre on it. I dropped the kind of English that was being grafted on me at Chigwell and reverted to cockney. Becoming a language chameleon helped me in later life to pick up languages from the local air. Last ditch defenders of teaching Latin and Greek argued that it was good for the soul, exercised the brain and encouraged you to speak and write good English. It may be so but no one can judge. Certain it is that I cannot recall more than a few phrases of the classics but now after all those decades I can still get around very well in French, the one 'modern' that they reluctantly and sparingly taught in Chigwell.

On Mondays, Wednesdays and Saturdays we had to change and play cricket or football all afternoon. On the other three

Studious Purgatory

days we also had to change and play for an hour before lunch. Some boys fainted from hard exercise on empty stomachs and some had to be carried off the field because of hard exercise on full ones, but the main purpose was served of keeping them occupied during every second when they might otherwise get into mischief.

And there lay the rub or one of them, due no doubt to our being only a Good School and not a First-Rate School, for we had both boarders and day-boys. Boarders tended to look askance at day-boys while actually envying them as they left for the warmth and freedom of home each day.

We could listen to the wireless on our home-made crystal sets, sometimes go to the silent cinema, stay up late, read in bed, have things like sausages and kippers for tea; all impossible luxuries for those rich imprisoned boarders. But more, much much more.

Outside on warm summer evenings or dark winter ones, pert schoolgirls clustered in gym tunics – the original mini-skirts – long, black-stockinged legs and wide-brimmed straw hats that were their uniforms; who could often be enticed into dark corners, vacillating, demurring but eventually going, moved by the same urges.

Adolescent excitements of this sort were not for the boarding boys who had been incarcerated by their parents' wish not to be bothered with bringing up children and their ability to pay. That monastic life froze their sexual interest before it included the other sex and fixed them into a lifelong sexual strait-jacket to complement the other English vice.

My brother Dick had been slightly luckier than I, for his school (paid), though a Good School, was more modern and he did not have to waste most of his time on classics, games and Divinity. We both emerged from those institutions into a sea of unemployability. There was in any case no possibility of going on to university.

The idea was that we should train to be Chartered Accountants which would involve years of the most stupifyingly boring activity yet invented by man.

But already the tide of unemployment was rising fast and well-spoken, well-dressed men knocked on the door selling brushes or vacuum cleaners and in conversation it turned out that they were unemployed Chartered Accountants or other qualified types. No incentive here to dash out and article yourself for years to become, if all went well, another out-of-work Chartered Accountant.

My father's hopes of respectable careers for my brother Dick and myself disappeared in the depression without our needing to cause him any offence. This was a relief to us for he was an admirable man and father, and enormously tolerant despite the conservatism of his own ideas. During the next decades when Dick got arrested for Communist activity and Members of Parliament were demanding I be hanged as a traitor, my father never changed his attitude of easy tolerance or tried to get us to alter our ways; always regarded our opinions and consequent actions as our own affair and seemed to enjoy Dick's later fame and my own notoriety with equal amused zest. He accepted my mother's agnosticism, irreverence about the establishment and the fact that she voted Labour to cancel out his Tory vote. (He would never agree simply not to vote if she did the same.) He took a drink a few times in a year, smoked ten cigarettes a day and I never heard him swear. Despite his tolerance he was a man of very strong principle and very honest. My mother put on his gravestone only the words: A Gentle Man.

The future had a solidly hopeless look. A little more than a decade had passed since my beloved Uncle George – youngest son of my chitterling-eating grandfather – had been killed at my own age among the artillery in the First World War; six million were dependent on the dole amid wretchedness worse than had existed a century before, caught in anonymous misery that it seemed would never end.

Even those of us who like Samuel Johnson despised the word patriotism as it is commonly understood, felt humiliated that our talented people had sunk to so little measure that a man as despicable as Ramsay MacDonald was being offered as our saviour.

Something was manifestly wrong but it was also easy to believe that the same thing had always been wrong – people, human nature, unchangeable and rendered more vile by every enhancement of its power to be so. There had always been the poor, there had always been wars. It was Life, the survival of the fittest, though the fittest in this sense seemed far from the nicest and appeared not to include Dick and myself.

So the depression became our university. John Freeman once commented in the *New Statesman* that the salient feature about a university was that it provided the only time in life when those lucky enough to go there could spend three whole years reading anything that they pleased. '*There's* privilege indeed,' he commented. Library books were free in unlimited numbers and we made use of this privilege. Dick had always shown talent as an artist and whenever he could afford decent paper, nibs and ink, he drew and he drew and discarded. I began a novel which I never finished. It was a good idea and still is, but far beyond my ability then. Maybe now too.

In the early part of the depression there was a belief among some, based on hope, that it was a sort of industrial and financial colic which would pass away, probably giving rise to a boom. This optimistic view enabled both Dick and myself to get jobs, by an extraordinary coincidence and without either knowing, with connected companies.

He worked as a representative – a euphemism for salesman – in Cardiff for Hall and Pickles Ltd., purporting to sell high-speed steel, and I with an associated firm, the Chatwood Safe Co. Ltd., in Leeds. We never sold anything but that was not the idea. We were working for optimists. Both companies having a fairly short list of potential customers, it was thought by them better to have personable young men calling round on people who might one day buy steel or safes, chatting them and their secretaries up, leaving engraved cards, sometimes buying a lunch, impressing the names on them so that later when the economy again took off with a whizz they would recall where to turn for tool-steel and banking equipment. We got low wages, some expenses and were cheaper than maintaining steady newspaper advertising. It couldn't last and we arrived back in London at about the same time, jobless but more experienced.

It was summer in London's unbearable workless streets and we set off into the country busking, drawing people's portraits for whatever we could get. Fairs and holiday resorts did not appeal and we sat instead in pubs with our pints and sketched customers who were usually keen to possess the drawings. I was good enough to draw a passable likeness but Dick was already brilliant; too good in fact, for the trend to caricature in his work was already strong and ironically my far inferior drawings were often preferred.

It was a happy interlude, walking round England's since departed countryside, sleeping in haystacks and dutch barns or sometimes being invited to stay overnight, eating well, lending a hand with the farm work. Then it got cold and boring and we went back to London and to our worst jobs yet.

I have forgotten how Dick got himself a job as a demonstrator of Heinz tinned foods, holding sampling sessions in grocers' shops and dressing their windows. His sole defence against the horrors of this was to treat it as fun. Complaints went back to the head office in Harlesden that his window-dressing was 'futuristic'. On one occasion he cleared the grocer's window, lined it with black velvet and installed in simple glory a single tin of baked beans. One grocer charged that he flirted with customers, another that he was mad because he declaimed 'Soup of the evening, beautiful soup' from Lewis Carroll's *Alice in Wonderland* to bewildered shoppers.

While Dick was working precariously for Heinz, I found an equally incongruous job in the Albert Dock Road as a shop assistant to a butcher who, when single, had sailed before the mast and possessed the most poetic ability to curse that I ever heard. Part of my miserable work was, in the bitter cold winter dark, to deliver vast orders of meat for local factory canteens. A favourite amusement of the factory girls when they found the chance was to stop the lift between floors, render one helpless by sheer numbers and perform a variety of unseemly acts, all in great good humour.

One weekend, when the shop was closed, the boss's son and I invited friends to a party there. We invaded the cold room, chose the choicest lambs and Scotch beef and feasted on chops, steaks and beer, got drunk, made a lot of noise and a neighbour phoned the boss. He came bristling. He was not, he said, having a bunch of Dutch-East-Indies striped bastards and other gits and pox-doctors' clerks with their bits of crumpet from Wapping Old Stairs turning his place into a knocking shop, whoring up and down the hall and ... and ...

Studious Purgatory

The fracas ended with pieces of meat flying through the air and the sack all round.

The dole was seventeen shillings a week out of which I paid seven shillings for a room consisting of a bed and a coin gas meter. Like most jobless I lived mainly on 'tea and two' the two being square slices of bread and marge. For protein I bought roast peanuts from Woolworths. Little remained for beer, tobacco, clothes or fun.

Talking about a similar period in his own life, though he is slightly older, Graham Greene once told me in Beijing that if he had not had success with writing he would have turned to crime. He did not say how much thought he had given to the problem of making crime pay. I gave a lot of thought to it, seeing my life otherwise stretching into the future on bread and peanuts. My knowledge of the East End, culled from the Albert Dock area, told me that there were not many fields of crime into which an unfledged amateur could penetrate without getting his face laced or finding himself in gaol, which must have been worse than the dole or more people would have opted for it.

Any would-be criminal must begin somewhere and I did not see myself in any imaginable criminal role from a shinner-up of wealthy drain-pipes to, at the callow age of twenty or so, a convincing swindler. Indeed I had been personally swindled out of five bob by a Petticoat Lane auction spieler. I recognised the feelings of Noah Claypole, rejecting one by one the risky criminal careers offered by Fagin.

Accidentally, an East London villain named Frederick Browne turned my questing mind toward making false money. He killed a policeman near my home and shot his eyes out, superstitiously believing as gangsters then did, that the retina would record a photo-image of the killer. The case became a sensation and Browne, to finance himself while on remand, ghosted a series of articles in a Sunday paper purporting to tell how he had counterfeited half-crowns in prison during one of his terms.

He had done no such thing. Nobody could have reproduced a coin in or out of gaol by the methods described in these articles, as I found out when I tried. Perhaps Browne had heard how the real coiners were doing it, for there was enough fact to set me experimenting and in a short time I was able to counterfeit any 'silver' coin well enough to pass normal handling. I had found what Fagin would have called my lay.

In those days a shilling bought twenty cigarettes or two pints of beer. The largest coin in general circulation was the half-crown, twelve-and-a-half of today's pence, two-and-a-half shillings. Faking half-crowns was more economical of time but they tended to come under closer scrutiny. In professional coining circles, the half-crown was the usual coin produced and the coiners mostly sold them 'to the trade' at about half their face value or less. In doing so they put their fate in unknown hands. Too many people were involved. Once a passer was nabbed, the police could usually trace the whole chain of production.

My own mode of operation, which I will not disclose, was safe for various reasons, mainly because I let no other person into the secret. I was satisfied with modestly supplementing the dole while I continued to look for a real job. Without doubt I was a criminal and could, I thought, have got up to fourteen years gaol for what I was doing, but morally I had no qualms. The government, too, was in the business of adulterating the coinage of the realm; had been for centuries indeed and still is. My products were not intrinsically of less value than the government's, they were merely unofficial. My only worry about coining was the remote possibility of getting caught.

Amid the encircling suburban gloom of tennis, cricket, churchiness and conservatism, Dick and I were very close, preferring each other's company, using the less jolly-boy pubs, hitch-hiking into the countryside, borrowing each other's clothes and endlessly debating. What kind of district it was may be imagined where the local leading funeral director tried to horsewhip some simple chap who had sung 'I'm young and healthy', for being indecent.

I kept my coining activities secret from Dick. It had not been his decision and knowing about it, I felt sure would worry him, he being a far more sensitive person than I, though mentally tough and intellectually stubborn. I felt too that it would make him an accessory unless he denounced me to the police. It would have been unfair to tell him but the alternatives were to give the whole thing up or devise some explanation for extra money I now had.

I embarked on a delicate affair with a non-existent married woman named Lois Brown whose husband was a well-britched business-man given to spending time elsewhere and so facilitating our dalliance. It had to be kept most hush-hush since the husband of Lois was suspicious. He was also mean. But she did what she could out of the housekeeping money, and it was her generosity that enabled me to pass on to Dick the odd pound note and St Bruno Flake tobacco which both of us smoked all our lives on the advice of our chitterling-loving grandfather.

When Dick was about sixteen Grandfather George took him aside as Polonius took Laertes and gave him some precepts on smoking which were well in advance of their time.

'Whatever anyone says, you will surely smoke. Now here is a good briar pipe quite plain and straight which I have personally smoked. It is cool and mellow. And here is my own favourite tobacco – St Bruno – strong but not as strong as plug. Never inhale smoke directly into the lungs. Never smoke cigarettes. If a pipe tobacco is too weak for you, it will burn your tongue. If it is too strong it will make your stomach uneasy. The right strength will taste better all the way down the pipe and won't make it too hot.'

Various commentators have suggested that there was a mystery about how Dick 'broke into the newspaper world', as though this were an unheard-of achievement instead of being almost the only way. Except for sons and daughters of people with a lot of pull, everyone in Fleet Street on the editorial side, breaks in. Rather, Fleet Street is where the pendulum stops. There never was any mystery in Dick's case. He was a rarity otherwise, even unique, but that was all.

We agreed that newspapers offered almost the only chance for people like us with no other qualification than literacy. We had no respect for newspapers and little idea of what went on in them or where we might fit in but felt that they could not be as bad as baked beans.

Our enquiries told us that there were various ways of getting into newspaper work of which the one to be discarded without further examination was via any of the proliferating journalistic schools which often began their advertisements with: 'Send us a five-hundred-word sample of your writing and we will tell you, without obligation, whether you have the ability to be a writer, journalist, etc., etc.' Practising journalists regard such schools as equivalent to learning to be a surgeon by correspondence course and a certified method of getting shown the door by any one in a position to employ you.

Another method, possible and indeed common but dreadful, was to get a job on the local press reporting the death of a local horse or the weddings of local pregnant virgins, meantime phoning hopeful local stories to the national press or Press Association until someone recognised your worth. To start this laborious process, you had to have a job, which was what you were trying to find.

Not being quite destitute, thanks to Lois Brown, and fares being then negligible, we took to drinking in Fleet Street pubs rather than locally. Everyone in Fleet Street drank and could scarcely do their jobs in some cases if an ill wind blew them sober into the office.

The area from Ludgate Circus to the Law Courts and from Holborn to the river formed a city within a city – devoted to The Print. Other minor enterprises also existed but those acres conglomerated everything that was needed to produce billions of pages of print every day.

Fleet Street was rich in pubs alleviating the bottomless thirsts of many kinds of people enslaved to this perpetual paper loom. And it was a bastion which held out longest against the monopolising incursions of the great brewing interests. From their own standpoint brewers prefer pubs where every square foot is occupied by people elbow to elbow drinking and as they inexorably monopolised control they preferred to close down the little friendly, man-and-wife pubs. Brewers preferred one modernised pub to three old-fashioned ones.

It was harder to carry out this barbarous policy in Fleet Street where the clienteles were highly specialised. It took us time to learn even the main subdivisions. You would rarely find an editorial man in the great bars of the Mucky Duck (White Swan) or a lowly sub-editor in the pretentious Feathers. Stereotypers, compositors, sports writers, political commentators all had

Studious Purgatory

their different needs and tended to hang together. Partly this depended on hours of work, though when you knew The Street well there was no time of day when you could not get a drink

Our favourite quickly became The Clachan, a tiny, one-room Scotch house in Mitre Court between the Fleet Street post-office and El Vino's wine bar, then forbidden to women and overrun with snobs and gossip-mongers who pretended to despise pubs but could not afford to drink at the Savoy.

The Clachan was managed by motherly-looking, broad-beamed Mrs Rothwell who, for all her amiability, kept very firm control and was reputed to have been a prison wardress. She was one of the women – usually childless – on whom Dick produced an impression of needing care, though he was mentally very tough and stood in no need of protection. She adored him as though he were an only ne'er-do-well son. To be his friend was a plus-point with her and anyone she fancied he did not like got served with a down-turned mouth. Being his brother I was allowed to stay after closing hours and could leave messages with her.

These were the days before CO_2, pub carpets, 'hammered' copper and imitation lager with synthetic lime juice in it. Beers had their distinctive flavours. We drank our Scotch ale, mild and bitter, draught Guinness, Bass and Worthington at the Clachan, Bell, Mucky Duck and Mooney's and became part of the Fleet Street scenery.

As Dick sat sketching in the Clachan one day chance brought a *Daily Express* features man in, a rare thing for the *Express* people frequented the cellar bar at the Falstaff. Dick was drawing a caricature of some film star. After a few beers the *Express* man suggested that if Dick would do some half column drawings 'on spec', he, the *Express* man, would see they got into the files and whenever one got used it would be paid at 'the rate' which was ten shillings. Very soon his thumb-nail caricatures began to appear accompanying film reviews. Dick had the toe of his shoe in, though a decade passed before he got his real chance on the now dead *News Chronicle* to evolve into Britain's best known film critic who, uniquely, illustrated his own brilliant reviews with what David Low described as the best caricatures in Britain. But just then he was still drawing the dole, getting his St Bruno from Lois Brown via me and waiting for the ten bobs to dribble in.

It now seems strange that we took no interest in politics. Our talk was of books, art, music, the theatre and film. In this we were witless victims of the carefully cultivated belief that politics was the myth of oscillations between Tory, Labour and Liberal parties.

We saw Parliament as only shadow-boxing, the repetitious device of always having in stock some more acceptable figure to step in and take over from others who had become over-exposed when things had become difficult.

Fingers had been burned and there was widespread working class defeatism following the carefully provoked and ruthlessly crushed 1926 General Strike.

Labour was striving, by moderation and soft words, to prove that it 'would serve the nation in opposition as ... gentlemen' and could function better in the current tension, within the Parliamentary rules, as His Majesty's Government. It was clear that with millions of unemployed and dependents, safe Labour and trade union leaders could better head off trends toward dangerous extra-parliamentary activity by men and women in desperate poverty.

To keep these leaders steering into the wind there was the bait of office – to meet the Royals, dance with duchesses, take Mum to garden parties, occupy safe Parliamentary seats and end up with a peerage.

But we thought that was all. We did not see past the blinkers put on us all our lives by education and environment. Fascinated by our own discernment, we were like onlookers at a spot-the-lady spiel, too smart to stake on a card but getting our pockets picked while watching.

2
The Threepenny Manifesto

Crossing Lincolns Inn Fields one midday on our way to Fleet Street, we came upon a small open-air meeting being addressed by a stocky man with intense black eyes and eyebrows like George Robey's, as though they had been painted on. He was talking in a common-sense way which was simple but hypnotising. We both stayed to listen and Dick, who had to deliver a drawing to the *Daily Express*, left reluctantly. I listened till he had finished speaking and walked through to a Chancery Lane pub.

Someone took the next stool and asked for a pint of bitter in the Lancashire voice I had just heard.

'I was listening to you out there,' I said.

His pint came.

'Cheers,' he replied and drank most of it at one pull.

'Thirsty work.'

He grunted.

'You a Communist?' It was a silly question but to my knowledge I had never met one face to face.

'Pollitt's the name. Harry Pollitt.'

'Oh.' That much I knew. He was the leader of the British Communist Party, described by the press in its rare mentions as 'tiny'.

'There's something I'd like to ask you …'

'Sorry. No time. Got to be somewhere at one-thirty. How about reading this for a start?'

He pulled a folded pamphlet from his pocket.

The Communist Manifesto.

I took it.

He held out his hand. 'Tuppence, please.'

'It says threepence here.'

'It's secondhand,' he said with a little vinegary smile.

I gave him threepence. He finished his beer and said, 'Ta ta.'

A manifesto – what a word! – put out in 1848 was not likely to contain much relevant to the situation eighty years or so later. No doubt the enshrined dogma of a sect. I recalled my Uncle Ernie who suffered ostracism for being pro-Bolshie and talking zestfully of the blood of the rich running in London's gutters. Later he became a born-again Christian and, sanguinary still, spoke with equal zest of being washed in the blood of the lamb. He cycled all over the place spreading joy until he landed in an institution.

Mr Pollitt had given a contrary impression – of clarity, presence and humour. When the pub door had swung shut after him I took the pamphlet and another beer and sat on a leather sofa. It went at once to the point: 'A spectre is haunting Europe – the spectre of Communism.'

By the time the pub shut at three I had read right through it fast and gone back over some parts again. I emerged into Chancery Lane bewildered.

There was nothing old-fashioned about the manifesto. It was stylish, tight and abrasive; hurrying ahead with the assurance that its ideas were valid and no time was to be lost in fulfilling them. No words were wasted on challenging almost all the concepts I had acquired and been taught. Rather it ignored them disdainfully as though I, the reader, had presumably seen through the quackery of contemporary politics and wished to get down to reality.

It was sudden and shocking to find in an eighty-year-old document an entire new mental universe, a fresh and scientific explanation of the present world crisis of idle workers, idle machinery, squalid poverty surrounded by potential affluence. These ideas, diamond-cut and polished by Marx and Engels, as it turned out, could no more be ignored than a nail up in a shoe. They were uncomfortable, maddeningly self-assured, infuriating for being so credible.

Insofar as I had given it thought, I had classified Communism with the two aspects or incarnations of Uncle Ernie – as extreme egalitarianism established by revolutionary violence and from there relying for its success on everyone being morally born again – not as Christians but as persons whose social discipline would rule out self-seeking. Unlikely in a society where even giving up smoking was too hard for most people.

Remarkable to find that actual Communists – people like Karl Marx and Mr Pollitt treated such idealistic fantasies with as much scorn as I had always done but at the same time put forward a closely reasoned explanation of why socialism must emerge from the present social order, if it did not destroy itself.

Although there was nothing sectarian about *The Communist Manifesto*, the same could not be said of the British Communist Party, or those whom Dick and I told that we wished to become members. In the two years since we had first encountered Pollitt, we had read and discussed the major works of Marxism and the decision to take an active part in real politics as distinct from the parliamentary kind was a very big step for us. In this the Nazi seizure of power helped tip the balance as it did for so many of our contemporaries.

In the early thirties part of the rank and file of the Communist Party regarded the party as an élitist club for true revolutionaries and said harder words against the Labour Party and others on the left than against the capitalists, or at any rate said them oftener.

We found our way to a meeting of the Walthamstow cell, there being no Communist Party organisation then in Woodford or Buckhurst Hill. It met in unnecessary and romantic secrecy in a two-up-two-down Victorian terrace house with a holystoned step on the pavement and an outside lavatory. The cell leader occupied his position mainly because he was the tenant of the house.

A member whose duty it was to make newcomers feel at home and 'draw them into activity' was one of the last Englishmen I met who smoked black shag in half of a whistling clay pipe. He was morosely suspicious, addicted to punch-ups on demonstrations and unmarried on principle. At that time many Communists of this sort sneered at marriage as a bourgeois institution.

Also on principle, he refused to try to get work because, even if he could find a job, he would be making a profit for some bleedin' capitalist. For this reason too he barely tolerated 'real workers' let alone such soddin' la-di-da gits as Dick and myself, probably police narks or *agents provocateurs* – then a much favoured expression. He concentrated in his person most of the English Left-Wing Infantilism which Lenin singled out for criticism.

There were seven people including ourselves and we spent our first evening talking about distributing leaflets, which did not arrive, and who would speak at a street-corner meeting on Saturday. This raised some argument since most believed it was useless to stand in the cold addressing themselves. It was agreed to wait till the weather was warmer.

Daunting to think that this material was going to change the social order. Outside, Dick quoted the Duke of Wellington: 'I don't know what effect these men will have upon the enemy, but, by God, they terrify me.'

All over the country the organisation was probably no better. It took months to get a membership card. Meetings were not prepared and ended in the pub on the corner. One night, or early morning, Dick was arrested while he was painting 'Release Thaelmann!' (the German Communist Party leader arrested and later murdered by the Nazis) on a wall at Whipps Cross. When the police asked him why he had run away he said jokingly, 'I am rather shy.' A report of his case and ten shillings fine appeared in the local press under the headline 'Shy Early Morning Artist'.

Shortly before this my father had very untypically and without my knowledge urged a friend to get me a job with John Knights, the soap people. I had to take it though it was actually a worse job than Dick's baked beans venture. A day after Dick's arrest, which shocked Buckhurst Hill, I was invited to the office of the sales director and there on his desk was the local paper folded to display the report of his crime.

I was asked to state whether I agreed with what my brother had done. I said yes. Was I a member of the Communist Party? I said nobody had a right to ask me, but yes. Would I leave it? No. That was that. I felt sorry for my father.

Dick and I agreed that painting 'Release Thaelmann!' on London walls, where nobody had the least idea who he was, did no good for him or the British Communist Party. Dick did not attend many more meetings. He was simply not meetings material, not political-party material either, political as he was.

To the end of his brief life we remained close companions and he worked for the Communist party and supported it financially. He remained a Marxist always, as any study of his work shows, and played a vigorous and sometimes decisive part in getting Soviet films shown in London legally.

Together we watched an illegal showing of *Battleship Potemkin* in the Pindar of Wakefield pub in Grays Inn Road after being chased from place to place by the police.

During most of the time that he was Britain's most authoritative film critic, he was doing the same job for the *Daily Worker* under the name John Ross – being the first two names of J.R. Campbell whose sardonic humour Dick much admired.

Johnnie Campbell was a twenty-four carat Scot to whom the description dour applied in all its richness. He was a Marxist and a sceptic and a splendid counterbalance to Pollitt's ebullient energy.

Johnnie had trod a rough road. From afar he could be recognised by his jerky walk, as though he suffered from flat feet, bunions, ingrowing toe-nails, corns and tight shoes with nails sticking up inside. His feet had been mashed up doing some modestly heroic deed in the dreadful Battle of the Somme. A medal for heroism coincided more or less with his decision to join the Communist Party. He was an outstanding economist. I sometimes caught him looking at me in the way Scots look at Englishmen. It was not flattering.

He had accidentally triggered the downfall of the first Labour government, being then editor of the *Workers' Weekly*, forerunner of the *Daily Worker*, and had published an appeal, not written by Campbell, to soldiers not to shoot at striking workers. Sedition! In the ensuing row over whether he was to be prosecuted, the wobbly MacDonald government had collapsed.

Dick's strength lay in his erudition, in applying consistent political understanding, unusual artistic skill and writing ability to the critical observation of the medium he knew and loved best – the cinema.

For a time, while those factors flowed together with the liberal period of the *News Chronicle*, a paper with a circulation of one-and-a-half millions, he was able to expose some of the commercial misuse of the film and support what was creatively good in it. His work was widely respected. Augustus John described him as 'a brilliant draughtsman and true critic'.

How that changed comes out in his last letter to me during the war in Korea, shortly before his death. Among the chat, he wrote:

> I am back at work but the NC [*News Chronicle*] have a down on criticism of any sort and a hard fight has to be fought. We are now heavily involved with Uncle Mac of the BBC Children's Hour and he, with the Royal Baby, represents the NC's big drive for circulation ...
>
> To convalesce I went to Deal, a good spot with a lot of very fine pubs. There as elsewhere I found myself famous (or notorious) as Alan Winnington's brother, a state of affairs I most strongly deplore. Incidentally, I was interested in your account of an interview with the captured *Observer* correspondent Philip Deane (Gigantes) as I had met and liked him. Last week I met his wife. In case you should see him she sent her love ...
>
> I have got some writing to do for the NC Woman's Supplement and I would sooner do anything else in the world. I was all set to go to Ireland to do a story about a film Paul Rotha is making there but the NC wouldn't play. They suspect 'culture', than which only 'communism' is more dangerous.
>
> This is maddening as I have got *Public Opinion, Picture Post* and *Sight and Sound* all lined up for a piece about the film. If on the other hand I could find a nice human piece about a film star's baby the NC would fall over themselves sending me after it. If they only knew how many such stories I let slip by ...
>
> I will write again soon. Perhaps you will let me have a few lines
>
>   Yours
>   Richard.

He died soon after and the *News Chronicle* died soon after that.

I have told this at length because Dick, so well known then, and without doubt unique in blending visual and verbal

The Threepenny Manifesto

criticism, deserves to have the record straightened out. There are various newspaper versions of his relations with the Communist Party.

So, for the record: Richard Winnington did join the Communist Party, never got a party card due to inefficiency and drifted out, which in my view was just as well.

Far from having been expelled, he was greatly admired by the Communist Party and until his health began to fail in 1948 was film critic of the party's paper, though not a member.

He remained always, in politics and in general, as his great friend, and mine, Paul Rotha described him: 'A Man among men. A man who sought out honesty, who followed truth, who symbolised integrity.'

I would add that he was also a lot of fun to be with. It used to be said in The Street that there was no better entertainment than the two Winnington brothers having an up an' a downer in the Clachan. Only one other man had a comparable influence on me – Harry Pollitt.

3

Banners in Piccadilly

'You can't believe what you read in the papers' is and was the view of many British people, who nevertheless read more newspapers per head of population than any other people. But the same sceptics will also say, 'Well, I saw it in the paper,' implying an element of credibility. Propaganda is a complex business. A large part of the public, especially of the working class, recognised that newspapers were owned by people whose interests were in flat contradiction to their own. Press treatment of the unemployed and of the Hunger Marches also alienated a large part of the thoughtful middle class.

Readers might be aware that what they were getting was at least biased and probably straight lies, but where to get the facts? Any newspaper for readers who wanted more than the mass press gave – sex, crime and human interest – would certainly have been boycotted by the advertisers and would be the financial equivalent of a lead lifebelt. In British press conditions, a Communist paper would have to be supported, or price itself out of the readership it was intended for – working people partly on the dole.

Lenin was very strong on this point. 'You must start this paper,' he wrote to Tom Bell in 1921, 'not as a business (as usually papers are started in capitalist countries) – not with a big sum of money, not in the ordinary and usual manner but as an economic and political tool of the masses in their struggle.' He warned, 'The English government will apply the shrewdest means in order to suppress every beginning of this kind.' Nine years later this paper was still a dream.

That was changed when a more or less completely new leadership was elected at the 1929 Party Congress, establishing

Pollitt, Dutt and Gallacher as the leading core who at once set about starting a Communist daily paper, which appeared – only two months after the congress – on 1 January 1930. It was run on a shoe-string, boycotted by the wholesalers, sued for libels, charged with contempt of court and incitement and survived, being distributed, sold and financed by such members as could spare donations, for it sold at a penny like other papers but cost much more to produce.

There was no doubt that Lenin had been right. The paper was the rallying point for all those jangling elements and the party began to develop. When it appeared to be recognised that despite my accent I had not been sent in by the Special Branch of Scotland Yard, I was getting up in the dark to collect the *Daily Worker* from the station, rewrapping them and delivering them to newsagents by bicycle.

Unlike Dick, I decided to stay in the Communist Party, having come to the conclusion that the Marxian analysis was correct. What people do with a correct theory does not necessarily change the theory's correctness. Einstein cannot be blamed because Truman dropped nuclear bombs on Hiroshima and Nagasaki. Newton cannot be attacked because those bombs fell down instead of up.

If Marx, Engels, Lenin and the rest were right, I had the same responsibility as any other person to forward the advance of history in which Marxists, correct in broad, are likely to err in detail. I could not blame Marx for the Walthamstow cell, but only try to improve it.

Racked by their perennial fear of any action that might offend that mythical beast 'public opinion', the Labour and trade union officials rejected Communist Party proposals for united action against Sir Oswald Mosley's blackshirted fascists whose numbers had grown considerably since Hitler seized power. At first it had seemed that Hitler was only attacking the Communists and Jews, but then the Nazi terror was extended to Social Democrats, trade unionists, liberals, humanists. Still the Labour leaders hoped that if you ignored the blackshirts they would disappear. After all, it *was* Britain.

Unless the strength of the great labour movement, especially the trade unions, could be mobilised against the fascists, regardless of what the Labour leaders said, the British fascists would make big gains under police protection. Much depended on the first major confrontation. It would literally be fatal if the anti-fascist struggle dwindled into one between the Communists and fascists with the mass of the public standing aside.

This now became a severe test of the Communist Party's 1929 reconstruction. I suppose there were no more than 2,000 members in London when the Communist Party decided to take counter-action against a demonstration called by Mosley for 9 September 1934 in Hyde Park. We showered leaflets from buses, buildings in shopping centres, Oxford Street stores, but unbroken silence was maintained by the media.

Hitler had taken over with the secret backing of the bankers and industrialists. Sir Oswald Mosley was now getting help of the same kind. Against our tiny *Daily Worker* he had the backing of the *Daily Mail* and a backwoods crew of extreme right politicians. Labour's official paper, the *Daily Herald*, was silent.

Somewhere the silence had to be broken and it was in the least expected place, the Savoy Hotel, where the Savoy Orpheans dance band was Britain's most popular bedtime listening. Between dance numbers a pleasant voice suddenly announced, 'Come to Hyde Park on Sunday September 9 and help to smash the fascists.'

Everyone had heard it, the press could not ignore it. According to the morning papers a young man in evening clothes had crossed the dance floor from his table apparently to request a number for his girl friend, a common enough thing then. Instead he had coolly lifted off the microphone and made his announcement. The Communist counter-action had begun in earnest.

The same thing happened at the Queens Hall. Next, messages were cut into feature films and were flashed on to screens in London's biggest cinemas. 'A daring and brave man', according to the *Guardian*, scaled the Law courts façade like a mountaineer to hang a huge banner. Some friends of mine and myself hung ourselves with ropes from the high bridge across the Southend Road and painted the same message. London's attention was focused on Hyde Park and all we needed was a fine day.

My own turn came when a phone call summoned me to the London district office of the Communist Party, where the campaign was being planned. On the way I imagined myself disguised with a wig by Clarkson and clothes by Moss Brothers, doing some daring deed far beyond my capacity and finishing up in a police cell, blackening for ever the name Winnington in Buckhurst Hill.

I found my way to a bare room with no carpet and one desk at which a man was sitting in front of a small motto: 'Audacity, more audacity, always audacity – Danton.'

He was Douglas F. Springhall, known as Dave or Springie, and looked tough, with a shaven head like a cannon ball which seemed to grow directly from his shoulders, and eyes gleaming with fun and sharp discernment. He looked me over and nodded.

'Just what we need, mate.' He got up and walked round me. 'Nice whistle. [Whistle and flute, Cockney rhyming slang for suit.] Nice tie. Just the job. Now look. We want one or, better still, two banners hung in Piccadilly Circus at nine o'clock tonight. Usual thing – 'All to Hyde Park Sunday September 9.' Nine sharp. I've tipped off the *News Chronicle* exclusive.'

'How?'

'Have to leave it up to you, I'm afraid.'

'Where are the banners?'

'Not done yet. You go and have a look round. Soon as you know the shape, ring this number. It's the Camden Town studio. They'll make them to order in an hour.'

'Just me or who?'

'Just you. You're on your own. We've found it's better like that on this kind of job. Here's a number to ring if you get knocked off. Solicitor. Ours. Good luck.'

It took me an hour to inspect the area. At the now defunct Winston Hotel I managed to book a top room overlooking Piccadilly Circus and said I would go to collect my suitcase. At half-past-eight, back in the hotel, I wired two narrow, rolled-up banners, ten yards long, to the window ledge. They were kept rolled only by cotton strands between which I pushed cigarettes as slow fuse and at five-to-nine I lit them. Leaving my empty suitcase on the bed, I went out, plugged the cylinder lock with matches and crossed the Circus. At nine the first banner unrolled. For thirty seconds I wondered if the other cigarette had gone out, then the second banner dropped.

Breakfast with Mao

That Sunday was the start of Mosley's eclipse. Hordes of foot and horse police could barely force a way for the blackshirts through a crowd reckoned at nearly 200,000.

It had also demonstrated that the Communist Party was now a political force and from the hotch-potch of something more than 2,000 when Pollitt became secretary it became, by 1939, a party of 16,000 disciplined members of high quality, with its own paper and holding many key positions in trade unions and other bodies.

While I was looking for somewhere to hang those banners I had one other serious worry. Suppose I was arrested; suppose as a result they searched my room and found my coining gear. I could not tell this to Springie and I would have been regarded as a coward if I had not done the job. So I went realising that I was risking not just the maximum sentence, which a Communist was sure to get, but also dropping a big blot on the party itself.

I had been lucky and I decided that my innocent bit of coining had to end for good. I had not done any for some time, having got a dull job in Fleet Street with a photo agency. So I waterproofed my paraphernalia and buried it by night in Epping Forest.

My job held up and soon, in my spare time, I was secretary of the Walthamstow Communist Party, street-corner orator every Saturday, organiser of some small Fleet Street Communist groups, lecturer in political economy, member of the Printers' Anti-fascist Movement and of the National Union of Journalists.

Like every other active member I had to spend too much time, it seemed to me, collecting money to keep the party's financial nose above water. I said as much once to Pollitt and added in joke that with all the skilled printers and metal-workers at our disposal we could do well at my old trade, which I went on to describe.

He listened, his sloe-black eyes fixed on me as their expression gradually changed to helpless, amused disgust. The joke had misfired.

There was a longish pause.

'And you've kept all that stuff?'

I nodded.
'Show me your party card.'
He took it and put it into his pocket.
'Where is it?'
'In the forest.'
'Didn't forget to put your name on it, I hope. Daft young booger. When you can tell me it's at the bottom of the Thames maybe you can have your card back. I'll think about it.'

Harry Pollitt's personality had much to do with the cheerful, self-confident militancy of the left in the thirties. The Communist Party leadership was filled with powerful figures: Dutt, Gallacher, Campbell, Tom Mann, Rust, Arthur Horner, Hannington, Springhall, Bradley, Bramley, Kerrigan, Allison, Burns, but Pollitt's position as leader of the Party was never challenged. There must be plenty of people living today whose lives, like my own, were transformed by meeting and knowing Pollitt.

Strong self-discipline regulated the relations between Harry Pollitt and Rajani Palme Dutt during their thirty-five years of association, which was indeed a strange one. Raji, as his friends called him, was remembered at Oxford as the most brilliant student of his era. Pollitt, a boilermaker, born in Droylsden, Lancashire, left school at twelve. Intimates knew that their clashing personalities were blended with respect and never seemed to influence their political judgements and co-operation.

On my last visit to Raji in his Golders Green flat, shortly before his death, he said that there had never been any question in his mind that Pollitt, 'in spite of some theoretical weaknesses', was the man to lead the Communist Party. 'And lucky we were to have him.' My own relations with Raji, over some forty years, were always friendly, even warm, but never jolly as with Harry. I can't imagine Raji taking a drink except for political reasons, unlike Gallacher who would not do so for any reason, and refused even to enter the House of Commons bar until the party ordered him to. Raji and Pollitt complemented each other – the Yin and the Yang of the British party.

A great part of Pollitt's strength and attraction lay in his unpretentious Englishness. His hand reached back into history to shake those of the English poor who had marched on London with their home-made pikes to demand redress, who had been hanged and disembowelled. His strong, clear, Lancashire voice called our serf forefathers from their crumbled graves. When he spoke from a platform in the open-air, you saw Wat Tyler addressing his followers on Clerkenwell Green.

Pollitt's Lancashire dialect and unostentatious way of speech made him acceptable to Cockneys, Welsh and Scots. Generally I do not like orators. Mainly they lack the essential ability to react, to speak as an exchange with their hearers. However much Pollitt orated, he did not give this impression or seem to be speaking for effect.

He never allowed himself to be put on the defensive by challenges that Communism was something alien. He regarded revolution as a very English thing and Parliament, insofar as it had value at all, was a means toward the transfer of power to the working class.

'Communism,' I heard him say in answer to one challenge, 'is more English than the Royal Family, which is German. Our present day rulers want us to forget that three hundred years ago we cut off the head of the English king. Later they imported a foreign brand. Britons invented Communism. Manchester and London influenced the thinking of Karl Marx and Engels more than the other way round – more's the pity,' he added wryly. 'Think of it: six hundred years ago – six hundred – an Englishman, John Ball, said that "things cannot go well in England, nor ever will, until everything shall be in common." There is nothing un-English or foreign about Socialism or Communism.'

Truly great people are rare and Pollitt was one. Trevor Evans of the *Daily Express*, and no lover of Communists, wrote of him: 'Almost as obvious as his Lancashire warmth was his tremendous atmosphere of sincerity. One felt in Harry Pollitt's presence that here was a man whose private world was enviable in its strength and consistency.'

That inner strength and consistency were tested as they seldom are in any person when the Second World War began.

*

There was nothing clear-cut about the way the war broke out. People with memories knew that the Communists had opposed the policy of Munichism – of offering the Nazis bait to encourage them to find their 'Living Space' to the east. A glance at the list of 'inducements' makes clear how the Western powers had weakened their own position to strengthen Hitler's: Spain, Abyssinia, the Rhineland, Memel, Czechoslovakia, Albania – all handed to the fascists.

Each concession was explained by the need to avoid war and if the policy of Chamberlain duped the newspaper-bemused public of Britain it did not deceive the Soviet Union and the Nazis. Only one thing could have stopped the Nazis – collective security against aggression.

Moscow gave a number of warnings. Stalin said they were not going to pull the chestnuts out of the fire for Britain and France. Zhdanov warned that unless collective security were forthcoming, Russia would make a major reassessment of policy. It could scarcely be plainer. There was, seen as a playback, only one possibility for the Russians to avoid being pushed into war by the Western powers at the wrong time and place, and the same applied for different reasons to the Nazis.

Both took it, also for different reasons, and made a pact not to attack each other. It gave Russia what she needed – time.

The Soviet-German Non-Aggression Pact of 23 August 1939 (it was not an alliance) caused a lot of people to turn round and start running up a down-escalator. If it caused the Communists less surprise than some it was because they had seen through the Chamberlain policies from the first. Of course the British press tried to present it as a Soviet-German alliance but clearly Stalin had trumped Chamberlain's ace.

It seemed a little naïve of such an old fox as Neville Chamberlain to suppose that the Russians would wait to be attacked and then watch the Western powers quietly helping the Nazis by such legalistic tricks as they had used to support Franco and strangle the Spanish Republic. And in the end, the Nazis, having absorbed all the resources of Europe, could swallow their chief benefactor, Britain. One can work out all kinds of variations and a lot of people did. But what actually happened has gone into history.

Understandably, when the Nazis invaded Poland a week or

so after the pact, no chances were lost in London to convince people that the Soviet Union had joined the Nazis in bare-faced aggression. Actually this was not so. They contented themselves with recovering an area beyond the Curzon Line stolen by the Poles in 1920 when the young Soviet Union could not resist.

Nonetheless, there were people including Communists who concluded that Stalin had let the anti-Nazi team down and who became anti-Soviet overnight. Since then, similar objections have been raised in times of sudden stress, often by well-meaning people who would like to have international politics cleaned up and run under Marquess of Queensbury rules. Thus seen, it was unsporting of the Soviet Union, whom Britain had been double-crossing, to have signed a non-aggression pact with the Nazis whom Britain had also been trying to double-cross. Or something.

The muddle thickened when Hitler attacked Poland on 1 September 1939 and Chamberlain reluctantly declared war on the Nazis. Pollitt argued, and most members of the Communist Party's Central Committee agreed, that for the British people it was an issue of the victory of democracy or fascism. He said that it must be a war on two fronts: to defeat fascism and to defeat fascism's Fifth Column in Britain – in the first place the Chamberlain government.

Three weeks later, when the Central Committee sat on 24 September, D.F. Springhall, who had been attending a meeting of the Communist International in Moscow, brought to London the decision of that body characterising the war as an 'out and out imperialist war to which the working class in no country could give any support'.

During the three weeks between 3 September, when Chamberlain, in sorrow and with rare truth, contrary to his hopes and expectations, declared war on Nazi Germany, and we all ran to shelter as the sirens went off, being inexperienced, there was time to worry about Harry Pollitt's concept of 'a fight on two fronts'.

I worried in plenty of company. Most Communist Party members and their close allies – skilled workers and shop-stewards – were very unhappy about the idea of being led into war by an extreme, indeed *the* arch-Munichite in person;

who had presented the Nazis in Czechoslovakia with a powerful military state, thirty-five divisions, the Skoda arms works and a mountain fortress line that had required the deployment of most of the Nazi army. And at that, to go to war for 'democratic Poland' which, politically, hardly differed from Hitler's Reich.

Communists of my generation were reared in the aftermath of the 1944-1918 war when the parties of the Second International – pledged to overthrow their 'own' governments in the event of war – went back on their vow overnight and voted for war credits.

The sole exception had been the Bolsheviks who had opposed the war, kicked out the Tsar and established the first socialist state. Harry Pollit's war on two fronts – support the war but change the government – had a smell of 1914 about it.

Hitler's attack on Poland and Chamberlain's plaintive war declaration had not changed anything basic. Hitler was moving in the right direction for the Munichites – toward the Soviet Union. Given a bit more pressure and encouragement, he might attack the Soviet Union with British support. Our job remained the classic one laid down by Lenin.

I welcomed the declaration of the Communist International and felt that they were more likely to know what they were doing than Harry Pollitt who had, I thought, no doubt with excellent intentions, been affected by working-class nationalism.

At the meeting on 24 September there were only two votes against the policy of the Communist International – those of Harry Pollitt and J.R. Campbell. Soon after it was announced that, in view of the difference of opinion, the Central Committee had decided that Harry Pollitt should no longer continue as General Secretary.

This hit him very hard. When he was elected to that position in 1929 he said that all previous experiences were only 'steps in my training, serving my apprenticeship until my comrades considered I was fit to become their Secretary'.

He did not make any statement except by letter to the Central Committee affirming his 'unreserved acceptance of the policy of the Party and the Communist International' and pledging full support in 'explaining, popularising and helping to carry it forward'. This promise he fully honoured.

For him, not to have supported a party decision with which he disagreed would have been like blacklegging on a majority decision to strike no matter how ill-judged he might think the strike to be.

During his time out in the cold, I met Harry by accident in Fetter Lane, walking over the broken glass after an air-raid. It was the first time I had seen him after he had been sacked as General Secretary and he told me he was back at his trade as ship's plater. I felt uncomfortable but he behaved as though nothing had happened.

It was a hot day and hard to find a pub where nobody would recognise him, but we found a dark corner in The Cock.

All the world was talking of the arrival of Hitler's deputy, Rudolf Hess, by plane in Scotland. The tale was that Hess had flown there without the knowledge of Der Fuehrer, but it was pretty obvious, I said, trying to get a reaction, that his real aim was to do a bargain with the British to ally themselves with the Nazis against the Soviet Union.

He thought it very likely.

I asked him, 'Harry, do you still think that this is a war which we should support?'

'My opinions haven't changed,' he said. 'The war hasn't begun yet. Resistance to the Nazis is growing everywhere. That's the side we have to be on. And against anyone or anything that helps the fascists. Suppose Hess wants to do a deal – whatever the British government does, the fascists will still be the enemy. If Churchill connives with Hitler his head will go in the noose too.

'Don't quote me,' he grinned and went off down Fleet Street, energetic, the glass crackling under his feet.

Whenever some kind of anniversary comes round the debate, usually with partisan overtones, tends to be reopened about who was right in 1939. Is the picture of Harry Pollitt alone bearing the banner of rectitude into the gale a true one? The only man in step? Was the Communist International right or wrong? Or did changes that took place during the war have the effect of making people right later who had been wrong earlier, and vice versa? Was the decision of the Communist

International biassed by the fact that when the war began the only powers at war were imperialist ones and that remained so until the Soviet Union was attacked – thus fulfilling the dreams of the Munichites too late, since by that time the Nazis had become the greater threat also to the Western powers?

In Britain, the Communist-led opposition to the war, contributing to Chamberlain's replacement by Churchill, and the growth of the Resistance throughout Europe changed the balance in one direction while the attack on the Soviet Union changed it in another.

Is there in fact an answer to the question: who was right in 1939? Was anyone?

The Communist International dissolved itself in 1943 without giving an opinion. The Communist Party of Great Britain has never given an opinion either. Stalin, who did not personally comment about the decision of the Communist International in 1939, said in 1946 that 'the Second World War from the very outset assumed the nature of an anti-fascist war.'

Pollitt said in 1956: 'In 1939 I thought it was an anti-fascist war. I thought it then and I think it now ... but I was outvoted by my Party and as I am a democrat I accepted the decision.'

Among the stories spread about at the beginning of the war to discredit the Communists the most persistent was that the message brought from Moscow by D.F. Springhall to the British Communist Party did not come from the Communist International at all but was a personal directive of Stalin: a rumour so persistent that there are to this day people retailing this tale to anyone still, after forty years, willing to listen.

After that business of hanging banners in Piccadilly, Dave Springhall and I became friends and for some years we gathered occasionally in Henekey's wine lodge in Holborn with Ben Bradley, who was sentenced to ten years in the trumped up Meerut conspiracy trial, and Wally Hannington the unemployed leader – all, as someone out of the Law Courts remarked, 'gallows material'.

For many years Henekey's remained one of the few decent pubs in London that was not tarted up beyond recognition. It preserved its wonderful long bar backed by gigantic wine vats, its intimate alcoves and its unique triangular stove of cast iron which seems to have no chimney.

We needed that warmth. The general air for Communists was clammier than ever with the Finnish war having begun and Chamberlain sending equipment to Mannerheim and preparing to launch British troops against the Russians on behalf of 'gallant little Finland'. Switching the war in fact.

Springie had a special burden, having personally brought the message from Moscow. He was also very easy to recognise with his round face and slit eyes, the whole now accentuated by his having been shot through the cheeks in Spain. He was always likely to be waylaid by fellow-travellers still suffering from shock at all the sudden twists in events – sad or indignant men who demanded to know why, why, why had the Soviet Union let them down? And was it true that the directive to its sections about what sort of war it was had never been submitted to the Communist International but cooked up by Stalin and put out in its name?

It happened once while we were all leaning on the cast-iron stove enjoying a pony of the tenpenny Amontillado.

Springie screwed up his knowing eyes and said, 'Well, I'm a bit of a mug and easily bamboozled, but I supposed you know who the General Secretary of the Communist International is?' Without pausing for a reply he went on, 'It's Georgi Dimitrov. Do you suppose that Stalin or anyone else – God included – could put one over like that on Dimitrov? And if Stalin, Dimitrov and all the rest, right through to Dutt think the same …'

Only people who lived through the birth of the Nazi Reich can truly know what Dimitrov meant to us then. I was twenty-three at the time and not yet a member of the Communist Party. I used to wake in the night and imagine what might be happening to Dimitrov in his lonely cell in Leipzig, preparing to face the Nazi court next day – or perhaps to be shot 'while trying to escape'. His thoughts were of another kind – how to turn his own trial into the public trial of the Nazis before the world public. If ever there was a hero, Dimitrov was one.

When, a few weeks after I met Harry Pollitt in Fetter Lane, the German armies smashed into the Soviet Union, Churchill broadcast Britain's aim of destroying the Nazi regime. Stalin welcomed this statement as 'historic' and Harry Pollitt was restored as General Secretary, giving the impression that he had been right all the time. He declared, 'The war for the defeat of Hitler is now the supreme issue before the whole of democratic mankind.'

Much as I agreed with that sentiment, Munich it seemed to me was still alive and flourishing. It had to be, whatever form it took. Churchill could only be a treacherous ally. Britain's new posture meant no more than that Hitler – the Axis – was a more immediate danger to British imperial interests.

The Chinese have a saying about the desirability, as a policy, of sitting on the mountain peak and observing the tigers fighting each other in the valley. Churchill had moved a little way down the mountain and was verbally supporting one of the tigers – the bear might be more apt – but until the British forces were playing a comparable part it was a refined version of the Munich policy.

If that estimation seems over-suspicious or even cynical, it was a view held by a large slice of the thinking workers whose distrust and detestation of Churchill – based on his record since the events in Tonypandy and Llanelli in 1911 – was shown at the end of the war. The great war leader was totally spurned by the electorate.

Naturally Stalin had welcomed Churchill's support and obviously we had to support Churchill and try to force him into a genuine fight against fascism. But it was far more realistic when Churchill's Minister for Aircraft Production, Colonel Moore-Brabazon, told a private meeting he hoped 'the Russian and German armies will exterminate each other'. This had been the aim all along. Moore-Brabazon was not dismissed from this vital ministry.

The *Daily Worker* – banned six months earlier – remained banned. We quickly gave up producing an illegal, duplicated substitute, though for a few days I was able to get five pounds a copy for the funds from sympathetic journalists or simply as a collector's item. We had better means of propaganda than a few hundred sheets produced as a gesture and likely to land us all in gaol.

The Moore-Brabazon-Churchill-Citrine policy, which in essence was to delay military action in the West leaving the

Nazis to deploy all their forces against the Soviet Union, cost the Russians millions of lives. General Jodl, Chief of the German General Staff told a meeting of Nazi gauleiters '... It is totally incomprehensible that the Anglo-Americans should have avoided forming the second front in the West.' Eisenhower wanted to strike across the Channel, Churchill prevented it.

Hope that the Russian armies would be exterminated was extinguished at Stalingrad and Kursk, where in Churchill's words, the guts were torn out of the Nazi armies. A fear began to dawn among the Western allies that further Red Army advances toward the Atlantic coast would present an urgent problem. On 6 June 1944, British, and Canadian US forces landed on the coast of Normandy.

Churchill had played for desperate stakes. But for the strength of the Soviet Union, the old world, very likely all the world, would have fallen into the hands of Hitler, Hirohito and the other barbarians. Strange that nonetheless the objective role of that ruthless reactionary was positive.

4
Professional Communist

Soon after the Nazis invaded the Soviet Union, Harry Pollitt phoned and asked me to call in for a chat. In those days it cost one penny to go from Fleet Street to Charing Cross, and buses passed those points every few seconds. In a matter of minutes I was sitting opposite him, back in his old room with the picture of Lenin on one wall and Ralph Fox, who was killed in Spain, on another.

'I suppose you do alright down The Street?' he asked.
'Pretty good.'
'What do you make? Ten? Twenty? Thirty?'
Somewhere between the lower figures, I told him.
'Without foreigners?' He wore his little dry smile as though he had sucked a lemon, 'foreigners' then being articles in short supply made on the side in factories for sale privately.
'Well, God knows how long it's going to take to get the ban lifted on the *Worker*. We've decided we need a press officer. If you'll take the job it's four quid a week – nett. Think it over. Take your time but not too long.'
'No need. The answer's yes.'
'Dead sure?'
He leaned over and shook my hand. 'Go and talk it over with Emile Burns.'
So I became a professional Communist and have remained one ever since. I recall it as the proudest moment of my life and through all the vicissitudes, disputes and disagreements have never regretted that decision.
Back at home, balefully official in buff and smudgy black, my call-up papers into the air force lay on the mat. Next day I told Pollitt that he'd better find another press officer. 'Get the

press office started and we'll see what happens. You never know what those sods will do,' he said.

I had little enough hope. The casualty rate in the air force was high and they needed men. Apart from being a Communist I had the right qualifications. Although the Churchill government was officially the bear's ally, the resulting growth in Communist influence due to Uncle Joe being on our side was not welcome. Especially in the aircraft factories and other war industries the Communists quickly showed that they were able to exert an influence on the workshop floor quite out of proportion to their numbers. This was disconcerting for the 'neo-anti-fascist' Munichites.

How Communists were handled by the armed forces varied greatly. Some were enlisted in the hope that they would not survive the war. Others were kept out to give them no chance of subverting the troops. A few liberal officers considerd that Communists, being intelligent and motivated, would make good officer and NCO material.

A special case had been made of the *Daily Worker*. Although journalists were in general exempt from military service, as soon as the paper was banned twelve of its best journalists had been called up. Herbert Morrison, whose hatred of the Communists amounted to illness, tried in this way to make sure the paper could not come out even if the ban were lifted.

My own case was in the future. I went off, to Cardington I think, and enlisted as a trainee fighter pilot. That meant going home again to wait for calling into a training unit. I had a military number stamped all over my green civilian identity card and was, for some reason, paid four shillings and ninepence, which bought a round of drinks in the Clachan.

I opened up the new press office in Bedford House, Strand and tried to forget that I was a soldier, living on borrowed time. That was not entirely plain sailing with those numbers stamped in my card. Very late one night I was having a saveloy or something in an all-night café in Aldgate full of AWOLs and questionable types. One of them offered to sell me forged ration coupons and another a bulk supply of badges to show I had been discharged from the forces honourably. I had my first forkful and there was a police raid and a rush for the back door.

Professional Communist

A plain clothes policeman examining my identity card said, 'Have a look at this, Percy.' It was my military number. Percy came along and from over my shoulder said, 'Hallo, Alan!' He was a childhood neighbour, now an officer in the CID. A few minutes after, the police left and left me with the problem of getting out of that café. I did not waste any time, abandoning my sausage and change from ten shillings.

It was the first of many occasions when that military number brought me to the edge of trouble, because I had it throughout the war. Three months after enlisting, the twin of my call-up paper came through the door. This time the message was 'Services No Longer Required'. I was not RAF material.

No doubt each of the hundreds of street-corner meetings where I had spoken had been reported by the men in raincoats and my dossier had become so thick and heavy that a single glance had kept me from flying a Spitfire or any other means of pranging the House of Commons.

My stint as the first Press Officer of the British Communist Party came to an abrupt end nonetheless when Herbert Morrison was compelled by mass revolt within his own Labour and trade union ranks to lift the ban on the *Daily Worker*. In its absence half a million people had placed orders for it. Most of its skilled staff were in the services.

It was fairly obvious why Pollitt called me to see him. The Secretariat had decided, against Pollitt's opposition, so he said, that I must work at the *Daily Worker*. It was a desperate situation over there.

'I promise you solemnly that I'll get you back to work at the Party Centre at the first possible moment. Here's my hand on it. I never break a promise.'

Most of all I deplored crossing over to the *Daily Worker* because of the success of the new press office.

One of the most zealously spread verities about the British Communist Party was that it was kept afloat on a torrent of 'Moscow Gold'. If that were so, I never noticed its effects either in the standard of life of its leading figures or the condition of the linoleum which was in many places worn to the canvas.

Pollitt had an unusually developed ability to convince you that the impossible was a myth, or at any rate grossly overrated

– it was merely a little more difficult than the possible. In the case of the press office, the rent, light, postage and wages for myself and one assistant would come out of the kitty. For the rest, I was on my own.

On this basis there was little room for launching press statements with cocktail parties or any of the usual activities of the more well-endowed PRO. This in Pollitt's view was all to the good. There was the press – national and local – there was the Communist Party and its fellow travellers. Use one to penetrate the other – simple. Well, not simple but far from impossible.

The local press is far more carefully read, more intimate, more easy to approach with readers' letters, news items, reports of events, than national papers which are impervious to anything except what they think will sell papers. We rapidly set up a chain of local 'press officers' in party branches who were responsible to the central press office, and who to a considerable extent financed it.

From the Strand, we supplied much of what they needed to break into the local press – handouts, biographies, stereo blocks with portraits of visiting speakers, ideas or drafts for readers' letters, sample reports and a lot of enthusiasm as the people in the branches saw the column inches growing.

Fleet Street itself became our armoury. Through the Communist Party groups and anti-fascist sympathisers we had the run of newspaper libraries, art rooms and to a tiny extent their columns. Whatever we wanted, maps, drawings, posters, photographs, lettering, retouching, block and stereo making was all at our disposal free. The stereos we sent to the local branches were cast, quite improperly, by the process workers of national papers who would have gone on strike if asked to do the same for the employers.

It was hard to leave all that to become a journalist, which breed did not delight me though in those days they had not become so thick-skinned as they have today under the pressure of technique and competition.

Only one person could get me off the hook, Bill Rust, the *Daily Worker*'s editor, whom I had so far met only on the stairs. He was reputed to be cold, dour, able and domineering but, withal, had reported in Spain with the International Brigade. I went to him to make a final effort to escape. He was always well-dressed in hand-made suits passed on to him by a sympathetic business man.

I told Rust that I was not a journalist, had never worked on a newspaper but only a photo-agency, would be a drag on the paper and ought to stay where I was.

He heard all this with his tight-lipped smile and commented, 'Half a loaf is better than no bread.'

My misgivings were a lesson in how rumour can mislead. Rust and I never became friends – that was plain incompatibility – but I found him a good man to work with. I imagine that in Spain he was right up front there where the bullets were buzzing.

I had to readjust my opinions about journalists too. These, who had sacrificed good jobs for the sake of writing to suit their consciences, were among the best that Britain possessed, to mention only Claud Cockburn, Walter Holmes, George Sinfield and Allen Hutt.

This last was the best all-round journalist I ever met. He was a typographical phenomenon, a swift and certain editor and sub-editor and enormously erudite in everything related to print. Compositors, then the aristocrats of print, stood in awe of him. 'Our Al,' a random-hand once said to me, 'he only has to pick up a stick of type and look at it upside down and italic and says, "Ah, yes, old boy. Nuremburg 1857. Copied, of course. Has a bastard lower case J." He's a bleedin' miracle.'

In two terrible and almost sleepless weeks Hutt trained me as his deputy in the most exacting and expert editorial job of all – chief-sub-editor – usually regarded on the British press as needing years of tempering. After that, during the whole war, air-raids, buzz-bombs, V2s, 'the two Als' alternated in the chief-sub's chair, six days a week, forty-eight weeks a year, allowing each of us two weeks' holiday while the other carried all editions.

Our local was the Pindar of Wakefield and we would unwind there as the shrapnel tinkled in the company of Elsie, a cockney girl who spent her evenings and wages as a street sweeper downing brown ales. She was a barometer of public morale.

'Buzz-bombs,' she snorted once as a V1 landed not far away. 'Nasty unnatural things. Give me the old-fashioned blitz every time.'

Bill Rust was one of the rare political leaders who made a serious effort to understand the practical side of newspaper work and was lucky to have as his mentor a unique newspaper expert such as Hutt, who turned down many tantalising offers to cross over to the opposition press.

As a species, politicians appear to believe that there is really nothing to understand in journalism, architecture, art and indeed everything else except politics. One criterion seems to be that architectural grandiosity reflects success and being accustomed to ride about in cars, they prefer vast vistas where pubs don't exist and you need a moped to get from one shop to the next. One example is the dreadful ruination of Beijing's ancient glory. But Prague is a notable case of renovation done with love by architects.

When laymen dabble in journalism horrible things can happen. On the night that Mussolini abdicated, copy was pouring from the tape-machines, inundating the copy-taster – Duce's life story, military role, Berlin-Rome-Tokyo Axis, new leads, snaps, snap and pulls, rewrites.

Rust was out of town. There was just myself and one late sub-editor to re-jig the whole of page one, and no hope of rewriting the leader.

A swing-door banged and in came Claud Cockburn, known to our readers as Frank Pitcairn, saying in his slightly nasal Oxford honk, 'Big stuff, huh. Need any help?'

Before he came to the *Daily Worker*, Claud Cockburn had been Washington correspondent of *The Times* from which he had insisted on resigning, overriding the pleas of its editor, Geoffrey Dawson. He was a gifted writer with an intense and complex political brain, enormous charm, a fascinating raconteur and even more important, able to hold his whiskey far beyond the requirements of duty and still recall what had happened. He was constantly bringing in scoops which were mostly stories which other journalists dared not offer to their own editors.

He had heard the news on the eleven o'clock broadcast and left his Hampstead home at once. An engaged taxi came along and he stood in the road waving his arms to stop it. Ignoring the furious driver, he leaned in and said to an entwined couple, 'Frightfully sorry. Urgent ministry business. Simply must get to

Kings Cross. Could you? Would you?'

He was wearing as usual a frayed suit, scuffed shoes and reeked of alcohol and garlic which he got from the Free French, being friendly with de Gaulle. But it was dark and even in the dark, Claud had presence.

Now he sat at the subs' table, one knee under his chin, a cigarette drooping.

Harry Pollitt came in, bubbling with good cheer at the news.

Claud waved to him and went on turning out sides of copy, perfectly typed with one or two fingers and needing only to be marked up for the compositors.

Pollitt read the galleys and wrote changes on the side. I took them out to the comps very seriously and told the night printer to ignore them.

Claud's last side went through the slot.

'Headline?' I mused. ' "Mussolini Abdicates", I would say.'

'Simple and clear,' Claud said. 'Our readers are early birds. Won't have heard the late news. The fact is big enough. Doesn't need bells on it.'

Harry would have none of that. Such a big fact needed hammering home. He was drafting headlines full of honest anti-fascist fury.

'Hitler Next?' was his offering.

The night printer came in with a constipated look and asked sharply, 'How about the splash head, Al?'

Pollitt said, 'A few moments.'

'Think of the train, Al,' the printer said.

'This is no time to pull rank, Harry,' I said.

It was a difficult situation.

'This is good,' Harry said. ' "Duce Mussolini – The End".'

Claud and I shuddered. 'It isn't even true,' I said.

The printer decided, picked up the headline and queried it with an eyebrow. I nodded.

Next day we had the worst headline in Fleet Street over the best story. Mostly the headlines ran straight 'Mussolini Abdicates.' Rust rightly cursed me for allowing myself to be overruled.

I rang Harry and said, 'What a lousy headline!'

He laughed ruefully. 'Ah've learnt me lesson,' he said.

*

Six years of chief-sub-editing was enough for me. On an English paper the chief-sub has control, subject to rare intervention of the editor; he steers the paper through the writers, sub-editors and compositors until the last line of type drops into the forme – or that's how it was. A chief-sub knew how much capacity he had on the linotype machines and whether he could cope with an emergency without losing trains. He steered the boat over rapids for which he developed extra senses. Each day there were challenges.

Bill Rust never interfered with the judgment of Hutt and myself, but J.R. Campbell, Rust's deputy, and others who occasionally took that chair were ditherers, as many editors are, failing to realise the value of split seconds.

News of the Hiroshima bomb flashed over the tapes at about twenty minutes before deadline on a slack evening. With all those idling linotypes we could have changed the page-one lead with minutes to spare and I buzzed down to Johnnie Campbell who was on duty that I was going to do it. He came bustling upstairs, dithered in a Scottish kind of way and – too late – said go ahead.

We came out with the story of the bomb that was to change the world, as a single-column 'top'. I could have wept. Rust would have said 'okay' and started to write the second edition leading article. Admire him as I did, we parted on bad terms.

Work in a newspaper office can also be dull. Once you have mastered its complexities, it goes on much the same from day to day. I did not want to be in it and now I wanted to be out. It was possible. The war was two years over, staff had come back and I told Rust – it seemed polite – that I intended to ask Harry Pollitt to keep his promise.

Rust was a choleric – he died of a stroke a year later – and always put the paper first. He blew his top and, while Pollitt was away, got some kind of decision made that I must stay at the *Worker*.

I kept my fury till Pollitt was back. 'The saucy booger,' he said, somewhere between amusement and challenge. Rust fancied himself as next General Secretary and missed no chance of staking his claim.

Obviously I couldn't work with him now, I told Pollitt. Pollitt said there's more than one way to kill a cat. 'Go back to the *Worker* and leave it to me. I'll think something up.'

I wondered what. It would be absurd and wrong to clash with Rust over me. A few weeks later Harry sent for me.

'How'd you like to go abroad for the party?'

Other than those who went as troops, relatively few British people had been abroad. Those who could afford to were of specific types which had created throughout the world the image of the reserved, haughty Englishmen with unusual sexual habits and a habit of talking loudly in English wherever they were.

British Communists were in demand in the socialist countries to staff English-language news agencies and radio stations. Well, that would make a change. I nodded. 'I suppose that when I get back I can come back to King Street.'

Pollitt ignored that. 'You may not have the same feelings when I tell you where. It's a tough and dangerous job.'

He let that soak in. 'I can't so easily think of anyone else we can send and you wouldn't have to leave the *Worker* after all,' he added with a wicked smile. 'You could double as a correspondent.'

Pollitt's guile was flattering though transparent. It was a tough and dangerous job and he had immediately thought of you because you had the courage and talents needed which, it was implied, were not present in every Tom, Dick and Harry. It needed courage and loyalty and settled the other problem too …

'What, where, when, how long?' I asked, expecting 'Hungarian News Agency' as the answer.

Pollitt fixed my eye.

'China.'

I blushed, transfixed.

My God. The caves of Yenan; names like Mao Zedong, Chu De, Zhou Enlai, Lin Biao; veterans of the Long March; the Eighth Route Army.

'You mean it?'

'You'll have to decide fast. I've got them coming tomorrow. Well?'

'Of course. What's the job.'

'The Chinese Communist Party has asked us to lend them an experienced man to act as adviser or something to their information services. That's you.'

'How long?'

'No idea. Reckon at least six months. From now on you're in their hands.'

The next day I met a tall Chinese man and his woman interpreter. This definition did her less than justice since she, like him, had been working underground in Shanghai, dodging Chiang Kaishek's secret police, risking certain death if captured and death from torture at that.

He had an equine, lugubrious face like a shoe box, of which half was a narrow forehead. This was Liu Ningyi, illegal leader of the underground trade union movement in China. His colleague, a beautiful mother of two children whom she had to leave in Shanghai, spoke almost perfect English. Her name was Yü Zhiying.

They had brought off a quite extraordinary coup. Lying low somewhere in Soho, hiding from Chinatown thugs, was no less than Chu Xuefan, head of Chiang Kaishek's official 'trade unions' – the Chinese Association of Labour.

Chiang Kaishek had decided to try to rally support by calling his 'National Assembly' and among the most important delegates was to have been Chu Xuefan to represent the working class. Chu had long been collaborating with the Communists and agreed to disappear – indeed things were getting a little tense.

He, Liu and Yü escaped to Hongkong, where Chu barely escaped with his life from a staged motor accident. On their way through London on faked papers, they had instructions to pick someone up and I happened to be lucky.

They were going via London, Prague, Moscow to Harbin in Manchuria, the largest Chinese city then in Communist hands. Facing each other across the Sino-Soviet border on a branch of the trans-Siberian railway were a little Soviet town called Otpur and a Chinese one no bigger called Manzhouli, which Liu Ningyi assured me was managed by a Mr Chang, to whom he gave me a letter.

He also told me that in Gerrard Street lived a Mr Ching who would buy me a plane ticket to Prague and give me £25 – the maximum one could take out of post-war Britain. This was expected to get me to Moscow from where the Soviet trade unions would look after me and get me to China.

My Chinese colleagues had overlooked a vital fact: that the Soviet government had diplomatic relations with Chiang Kaishek's authorities. There was, in fact, no Chinese Communist government at that time.

An extremely helpful Soviet embassy official said that they would do all they could to help the Chinese Communist comrades, whom they loved, and the British comrades whom they loved too, but a Soviet transit visa, stamped into a British passport, permitting me to cross into a Communist-held Manchuria, would be international dynamite.

'Suppose,' he said, 'you died on the journey or, even worse, had your passport stolen.'

He thought for a moment and went on, 'I have a suggestion. You could easily get a Kuomintang visa to enter China at Shanghai. Then I could give you a transit visa to cross the Soviet Union by the trans-Siberian, leaving by sea by the northern route via Khabarovsk and Vladivostock.'

'But,' I said, 'that will not take me to Harbin.'

'Once you are in Moscow, Comrade Winnington, you must use your initiative.'

5
En Route to China

Whether or not you are superstitious, there is a case for believing in luck, whatever it is. An old Cockney friend would say on occasion about a third party, 'Luck, Al. Stone me, luck. If 'e was to fall into a karzi [toilet], 'e'd come up wiv a pianner rahnd 'is neck.' Why piano? I took it that in his day, a piano represented the peak of upper-working-class status.

As the next period unrolled, I felt a certain kinship with that lucky piano finder. My transit visa for Vladivostock was delayed. Never mind, it finally came at a lucky moment. Twice I reached the end of the runway and was turned back. Trouble in Prague. The twelve Czechoslovak bourgeois ministers had resigned in a trial of strength with the Communist-led government.

On the third attempt, the plane lifted and I, my two suitcases and duffle coat converged on Prague ten years after Munich and at another historic moment. Workers were jamming the streets, armed and determined to ensure that Benes would not sell the country again, this time for Marshall Aid.

I knew nobody in Prague, nobody's address anyway. During the war a quiet, charming Czech refugee had wandered round the *Daily Worker* office helping to advise on European affairs. He was Ludwig Freund and I think he was the first Communist elected to the Czech parliament before the war.

I found my way to the Communist Party's office and was standing forlornly among my suitcases in the middle of a revolution wondering what to do when I felt a tap on my shoulder. It was Ludwig, now in charge of economy and 'able to pay back a little of what you all did for me'.

At the bottom of the Wenceslas Square we heard Klement

En Route to China

Gottwald announce that President Beneš had, under pressure but without any violence, formed a government with a majority of Communists and Gottwald as premier. Ludwig drove me round to the back entrance of the main telegraph office and told the staff that the first cable on this piece of history must be sent by the *Daily Worker* correspondent. It was also my first ever cable to the paper and it was a world-wide exclusive for a few minutes, though as such useless to a daily paper. But Ludwig was happy.

'Moscow by train,' Ludwig scoffed. 'Three days on hard seats in sub-zero weather. No restaurant car. There's been a war, you know. Your £25 dropped into the right hand ...'

We spent the evening in Prague pubs and wine bars, dancing and embracing with hilarious citizens who ten years earlier had lived through the bitterness of Munich.

It was still dark when Ludwig woke me in my dingy hotel near *Rude Pravo* and pushed me, unshaved, into his official car.

'I've done it,' he said. 'But for God's sake keep your head down and your tongue still. Not one word. If anyone speaks to you, don't answer. I'm going to smuggle you on Zorin's own plane.'

V.A. Zorin, who had been the Soviet ambassador in Prague from 1945 to 1947 and was now Deputy Foreign Minister, had been in Prague during the days of crisis and was flying back to Moscow.

From the rear of the unheated military plane I waved my last goodbyes to my old friend and fellow worker on the paper. His ghost haunts many of my favourite pubs in Prague and London. He was executed soon after – a victim of Beria in the infamous Slansky affair.

Zorin and the rest of the brass in front occasionally opened a bottle of vodka to wash down the salami and smoked fish. By general consent I was invisible, thanks to Ludwig no doubt, sitting in the last seat. They were huddled in fur hats and magnificent coats, sunk in their seats, but still the cold got to them in the unheated plane. My English duffle-coat was good, but not good enough.

At dusk we landed. I remained unseen, standing watching as

Breakfast with Mao

my fellow travellers and crew were driven away in big cars, leaving me on an apparently deserted airport in a blizzard. The airplane made little noises as it cooled. I jumped up and down and ate some snow. Two hundred yards away, just visible, there were some buildings.

On the way I had to keep putting down my suitcases to rub my ears. I padded round, pushed open a door and fell inwards. I kept shouting into the dark silence until some astonished guards came tumbling out of somewhere warm and light, hurrying into great-coats and readying machine-pistols.

They brought a girl, seemingly the sole civilian staff and she spoke a few words of French. It was hard going but she slowly gathered that I was an *Anglichyni* wanting to get to Moscow. An hour or so passed.

She came back with the horrifying information that a '*machina*' from the British Embassy was waiting in the snowstorm outside to take me to Moscow. I had failed to tell her that I was travelling under cover.

She was rightly expecting a pat on the back for her success and became amazed and indignant at my unexpected cries of '*nyet*' and '*non, non, non, je vous prie. Je suis un Communiste Anglais,*' and so on. Luck stayed with me. I had not given her my name and she finally agreed to try again.

Much later she came back, '*Intourist? Machina Intourist? C'est bien?*'

For the first time I smelled that oniony petrol that I came to associate with Moscow. There weren't many lights about, post-war no doubt, till we got to the warm, plushy interior of the Savoy Hotel where there was a reception committee of three. Both men said nothing; the woman who sat at a big desk, could only be described as formidable. She was statuesque, clad in black with a large high bosom, black hair parted in the middle and coiled over her ears.

She did not ask to see my passport.

'I am here at the invitation of the trade unions. Name Winnington. I would ...'

'Nothing can be done tonight but you may stay here. If it is a trick, I shall inform the police. One of these gentlemen will show you to your room.'

'I am very hungry and I have no money.'

'The restaurant is there,' she waved a hand and a waft of perfume followed.

We dumped my bags in the suite by the famous stuffed bear and I went into the restaurant. It did not shame its namesake – polished silver, cut-glass vodka carafes, starched linen hard to unfold, a fountain, a band playing old-fashioned dance music to which soldiers, mostly of low rank, danced with girls in their best clothes. They brought me caviar, smoked salmon, Russian salads, half a dozen kinds of bread, a carafe of vodka on which the frost was forming, beer, wine.

Now that I was here, I supposed, Intourist had decided that I should have my way at the table and when the world woke up, I would either be thrown to the sharks or given a medal.

I was wrong. Restraining my appetite to leave space for the main dishes, I looked up and saw a young woman standing at my table. I stood up, full of curiosity and hope, and she said in English, 'May I sit down?'

She refused a drink.

'You are Mr Alan Winnington?'

Her handbag was on her lap and she opened it.

'Please be so kind as to lean forward and put your hand under the table.'

She too leaned forward and I felt a thick roll of paper pressed into my hand.

'Please do not look. It is money. Enough. Please do not discuss your business with anyone except Comrade Zuzin of the trade unions who will come and see you after breakfast which I suggest you take in your suite.

'By the way, there is a performance of *Swan Lake* at the Bolshoi Theatre tomorrow evening. Would you like to go?'

'Indeed, yes. Perhaps you could keep me company.'

'So sorry. I have an appointment with my husband. Comrade Zuzin will go with you. Goodnight. Pleasant dreams.'

'Is this a dream?'

She smiled, shook hands and went.

Long live Liu Ningyi and Comrade Zuzin, I said, steadying myself on the stuffed bear as I went to bed. It was not forty hours after I had left London.

The Soviet trade unions gave me a wooden box filled with

black bread, salami, cheese, butter and ten bottles of vodka – the old sort with tiny corks which fly out if you smack them hard on the bottom. Reassuring himself, I think, Comrade Zuzin said, 'This train has no restaurant car but there are restaurants at the bigger stations.'

Splendid restaurants they were, serving splendid food, but never once did I get a meal in one. The trans-Siberian's longest halt was forty minutes. Russians eating out don't go for a quick snack, it is an event, among potted palms and six-piece bands and the service is geared to this. Citizens with all the time in the world sat enjoying great portions of this and that while I waited for my soup. Sometimes it arrived just before the train started screaming at us to get aboard, usually synchronously. I still wake in panic recalling when the train once suddenly disappeared with all my possessions and passport. It had gone somewhere to see a man about a dog, but came back. I never let it out of reach again.

It ought to be counted as a miracle that the trans-Sib ran at all – with heated international-class compartments – so soon after the war. A restaurant car would have made it voluptuous.

And if ten bottles of vodka does not amount to much on a ten day journey over endless snow, there was always a woman parading along the corridor with a pail of vodka and a *stogram* ladle.

At Chita I left the main line and took a train to Otpur, now the last station before crossing the border to Manzhouli in China.

At Otpur the trade unions apparently ran out of clout.

There was a dapper colonel of the border guard with the world's biggest book of phrases in six languages compiled before the revolution. He seemed to like the useful phrase 'Wherrr iss your rrrevolverrr?' In that book a gentleman carried a pistol.

I drew his attention to Manzhouli, a mile or two away through the barbed wire. It did not exist. Tovarich Chang did not exist. Liu Ningyi did not exist. He did not even query why I had no Soviet entry visa. I had to go via Vladivostock and that was reached by Khabarovsk. Thus, I must return to Chita. The train was waiting and I must be on it.

As talismans, I suppose, and in fury, I left my suitcases with the colonel and arrived at Chita's sole hotel without a change of clothes and with nothing to read. There was no bathroom and the toilet proclaimed its presence far afield.

Chita was pure *Anna Karenina* – giant wood-burning locomotives hissed steam, log houses with fretted eaves lay almost buried in unsullied crackling snow. How I regretted my books! Each day the Chita Communist Party secretary came for his second breakfast and shook his head. I went to the barber shop, then to the tiny cinema to see the same film again. The bookshop had two English language tuition books, each of fifty pages: *Huckleberry Finn* and *Nicholas Nickelby*. Each evening a six piece band entertained the guests and after a long meal I could stagger up to bed and hope to sleep.

After eight days of this I had come to the conclusion that something had gone wrong. Somewhere along the line a voice had been raised in query: what is this man about – wandering round Chita without luggage in an English duffle-coat, Russian hat and felt boots and with wads of roubles? He came in on V.A. Zorin's plane with other Soviet officials, he has never gone through our passport control, the whole thing was arranged by a Sudetan German *émigré* from Britain where they were close colleagues and he is trying to get into Communist-held Manchuria.

But then the scene changed. The local Communist Party secretary came in smiling. Everything had clicked into place. The Otpur colonel recovered his sight. Manzhouli appeared on the map. Once more he asked to see my rrrevolverr and did not expect a response. But he brought vodka and black bread and we solemnly shook hands. He took my roubles and gave me a receipt. I looked inside my passport. Nothing had changed. I had, officially, neither entered nor left the Soviet Union but had an unused Soviet transit visa and an unused Kuomintang entry visa.

Looking through rows of barbed wire toward Manzhouli there was no sign of a road or a vehicle and I would need, I thought, to haul my two suitcases along the track. Then the huge locomotive hissed forward, unhitched from the train; an open truck was hooked behind and in the middle of that they put a kitchen chair and my suitcases. I rattled eastwards through no man's-land, the personal heir of Genghis Khan.

Breakfast with Mao

Five minutes later we stopped at a deserted railway station and the driver climbed down to help with the cases. We split the rest of the vodka and the great machine rolled back into the Soviet Union, emitting some whistles as it went.

6
Arriving at Nothing

Not one of China's then reputed five hundred million people was to be seen. Not a bird sang. Not a sound disturbed the frozen sunlight. I expected nothing particularly but I did not expect – nothing. It was anti-climax but it was cheering that the Russians and the Chinese Communists now felt no need to guard this long disputed frontier. It seemed to confirm that, diplomatic needs apart, the Russians' hearts were on the side of the People's Liberation Army.

Heaving up my suitcases, I went toward the station buildings, looking I suppose like a Russian with my Moscow fur cap and felt *valinki*. Two Chinese soldiers came out, saluted, and said something. They wore big hats of dog or wolf skin; washed-out, khaki quilted-cotton uniform, puttees and padded cloth shoes. I held out my letter for Mr Chang.

Before they had a chance to take it, a flat-topped cart pulled by a Mongolian pony came racing into the station, driven by a similarly dressed man, standing on the rocking platform.

Mr Chang in person.

He read the letter and said '*Hao*'. There our conversation ended. He made signs for eating. I made signs for taking a bath and he led the way into the engine sheds, picking up some soap and two not very clean towels on the way. We stripped and he stepped between the rails, turned a handwheel and with a screech leapt from under a scalding shower used to wash the carriages. One side of him was bright red. When he got the temperature right I had my first bath since Moscow. There was nothing to see in Manzhouli and we ate at the only restaurant, where a clockwork gramophone ground out two old foxtrots and two White Russian women offered to dance, probably also being available for other services.

Nearby a locomotive was oozing steam at all joints. A single closed-in goods-wagon was hooked on and a soldier was guarding it. Inside were two beds, one for my guard, a table, a washbasin and a small towel. My brief acquaintance with Mr Chang ended there.

We rattled through the inner-Mongolian night. Japan had been defeated over two years ago and was now – no longer as an enemy – helping the Americans and Chiang Kaishek to fight the Chinese Communists. To ease Chiang's path, Washington sent General George C. Marshall as mediator.

Stalin was reported to have commented drily that if any man could mediate the situation in China perhaps it might be Marshal but not even he could bring the Chinese together under Chiang Kaishek.

It hardly needed the brain of a Stalin to see that Marshall's job was to delay while men and arms were redeployed against the Chinese Communists. But later evidence showed that Stalin also knew that the Chinese Communist Party leadership was split along a fissure that was constantly to open, close and reopen through the decades, and always on one side were Mao Zedong and Zhou Enlai.

Most of the Chinese Communist Party leaders ridiculed the view that mediation was possible with 'the US imperialists'. Meetings with the Americans caused ground to be lost said people like Chen Yi (later Foreign Minister) and Peng Dehuai (later Defence Minister). America wanted to keep Chiang in power as an instrument against the Soviet Union.

In an interview with an American diplomat, John S. Service, Mao Zedong had strongly emphasised the common interests of America and China. Service reported Mao as saying:

> America needs an export market for her heavy industry and these specialised manufactures. She also needs an outlet for capital investment. China needs to build up light industries to supply her own market and raise the living standard of her own people ... America is not only the most suitable country to assist this economic development of China: she is also the only country fully able to participate.

Mao held out the prospect of fifty years of a 'democratic'

China with strong capitalist features. Russia, 'licking her wounds', would not be in any condition to help the Chinese Communists, he said.

He and Zhou privately suggested that talks in Washington would be useful but the Americans simply ignored this, evidently preferring to stay with the devil they knew.

It would have taken political foresight of the highest level to predict that Chiang Kaishek, having American support, could be defeated by unkempt guerrillas and even if that estimation had been made it would have needed a political wizard to get the idea of co-operation with Communists accepted in the US.

The Mao-Zhou proposal must have seemed like a diversion rather than an offer of that collaboration, which had to wait almost thirty years for Nixon to seal it, with Mao gaga, Zhou a dying man and China in chaos.

Throughout, the Communist Party went on with its stated aims of preparing for a real coalition with Chiang if it could be got or to continue fighting if it could not.

Seen through American, Nationalist Chinese and Japanese eyes, there could be little doubt that, as soon as everything was mediated into position, the annihilation of the Communists would not present a problem. The Kuomintang warlords who had been sitting out the war against the Japanese could turn all their energies and American and Japanese weapons against the Communists and restore their control over their domains.

Some counting of chickens seemed justified. America still had a monopoly of the atomic bomb. This would be enough to ensure that the Russians must pull out from Manchuria according to agreement. Chinese Kuomintang troops would push the Communists out of the spaces left by the Soviet withdrawal and Washington would control, through Chiang Kaishek, the entire Chinese land mass and its 4,000 mile border with the Soviet Union. As the US Military Attaché to Chungking summed it up, 'The Chinese Communists are no match for the Central Government [Kuomintang] troops acting with American assistance.'

Who could doubt this? By 1946, Chiang Kaishek had 4.3 million troops with modern arms and an area with an estimated population of 300 million – actually more. The Communists had built up their regulars, with variegated captured arms to about one million, plus local militia of perhaps two million, 'armed with gaspipe muzzle-loaders and sharpened sticks' a US adviser said. The areas they controlled were scattered and reckoned to have 135 million people.

After the Japanese capitulation, Japanese troops were ordered on no account to surrender to Communist forces. Overnight, Americans, Nationalists (Kuomintang), Chinese warlords who had collaborated with the Japanese and the Japanese enemy themselves had joined forces. The sole enemy was the now Chinese People's Liberation Army (PLA).

But the farcical mediations were still going when, on 22 July 1946, the forces under Chiang Kaishek began an all-out civil war, moving into the Communist-held areas behind American bombers, tanks and artillery.

The PLA faded from the towns into the countryside, keeping on the pressure. They even abandoned their old headquarters at Yenan. Chu De later said to me, 'Towns can be recaptured, lost troops are lost.' Entire Kuomintang units took their weapons and crossed to the PLA which was arming itself with the best weapons originally intended for use against the Japanese. With the PLA went the land reform. Peasants joined the militia.

As General Chu De left Yenan to the blockading Kuomintang army under General Hu Congnan he told some older peasants remaining in the deserted town, 'We shall not be gone long.'

By the time my luxury cattle-truck rattled into Harbin late in March 1948, the Kuomintang forces had been reduced to 3.6 million. The PLA had grown to 2.8 million and held 529 of the towns that had cost Chiang so many men and so much equipment. Chiang still disposed of more men – better equipped men – but he had almost no idea what to do with them.

Meeting my train, Liu Ningyi and Yü Zhiying had brought with them General Lin Biao, Commander of that most famous PLA force – the Eighth Route Army. They were all very cheerful.

This storm had been centuries gathering. From time to time its component elements had coalesced and been dispersed, elements which were the essence of China's life, vested in the downtrodden, misgoverned, frugal, courteous, hard-working, patient, cheerful, tolerant and basically democratic peasantry. Now they were flowing together.

Arriving at Nothing

The lot of the Chinese peasant had not always been so grim as in the recent centuries. For almost two thousand years until the end of the Ming dynasty, China's population had been almost static at fifty or sixty millions. Its peasants, downtrodden as they were, could still subsist after their feudal betters had taken the cream.

At about the time that King Charles lost his head, the Manchus swarmed south and conquered China. At the end of the Manchu (Ching) dynasty in 1911 the population was reckoned to be over four hundred million. Pressure on the land became unbearable, creating extreme economic polarisation.

There had been endless encroachments by imperial powers, the forced import of opium – hitherto unknown in China – and export of silver to pay for it; the destruction of Chinese crafts by cheap manufactures; a chain of revolts leading to more severe repression.

The Taiping uprising that swept through China in the middle of the last century was at once the last of the peasant wars and the first of the modern struggles which culminated a hundred years later in the Chinese People's Republic. It began near the Vietnamese border, advanced to within reach of Beijing and Shanghai and into Tibet, establishing the Taiping Tian Guo (The Heavenly Kingdom of Great Peace) with its capital at Nanking. Its leader, Hong Xiuchuan, had come into contact with Christianity and declared himself to be the younger brother of Christ.

After fifteen years the Taiping Revolution was drowned in blood by a combination of imperialist powers and the Manchus, but it gave rise to a tradition that inspired Sun Yatsen in the belief that the future lay with the common people.

In 1948 the fruits of long struggle and 'eating bitterness' again hung heavy on the bough and it seemed that the military successes of the Taipings were about to be repeated in a new form, bearing a similar message. Where the Taipings had gone they destroyed the authority of the regime, deposed its officials, distributed the wealth of the exploiters to the poor, created a popular army which worked when it was not fighting, abolished slavery, stopped prostitution, footbinding and the sale of women in marriage.

Although Hong Xiuchuan called himself Christ's younger

brother, the Taiping Tien Guo was not religious. In Chinese tradition there was no idea of waiting for a Messiah but rather for a Robin Hood, a daredevil bandit who would take from the rich and give to the poor. They saw that figure in every grey-green PLA soldier with his rifle stopped with a plug of rag, his bag of parched meal, battered tin-cup and spoon, towel drying on his belt and often a pen in his breast pocket.

Chinese lore is of popular heroes, tiger-killing supermen, leading the downtrodden, strong in the blood-brotherhood of outlawry. Those who joined the PLA saw themselves in the light of that epic Chinese romantic novel, *All Men are Brothers* or *The Water Margin*. In contrast to the marauding Kuomintang soldiery, the disciplined PLA paid their way, left a village cleaner than they found it, dug irrigation works, reclaimed land, helped with harvesting and never took 'a needle or a piece of thread' from the *lao bai xing* (Old Hundred Names – the common people). In the tradition of Liu Pang, peasant founder of the great Han Dynasty and Kuan Kung, the innkeeper, who became a famous general during the Three Kingdoms; PLA soldiers sought self-sacrifice, despised danger, took pride in honesty and loyalty. It was so. Such exaltation is rare in life.

The Soviet forces which had demolished the Japanese Kwantung Army had left Manchuria two years before I arrived there. It was the hiatus between Hiroshima and the development by the Russians of their own atomic bomb – a time for walking on tiptoe. Western hawks, and even muddleheads like Russell, argued for the threat or use of the A-bomb to gain ascendancy for the West while there was time and Russia was 'still licking her wounds'.

Amid the talk of settling with Russia now, suggestions were made that if Chiang Kaishek's troops happened to clash with Soviet forces, there would be a clear case for making use of America's atomic capability. For the Russians nothing was to be gained by waiting about in Manchuria, so they withdrew in March 1946, taking with them the enormous military arsenal which the Japanese had established for invading the Soviet Union and which Moscow had no intention to leave, possibly to fall into the hands of Chiang Kaishek, the Americans or even the Japanese forces they had just defeated.

Arriving at Nothing

Manchuria was not part of China formerly. It was a barbarian area outside the Great Wall. Beijing's 'historic' map-drawing is not always convincing therefore. The 'uncivilised' Manchus who conquered China and established the Ching dynasty prevented the Hans – the majority of the people known as Chinese – from migrating to the rich Manchurian plains. The Hans only flooded northward after the overthrow of the Ching Dynasty in 1911. They soon became the majority of the Manchurian population which otherwise consists of Manchus, Mongolians and Koreans.

Harbin was the biggest town in Communist hands – a big rail hub built by the Tsars, much fought about but hardly damaged. It was an exciting town, especially at night, snow-padded, mournful with the sirens of shunting engines, ice creaking and exploding out on the Sungari River. Sometimes Kuomintang agents loosed off a burst of automatic fire, unconvinced and unconvincing.

Spring came and remnants of snow piles trickled dirtily. Women sat in the sunshine, spinning, making quilts, stitching shoes for the army. Grey-green haystacks of uniforms grew in every open space. Bronzed peasants – become landowners under the new reform – drilled, bayoneted sacks and squatted listening to instructors. All day long, potato-masher grenades arched overhead.

The dusty shelves of the British Consular Club in Harbin housed thousands of jolly good solid books to help me through the lonely evenings; a hard tennis court and some soft racquets provided an occasional game of pat ball; there was a bar with no drinks and a dance floor. Most of the top people had acquired the habit of Saturday night dancing in Yenan and on my proposal – dreaming foolishly of making feminine contact – we spent one evening shuffling stiff-armed round to the music of an old wind-up gramophone, sipping hot water and nibbling sunflower seeds.

The men were high-up political and military figures and the women were powerful young army girls, ruthlessly energetic and built like Mongolian ponies. They did the inviting, sweeping you straight on to the floor and maintaining a spinning velocity without time or rhythm. Feminine contact was markedly absent; it was an extension of road-work.

There was one exception, Mao Zedong's third wife, Ho Zizheng, who had spent some time having medical treatment in Moscow and seemed to have learned to dance there. She looked quite frail but they told me she could use a pistol equally well with both hands. She bore five of Mao's children, one on the Long March, and he divorced her over the objections of the Political Bureau to marry Lan Ping, a minor Shanghai film actress, whom he renamed Jiang Qing – later the termagant leader of the Red Guards.

This dance party was not repeated. Disciplinarians launched an attack on the event as frivolous and likely to bring the Communist Party into disrepute since dancing was associated with prostitution. Sackcloth and ashes were noisily donned and the spartan life was resumed.

One of my jobs each day was to edit the morse-cast from far away North Shensi, get into a droshky and trot round to the radio station to read it. There was no way to find out whether anyone was receiving it. Many years later I met Guy Burgess in Moscow and found that he had read my Harbin reports in the Foreign Office in London, where they found them 'accurate and objective' he said.

We *ganbu* (usually translated as cadre) ate according to three ranks, the great majority in the bottom one, eating the same food as the army rank and file – boiled sorghum or millet porridge or steamed cornmeal loaves as heavy as stone, some pickles, vegetable soup and a little soya bean curd (*dofu*). Being intellectuals, most of the Xinhua News Agency people had digestive troubles but the fact was that they were eating not only better than the *lao bai xing* – they were eating.

The chief of my office was a young martinet whom I will call Liu Sun, whose rank put him into the middle 'kitchen' where there was a little meat. I was in the top rank, like a general, with rice or noodles and two dishes to each meal. What I missed was alcohol.

Liu Sun's wife had been caught by the SACO – the Sino-American Co-operation Organisation – which was run by Chiang Kaishek's Gestapo with US help and therefore had scientific methods of torture. She had been picked up while working underground against Chiang. Capture was the worst thing that could happen to a Chinese Communist cadre. Either they died under torture or if they did not die it was assumed that they had talked and therefore they would never again be trusted. Catch 22. She did not die and was set free by the PLA. But it was common, when the Communists were advancing, for SACO and other Kuomintang people to try to save their skins by treating their prisoners well. It did not help her. She steadily denied having broken down under torture; indeed she said she had not been tortured at all owing to her captors trying to ingratiate themselves. But Liu Sun insisted on a divorce.

The chief medical officer of the most famous PLA Army – the Eighth Route Army (officially the North-East PLA) under Lin Biao – was not a Chinese at all. He was a urologist, an Austrian Communist and a Jew. Understandably he fled to Shanghai but he wanted to do more than sit the war out. Helped by the Chinese Communists he got to Cheefoo in Shandong, landed in Japanese-occupied territory disguised as a high Nazi officer and got through the lines.

I met him by accident as I was clopping along the Harbin cobbles in my droshky. A jeep passed me containing not merely a 'big nose' (as I was too, in Chinese) but a man whose nose was big by any standards. He was dressed as a Chinese general and his personal guard was of high rank. We were all amazed.

He was Dr Jack Rosenfeld and became a friend of rare congeniality, knew everybody, spoke English and Chinese and, according to General Lin Biao, had a natural genius for organising military medicine as well as many connections with Shanghai – both among criminal criminals and official criminals in the higher ranks of the Kuomintang.

From them, anything could be got for gold bars. Drugs made the difference between life and death in battle, but they were regarded as far too valuable to be squandered on press-ganged soldiery. Most American and UNRRA medicines eventually found their way to the Communist forces.

On occasions Dr Lo (Ro) organised entire train-loads of medical supplies through the lines or, acting on information, arranged for PLA forces to capture consignments.

He was also a competent surgeon but almost landed in trouble over a vasectomy he performed on Lo Runghuan, Lin

Biao's political commissar. Soon after, much to everybody's concern, the commissar's wife found herself pregnant again. I met Jack, rather perturbed, on his way to do a D & C. He explained how tests showed the commissar to be still fertile. It sounded feasible.

Dr Rosenfeld suffered from disease of the coronary artery and once described to me the pain and sweating fear of death when he awoke at night with an attack. He never rested in spite of this. A good deal has been written about the spectacular and irascible Dr Norman Bethune, and no doubt with justice, but there never seems to have been anything written about Dr Lo or a single word of official praise for him, though he just as surely gave his life for the Chinese Revolution by working day and night when his sole hope of prolonging his life lay in rest and care.

He was angry when he heard about my living conditions. 'Typical intellectuals. Trying to prove themselves holier than the pope. Harbin is full of captured American coffee, pipe tobacco, bourbon, all the things the Chinese don't like and I can't have with my weak heart.' He cited cases of PLA men opening coffee tins, throwing the coffee away and using the tins as cooking pots.

His intervention brought my first official visit from commander Lin Biao. Considering his reputation on the battlefield, he was an unimpressive figure, apart from his thick black eyebrows. He was followed by bodyguards carrying cases of beer, bourbon, coffee, corned beef, chocolates and tobacco and reprimanded Liu Sun for not taking proper care of a foreign comrade. Liu was told to provide any money I needed and not to wait to be asked. I was given the honorary rank of general and a personal bodyguard, a dour Manchurian named Jia Yulin who possessed a big wolf-skin hat and a long-barrelled Mauser with a wooden holster which turned it into a machine-pistol. Money was superfluous but my new status and wealth meant that I could throw parties and finance boozy swimming picnics on the Sungari River.

Jack realised that he could not live long and he worried that his heart might not carry him as far as the capture of Beijing. At that time, the summer of 1948, it was being assumed for public consumption that it would take up to five more years to finish the war.

I was at Dr Lo's place one day when Lin Biao called in. He

said, 'No. The Old Man [Commander-in-Chief Chu De] prefers to spread the idea of a long war and it is also what Chiang Kaishek wants to believe. But we can't afford to wait. Our worry is no longer Chiang but the Americans.'

'How long?' Jack asked.

'Not a year,' answered Lin Biao.

With Jack translating I asked Lin Biao, 'Couldn't the Russians help the Chinese Communists more?'

'That's the last thing we want. Direct military help would stir a hornet's nest. We want to go on quietly getting ready. The Russians can help us most by just being there and accidentally protecting our rear.' He gave a little smile.

'They wiped out the Japanese Kwantung Army and handed us over all those weapons; they provide a safe base for what is going to be our final drive. Make no mistake – but for the Soviet Union, we could not win.'

7
With the Chinese Red Army

Most civilians have probably sometimes wondered what makes a good general or even whether there is such a thing. Napoleon, when asked a question on such lines replied, 'Well, you join battle and then you see.' Ultimately there may be something of that sort involved, but stated just like that it sounds slightly haphazard.

The face of the man on our side whose job it was to join battle – C-in-C Chu De – gazed down from photos on walls everywhere: homely, craggy, full of simple good nature, like a lump of hurriedly modelled clay.

There was nothing to indicate why he was chosen as leader of an array of tested generals who had all achieved fame in decades of battles. That shy, diffident grin could have belonged to any peasant. But inside his brain must have been a changing picture of all the dispositions of men and material; the landscapes and possibilities of movement all over the map; the pattern of the war in its ebb and flow and totality.

Jinzhou on the map was a medium rail-town south of Mukden, heavily garrisoned but presenting no particular problem in the taking were it not for a single condition laid down by Chu De in an order to Lin Biao:

'TAKE JINZHOU ELIMINATING EIGHTEEN DIVISIONS AND THE CHINESE SITUATION IS IN OUR HANDS END'

On that September day in 1948 the starting gun was fired for the liquidation of Chinese feudalism.

Lin's assault on Jinzhou took the garrison unawares. In a few days the town was taken with a loss not of eighteen but of twenty divisions. Hardly pausing, Lin Biao pushed north and took Changchun. Shenyang was bracketed, its garrison fled, were blocked and surrendered.

In six weeks three major Manchurian cities had been captured and almost half a million Kuomintang troops had been put out of action. All links between the Kuomintang forces in Manchuria and those south of the Great Wall had been severed. The opposing armies had been equalised at about three million each. From the staff point of view, Harbin was finished: we left by every available means for Shenyang.

In Shenyang the merchants proved more tenacious than the Kuomintang army. Inside the blockaded city where the people lay starving in the streets, the godowns were full of grain and merchants were making paper fortunes in the new 'Gold Yuan', devised by Chiang Kaishek's son to skim another layer from the milk.

Chen Yun's job was to sort out the economic mess. He was a small bony man with a falcon's nose and laughing eyes and the sole industrial worker in the Chinese Communist Party's leadership. He had studied in Moscow and was the unchallenged economics expert in the Communist Party until the late fifties when he opposed Mao's Great Leap and went into obscurity.

Grain was moving toward Shenyang by every means of transport, even shoulder-poles. State grain shops were already opened and selling grain in any quantity at low prices. Well-heeled speculators were buying it, trying to corner it.

Chen Yun dropped in to see me at the Yamato Hotel (the city had been Japanese) and said that the grain merchants had no idea how much grain was available. 'It isn't much, though.'

'But can't you commandeer it?'

He said that would be possible. But what an operation! 'We'll have to see if they lose their nerve before our supplies run out. Much better to let them store it and sell it for us.'

The Gold Yuan was beautifully printed in the US but was already being used for toilet-paper. Chen Yun went ahead and bought it with People's Yuan, lowering its value too. But, as he pointed out, there has to be money and the people have to get it. So he paid a 'fair price' and, using his contacts with Shanghai gangsters, sent the Gold Yuan through the front where it accelerated the inflation in the Kuomintang areas.

With an event like the fall of Shenyang all to myself, I had a journalist's dream to carve up a package into suitable portions for my own paper and for the Chinese information services, taking all the time and space I needed. I was wrong. Chiang Kaishek was making the same mistake, too.

Down south, in a little village far below Beijing, Chu De was doing his sums and, having worked out what the enemy would forecast he, Chu, would do, went right ahead and did some other thing.

Not merely an unimaginative, arrogant dictator like Chiang Kaishek – whom General Stilwell dubbed The Peanut and others still more rudely Chancre Jack – but even farsighted commanders would consider it necessary for Lin Biao to sort his situation out a bit.

He had not paused to digest almost half a million surrendered Kuomintang troops who largely had crossed over to the PLA, plus the captured stores, weapons and other booty. He had not even met the North China commanders to co-ordinate plans.

In that situation Chu De picked up his writing brush and wrote a dozen characters which were transposed into one of those uncrackable Chinese codes and sent to Lin Biao:

'DO NOT WAIT. MARCH ON BEIJING AT ONCE.'

The Kuomintang general commanding the North China army was America's darling, Fu Cuoyi, the man and the area which had the best of everything available and which included Beijing.

Up to now Chu De's tactics had been classical – good but ordinary. Napoleonic perhaps. Now they took on the shape of genius.

To move the Manchurian PLA southward – with its booty and prisoners – and reorganise it for enormous battles on the North China Plain must have seemed to the Kuomintang and their American advisers a logistical task allowing them all the time in the world to prepare.

The Old Man, however, took into account features of the situation which General Fu and his advisers did not know existed and would not have regarded as important if they had.

By ordering a forced march of six hundred miles Chu De

could scarcely have struck a more encouraging chord. It recalled The Long March – that epic of the thirties. In the PLA there were those who had taken part in the Long March and the later comers who – unalterably – had not, and felt this as a defect. A Long Marcher had something of the aura of those who had fought in the International Brigade in Spain. The March on Beijing, too, had a fine ring to it; something to tell the little grandchildren.

Also overlooked by General Fu was that the prisoners were not prisoners, they did not regard themselves as prisoners and were not called prisoners but *jiefang-le* – liberated. They were peasants like the rest of the PLA. They had been press-ganged into the Kuomintang army and now they had a chance to fight their way back home and take part in the land reform when they got there.

Spirits were high as the exodus got under way, as though it was all a great celebration and a mere picnic to cover six hundred miles in twenty days and do so with their equipment on shoulder-poles or being hauled on carts.

Often, at one time, not waiting for the roads to empty, there were three or four green-clad columns flowing across the barren mountains down to the Great Wall and into the plains of North China, shoulder poles bouncing, shoving stubborn oxen, angry mules and carts along with them.

They loped, almost trotted, tireless; they wore hats of dog, wolf and fox, big, with earflaps usually untied and tails streaming, padded great-coats, padded trousers bound with puttees, and they were hung with rifles, machine-pistols, hand-grenades, trenching tools, knives, pots and mugs. They looked resolute and dangerous but curiously pacific.

We got browner every day in the bitter cold sunshine. Cooks, food and huge cast-iron pots went ahead and food, however simple, was hot. Villagers marvelled at the first army that did not steal or rape. 'So many men. Such fine clothes, so many guns.' From one village they streamed out with the marchers to the next, keeping them company with drums, cymbals, reed pipes and two-stringed fiddles, dancing the Yanko planting dance and handing them over ceremonially.

Being a foreign friend I had to struggle all the time for the right to walk. No Chinese will walk if he can ride, regarding exercise as madness. Nobody would believe me when I insisted that I preferred walking to being balanced on the top of an ancient Dodge lorry so decrepit that it could scarcely keep pace with the people on foot. In thirty degrees of frost this was a special kind of hell.

Overloaded, on springs chocked with wood and tied down solid, the Dodge crept up every incline shuddering in pain and often we had to leap out and push. Once over the pass, a thread of road curled down out of sight, the driver would switch off to save fuel and we coasted, swaying top-heavily round bends, squealing brakes patched up with iron wire.

Captured drivers were invariably morose and dangerous. A Kuomintang driver's job was an investment from which he got a lot of 'squeeze' carrying illegal passengers and goods. When they captured a jeep and its driver at Beibiao in Jehol I asked for the vehicle and got it. But I was not allowed to drive it because it was thought that to let a foreign friend drive was too menial and the army would lose face. Its complement was therefore myself and Yü Zhiying at the back and Jia Yulin in the passenger's seat next to the captured driver.

In Beibiao we slept in a former Japanese army brothel with one hundred cubicles, each just about large enough to hold two small people. Ordinary armies, some wit said, quoting Napoleon, march on their stomachs, but the Japanese army marches on its libido.

Two miles out of Beibiao, it was still dark, we were half asleep again and did not observe that the driver, who seemed to have some minor engine trouble, let the rest of the convoy pass until we were the last vehicle. It was one of those roads built up against flood like a railway embankment above paddy land and the driver coolly tipped the jeep over, stepping neatly out and leaving the rest of us on board. I still recall pushing myself over the open back as it rolled down. Nobody was hurt and the driver was amazed and aggrieved to find himself covered by our three pistols.

Some peasants helped to haul the jeep up on to the road again but nobody had noticed that we were missing. I drove now and the others took care of the driver.

When we caught up, people seemed less interested in what had happened than in the fact that I actually could drive.

Driving was seen as a profession in itself, which in a way it was, since drivers had to maintain their own vehicles. I even lost face because driving, though clearly needing some low-grade skill, was hardly an occupation for an intellectual, which I was supposed to be. The driver was shot. A search had uncovered two gold bars taped under the chassis and covered with mud. This explained why he made a desperate try. I kept the jeep.

Like birds gathering, the headquarters staff converged on a group of tiny villages east of Beijing and north of the Great Wall. They came with no fanfare. A fair was going on with peepshows, jugglers, tumblers and story-tellers and at dusk, the whole township gathered in the market-place, men, bound-footed women, children, squatting cross-legged, nibbling melon seeds and waiting till shadow-players rigged up their complicated, candle-lit puppet-theatre. Onlookers huddled in bitter cold, hour after hour, watching an endless ancient play, while men with shoulder poles went round selling soya-curd 'brain', *dan-dan mine* (peppery noodles) and home-made liquor.

Next day, I was invited to a nearby village with Yü Zhiying for supper and there, on the heated clay *kang* (bed) of a middle-peasant, with no more fuss than arranging a picnic, the taking of Beijing was organised.

Dr Jack Rosenfeld called for us and as we arrived Lin Biao turned up. He jumped out of his jeep, quite unlike his reserved self and embraced Jack and myself. Then, spotting my new model Canadian Browning he pointed it to the sky and pulled the trigger. Being automatic, it emptied itself, with shells showering round him. Minutes later, General Nie Rongzhen, Commander of the North China Military Region fresh from the conquest of Chengde, capital of Jehol Province, arrived. It was the first time they had met since these momentous advances and they hugged each other in a very un-Chinese fashion and did a little dance watched with embarrassed grins by their bodyguards. General Huang Kecheng, scheduled to be military commander of Tianjin, came next with his long knitted khaki scarf and the habit of now and again doing a few steps of *taijichuan* shadow-boxing along the *kang*. Then Lo Runghuan with the leaky *vas deferens*, now repaired.

Breakfast with Mao

While we waited for the meal, Lin Biao and Nie Rongzhen paced about in their socks on the huge brick bed tossing ideas to each other.

General Fu Couyi had already made too many mistakes to be remedied. Jinzhou should have been held. Even better, Fu Couyi should have insisted that Chiang Kaishek's troops in Manchuria – all of them – should have been pulled out south of the Great Wall to help hold North China.

Now all Fu's forces were stretched out along a line from Kalgan to Tianjin. The Old Man had been right so far but what were the chances of getting Beijing without damaging it?

Nie said that if Old Huang could take Tianjin really fast it would scare Fu as well as bottling him up.

But only if we first take Fengtai, Lin Biao qualified. 'Fengtai is the key. We take that, then Tianjin and then we can choose which day we walk into Beijing ...'

When the first dish arrived it was Peking Duck – one golden brown duck to each table. 'Symbolic,' as Jack commented. Lin Biao apologised for not serving it in the proper style. That must wait a few weeks. We drank to that, and then to Chu, Mao, Liu, Pollitt, Dutt, the army, internationalism, Stalin, Lenin and began the finger game as new stomach-lining dishes came. I was staying in a runaway landlord's over-furnished house. On the way back, under the frosty moon, the shadow play was still going on. Someone pulled off my Japanese felt-boots and shoved me fully dressed into my sleeping bag.

There were still a few days while the plan of attack on Fengtai was worked out and we were not far from the tombs of the Manchu Emperors including the notorious Empress Dowager Ci Xi. Her tomb and that of Qian Long had been robbed in the twenties by the warlord Sun Tianying and some of our advance patrols had surprised Kuomintang soldiers in the process of robbing the tomb of the Emperor Kang Xi and driven them off.

The main tomb was under an artificial hill and reached by a semi-circular tunnel – now cleared – just big enough for a slim man to creep through on his stomach. It was fifty yards long.

There was an argument whether I should be allowed in. Suppose I got stuck, suffocated, went gaga? Should I have a rope tied to one foot. Finally a PLA man led, I went next and Jia Yulin went last. It was horrible and six yards in I was running sweat and silently palpitating with claustrophobia, partly because there was no way to turn round.

The tombs had been opened by the robbers before they fled. Six of Kang Xi's favourite wives and concubines had been made to commit suicide to provide him with solace in the next life.

His favourite, a girl of twenty, had eaten gold – it was said – and so died. In the light of an electric torch she still looked lovely. The robbers had slashed her belly to look for the gold she was supposed to have eaten. Kang Xi himself was less well preserved. On one finger was a coral ring eaten away where his finger had curved over it during the centuries.

Outside the tomb was carved: 'Ten thousand mountains bow to the glory of the Emperor.' They were still there.

The Kuomintang's news service put out a report that we had robbed the tomb.

As I first saw it from a distance, with its high battlemented walls and many-storied city gates, Beijing against the morning foothill mists looked like a Tartar encampment done in stone, a fortified garrison of nomad bannermen. It was first laid down in that form by the Kublai Khan in the thirteenth century, though its first stones go back three thousand years. There has never been a walled city which could compare.

The Chinese Communists took great pains and time to capture the unique ancient capital peacefully and intact. It was, at that time, out of respect for tradition and on humanitarian grounds, no less than as a signal to the enemy of a desire to compromise. That was so as we prepared to march and remained so till the Red Guards were incited to vandalise it and create from its ruined glories a monstrosity in a fog of manmade dust. We who saw Beijing in its splendour were indeed fortunate.

If the essence of warfare is deception and the peak of military skill to subdue the enemy without fighting, according to Sun Zi, then the peaceful capture of Beijing was a classic military task. Lin Biao, walking about in his stockinged feet on the peasant's *kang*, chewing a drumstick of Peking Duck, had gone to the point at once.

To take Fengtai – vital rail knot – at night with a hand-picked spearhead of crack troops was a piece of audacity well beyond General Fu's imaginative capacity. But it would at one stroke unlock his whole front.

Men of the 42nd Army were hand-picked and intensively briefed by local informants till they could have marched to Fengtai blindfold. Weapons were muffled, cloth-soled shoes, thick North China dust and snow silenced our feet. The sky was light, the air cold and crisp. We were not heard as we crossed the airfield where the Kuomintang sentries seemed to be asleep.

We did not know – otherwise Beijing might have been taken that night – that General Fu Cuoyi himself was also sleeping not a mile from where we passed.

South of the airfield our road passed under a bridge at the same time as enemy troops passed overhead. Some of our men with southern accents called out greetings and were assumed to be their own men.

As the sky lightened, we raced into Fengtai firing into the air, with terrifying screeches: '*Pao! Pao! Ba Lu lai lo!*' ('Run! Run! The Eighth Route Army's here!'). Totally confused, some of Fu's troops were running, buttoning as they went, some tried to surrender but we wanted no prisoners getting in the way. 'Run if you want to live,' they were told. 'Drop your weapons and run.'

They ran toward the rising sun whose light was pinkly creeping over the rim. By the time it turned to glittering white frost, Fengtai was in our hands and General Fu's twenty-two divisions in Beijing had been immobilised. He could, of course, elect to fight, but he could not win. Or he could negotiate, which he began to do.

The man who had to deal directly with the tricky old warlord was General Ye Jianying himself a soldier with a long and famous history.

A curtain hung over the details of the negotiations but General Ye told me off the record some of what was at stake.

'Fu Cuoyi,' said Ye, 'is the best military man they have and the Americans consider him, even beseiged in Beijing, the best man they have available to build a 'third force' between the Communists and the Kuomintang.

'He could of course get away by air, but not with his army which is the best they have. Without his army he would be nothing – less than nothing, in personal danger. Fu Cuoyi's trading stock is Beijing. If he puts on too high a price, politically, we shall not pay. If we offer him too little and leave him no face, he would make us fight, destroy the city and himself. Also, we have limited time because of the Americans. He knows that.'

Unless he kept his face – *lien* – General Fu would certainly be prepared to wipe out Beijing and go down in its flames – that was understood.

Face, important as it is, can hardly be defined other than as status, or standing, or possibly self-respect, but it embraces many indefinables and is very easily damaged. From a person's earliest days, *lien* is of prime importance. There is no graver reproach to a child than '*mei lien*' – shameless (literally: not have face), or in company a mother may silently reproach an erring child by stroking her own cheek with a forefinger.

People without face in general included peasants, common soldiers, women, artisans – the *lao bai xing*. Each person in the feudal hierarchy belonged to an allotted place and ways of advancement were few. Those at the bottom had no or little face, must put up with treatment which no person with face would bear and had no redress against unbearable hardship other than to commit suicide and take revenge by shaming or haunting the oppressor.

Traditionally, common soldiers had no face. They were press-ganged and forced to live by marauding. PLA men, in contrast, lived by a strict code of conduct and took nothing from the people, not even the proverbial piece of straw. They protected the peasants when they took over the land.

Old China Hands – foreigners – even those hostile to the Communists – spoke of the discipline and courage of the PLA with praise and amazement, usually failing to realise that this was because a PLA man possessed face.

Possessing face carried with it the possibility of losing it – individually and collectively – and of gaining more. Out of this grew an army with *élan*, discipline and self-sacrifice. About half of the forces surrounding the city were former Kuomintang conscripts who had changed sides and marched from

Manchuria with the PLA. Now there was time to incorporate them into the PLA and imbue them with its spirit for they were very keen on catching up on face. So while General Fu and General Ye – through their delegations – bargained about Beijing, the fields around the city were full of PLA soldiers learning to write, training, constructing scaling equipment and listening to lectures.

It was Christmas Day 1948 in Fengtai. That is, it was four in the morning on that day and thus it was Christmas Eve in London. General Fu had chosen the moment to put up an artillery barrage and nobody could guess why, so they suggested that I move a bit south to Liangxiang, where staff was being assembled to take over Beijing.

Peng Zhen, scheduled to be mayor of Beijing and a survivor of everything so far, was the man in charge and gave me an effusive phony welcome when I arrived. Actually he wished me to the devil – a confounded big-nose landed on him when he had to take over the whole capital city. But this was because he took his guarding job too seriously and would not let me wander about as Lin Biao had. He was – and I suppose is – an unusual looking Chinese with a high, domed balding head and a sharp red-tipped nose.

Even Germans and Czechs are convinced that English cooking is the worst in the world and of course Peng Zhen too, with more reason. I agreed that Chinese was the best but enlarged on the Christmas board: the seven succulent meats on a turkey, the stuffing, ham, roast potatoes, gravy, bread sauce, sausages.

Peng Zhen shook his head and sent me three seven pound tins of American army turkey with the message that it was no surprise that the GI could not fight on that stuff.

It was indeed factory-homogenised protein, tasteless and with edible bones, impossible to imagine as a bird. My colleagues looked wondering. However, it was meat of a sort. We went on a tour of the little town and managed to find red pepper, garlic, soya, Chinese cabbage, peppery pickled turnip, sesame buns, dried fish and fresh-made, 60 per cent alcohol. So we blew up a fire in our billet and feasted on devilled turkey. Doctored up, it was excellent. Peng Zhen accepted a bowl and boasted that he had provided Ah Lan with a real English Christmas dinner and that it was quite good – like Sichuan cooking but not to be classed with Peking Duck.

Bodyguards in my experience have mainly a status value though they are useful for carrying things, may possibly deter nervous assailants and one cannot entirely rule out that they may accidentally stop the odd knife thrust or bullet by accident. If my own first guard, Jia Yulin, had any value it lay in his dangerous appearance which was shown to be false in unhappy circumstances.

That New Year's Day, while the Generals Ye and Fu were locked in argument, I was summoned south to the Communist Party, Army and Xinhua headquarters to discuss plans for press and information work in Beijing with Mao and the others, much to Peng Zhen's relief. He even came to see me off, lent me his own weapons-carrier and an escort for the three-day journey south through reputedly dangerous areas.

Jia Yulin gave a fine show of importance sitting next to the driver. Peng Zhen, checking, called him down and demanded to see his gun. Yulin took his long-barrelled Mauser from its wooden holster. He was blushing and in a moment so was Peng Zhen, with fury. The mechanism was corroded, the ammunition ancient and useless – it was a write-off. Face again. Rather a Mauser that was useless than a new Smith and Wesson.

Peng Zhen flung it to the ground and said 'Give him yours' to his personal guard.

The man was near mutiny but he slowly unbuckled his own gun. Yulin's eyes gleamed. It was a Spanish-made, blued-steel Mauser – the most coveted pistol among the guards. I only hoped that Yulin never needed to use it.

Headquarters was now at Ci Bai Po Village and the three-day drive was through no man's land infested with runaway enemy troops turned bandit, but the peasant militia had been alerted and we saw them on the hilltops dressed in forget-me-not-blue cotton with white towels for turbans knotted in front. We followed a single strand of copper telegraph wire over the hills, the track opened out into a wide river valley dotted with peasant homes and we were in the heart and brain of the Chinese revolution.

An evident westerner got up from his haunches and called in an American accent, 'You must be Alan Winnington. I'm Sydney Rittenberg.' He climbed into the jeep.

Rittenberg – who since then spent two terms in gaol totalling sixteen years – was a solemn young man, speaking perfect Chinese which he had studied at Stanford during the Second World War. He had arrived in China as an interpreter in the US Army Judge Advocate's Office and there were various versions of what had prompted him to work for the Communists or why, with his background, they accepted him. I never found out.

He was editing texts for the New China News Agency (Xinhua) and the radio. While I had been in China I had heard a woman reading English language news from this village in a tinny voice with an accent that showed she had learned it from an American. This was Wei Ling and she was married to Rittenberg.

It was a peaceful series of villages and did not seem to have noticed that the attention of the world was focused on it. Pigs scavenged on the unsurfaced roads, families squatted on their heels round the doors taking their meals or fanned grass fires to cook their food and warm their brick beds.

It seemed to be too secure to need personal guards. At any corner you might meet a walking fortune – a Communist bandit with a price on his head or hers. Chu De was instantly recognisable from the many posters and his kind, ugly smiling face, looking very carefree for the commander of an army of three million men scattered over a continent.

This much-wanted man stopped, stared and asked in surprise whether I was Ah Lan. He had expected me to be a woman because of my name. *Ah* is a diminutive and someone had concluded that the character for *Lan* meaning Orchid would go better than some other character pronounced Lan. There it was – Little Orchid. It caused confusion.

He pulled me to his house for a home-cooked lunch with Kang Keqing, his wife, and Deng Yingchao, Zhou's wife; just as we sat down news came that Tianjin had been taken in a swift assault. 'We did it to put a fire-cracker under Fu's arse,' Chu De said.

Work was mostly done at night to avoid interruption, owing to the tradition that a visitor cannot be hurried to leave, and so it was at night that I met Zhou Enlai. His working room was large, modernly furnished and with underfloor heating. It was extremely comfortable.

We spent several hours discussing plans for the takeover of the press and radio in Beijing, what to do about the foreign journalists there – mostly English-speaking – and how to set up the Xinhua News Agency, broadcasting news in various languages. It was all pretty straightforward and he asked me to draft various statements for distribution to the foreign journalists. There were a few embarassing moments when Zhou tried to show his knowledge of English, which was very slight, by correcting, wrongly, my interpreter's translations.

Mao Zedong invited me to breakfast, my second breakfast or lunch, since it was at midday. It was a normal Chinese breakfast of rice porridge (congee), salted peanuts, pickles and soup, all well spiced with red pepper, Mao being a Hunanese. His clothes were baggy, unlike Zhou's, with trousers wide enough to pull on while wearing shoes and sleeves that acted as a muff when necessary.

Through the meal and during our long talk he smoked without stopping – a Shanghai brand of cigarette made by the British and American Tobacco Company, labelled in English 'Ruby Queen' and packed in a bilious pink paper wrapping. I heard that this used to be a favourite working-class cigarette in Liverpool, equivalent to the Woodbine further south. Mao was trying to cut down his smoking on medical advice so he broke every cigarette in half and chain-smoked the halves. Since he smoked each half in a holder down to the last shred, the actual effect was probably the opposite of what he intended. This happened to him later in far more important matters.

Jasmine tea was served in the usual big mugs with lids and those delicious peanuts boiled in soya sauce and flower pepper.

One remark he made which I assumed at the time to be rhetorical was, 'The Americans have supported the wrong side.' It seemed a pointless statement since he did not enlarge on it but I did not know the then well-kept secret that he and Zhou Enlai had made approaches to the Americans and been rejected.

He went on ironically, 'It really is noble of them to show such keenness to get peace now for the good of China, after starting the civil war for the good of China.

'Chiang's armies are falling to pieces. But their political tricks are as transparent as their military tactics.

'We've seen enough of them. They want to talk to gain time, patch up their armies, stay on the stage by any means.'

'And Fu Cuoyi*?' I asked.

'He cannot harm us, but can destroy the city. We shall treat him well. Very well. It will give others the idea of coming to peaceful terms with us as we go south. Everyone now must think again: "Where do I stand?" Fu can have his place in the new China, the new republic, but first he must do something political for it, he must take a political stand.'

He broke another Ruby Queen in half and lit it with a rueful smile. We chatted a little longer and I said I must leave him in peace to work.

'Oh, I'm not busy,' he said in the polite formula. 'But no doubt you have a lot to do. Do you have all you need? Please give my regards to Comrade Ha-li Po-li-teh.'

He saw me to the entrance of the narrow courtyard.

'*Yi lu ping an (Bon voyage)*,' he said. 'See you in Beijing, soon.'

Enough has been written about the supposedly effeminate-seeming Mao and the suave, dapper Zhou Enlai. To me, what they appeared to have in common was a self-conscious desire to impress: Mao vastly calm, bland and seemingly sure; Zhou with the quick watchfulness of a blue tit, sharp black eyes under thick black eyebrows, studying the effects of his words and movements; both in their different ways inhibited, both detached.

The other three of what were then the Big Five – Chu De, Liu Shaoqi and Chen Yun put me at ease immediately. All were gentle, soft-spoken and friendly. With them I felt entirely at ease and with the other two, always circumspect, entering into the role in which they saw themselves.

Outside China, Liu Shaoqi was regarded as an *éminence grise* – a man who put into effect what Mao decreed. This derived in part from the fact that few outsiders had ever met him and

---

* General Fu Cuoyi became Minister of Water Conservancy in the Chinese People's Republic, and was very successful.

partly from his quiet manner. I spent most of two days talking with him and found him friendly, with calm wide eyes and a modest, almost bashful appearance helped by his large front teeth and small chin.

He was looked on as Mao's obvious successor. It can be said that Mao and Chu De mainly built up the PLA and Liu Shaoqi was the prime organiser of the Communist Party.

In a decade he was to be Chairman of the Chinese People's Republic and less than a decade after to be dying like a dog of a deliberately neglected lung infection in a Kaifeng gaol.

He went to Moscow to study in 1921 and was always since then an advocate of international communism and an opponent of the Great Han nationalism which was the fatal weakness bequeathed by millenia of the Central Kingdom.

Liu's first major work in the ideological and organisational field was *How to Be a Good Communist*, which stressed the need for absolute loyalty to the party and to overcome individualist tendencies.

Only years after, reading over my notes of these talks on the eve of the Communist victory in China, I could see some clues about what was going on in the top levels of the party at that time before the major divergencies became clearer — for the Chinese party is good at keeping secrets even for years, even when the whole country may be discussing a subject behind the gauze curtain of a fifteenth-century opera, totally incomprehensible to Westerners.

Paragraphs like these from my notes ceased to be so trite in the light of later events:

'We would be really stupid to suppose that the American imperialists would help the Chinese people to gain real independence.

'The aid of the Soviet Union and international communism is the most important condition for the success of nations struggling for national independence.

'The choice is between alliance with the Soviet Union and alliance with imperialism. It must be one or the other. *That* is the dividing line between patriotism and treason to one's own country, between revolution and counter-revolution.'

I turned back to those notes after reading some remarks of Chairman Mao, made but not published, just before the

Eighth Chinese Communist Party Congress, the first to take place after the revolution. Mao urged, 'We must not blindly follow the Soviet Union: we must be more discriminating. Every fart has some kind of smell, and we cannot say that all Soviet farts smell sweet. Everyone is now saying that they stink and we can say so too. We must study what is appropriate to China, including the good points of capitalism.'

Liu Shaoqi questioned me closely about Munich and the difference of views in the British Communist Party in September 1939. He commented, 'Comrade Pollitt's firm line of publicly supporting the policy decided by the Party and rejecting all suggestions to present his own opinions was in accordance with Communist views and practice.

'Agreement with a decision is a matter of personal opinion, but the duty to carry out a decision is essential if the Party is to act unitedly. It is the same with a trade union. Workers must act in unity if they are to win.'

It was a short visit. A message came from Zhou Enlai that I should hurry back to Beijing. That afternoon there was an informal send-off banquet which Chu De described in humorous imitation of Chinese feudal courtesy as 'a few mediocre dishes and a mouthful of watery wine'. Among them were pork, mutton, chicken, duck, fish, big soups, small soups, maybe twenty dishes.

Guests were all politicians in their own right which may have accounted for the absence of Mao's wife, whom I was keen to compare with his former one in Harbin, and the presence of those of Chu and Zhou. Mao, Chu, Zhou, Liu and Gao Gang were among the others.

This was probably the last time these men, who had all spent most of their lives with a price on their heads, sat together informally round a table, joking, relaxed, bubbling with success and impending victory. Soon they were statesmen and not long after opponents and rivals.

I was the excuse for the banquet and as such, the target to be got drunk which is ostensibly the Chinese object in drinking – making others drunk. Incidentally, only, they get drunk in the process too. I was indeed an easy mark for I was hopeless at the finger game* as well as being under the usual pressure to drink to Pollitt, Dutt, Stalin and a long list of other notables, all toasts being drunk in the usual moonshine called *baigan* and downed in one.

We said our farewells and I was told that a dance party had been arranged in a nearby village, as I was hoisted onto a docile horse which knew its way and took me to the dance which was in full swing with music from read-pipes, two-string fiddles, cymbals and a drum. Only Chu De and Gao Gang kept me company.

Chu, a kind old uncle, his face like a benevolent rock with its craggy smile. All the girls looked alike in short skirts with heavy boots laced halfway up their calves and short plaits sticking out behind each ear. Chu De was their target and they took turns to pull him on the floor. He shambled through every dance, waddling, legs-apart in his quilted trousers, smiling all the time, looking like a slow-witted peasant. It was when he was in thought that the power of the man who had ordered Lin Biao's army to march straight to Beijing became visible.

I was pulled on to the mud floor by one of the PLA girls and as I started to dance – or try to keep in step with her – I felt a tap on my shoulder and a guard whispered, frontier style, that all guns must be left at the door. Not unreasonable considering the type of people who came to these functions.

---

* The finger game: two contestants must simultaneously extend some fingers of one hand and call a number from zero to ten. The winner on each round is the person who first calls the combined number of extended fingers. The loser must drink a cup.

8
Beijing Changes Hands

It was not certain till the last moment whether General Fu would hand over the city, though after the fall of Tianjin he had no way of escape. But he kept the threat to destroy Beijing in hand and the suffering of the people to improve the terms.

Beijing's population had been under terrible stress for 48 days. Nobody knew which side the coin would come down and the mad preparations for battle to the last went on. Civilian houses were torn down to construct useless earthworks. Packs of diseased dogs scavenged the streets feeding on the corpses of people starved to death in sight of bags of flour being used as sandbags; lorries loaded with men and women denounced the previous day were driven to be executed at the eleventh hour. It was incredible, someone said, that people could sleep at night and even more incredible that they summoned the will to get up.

Outside the city the PLA men and women held meetings, discussed tactics, practised military exercises. As a lesson to General Fu that there was no protection in the city wall, the PLA put on a demonstration of how they would break through it, using tremendous small-arms fire for cover as engineers blasted holes through a nearby city-wall.

Fu Cuoyi capitulated officially on 29 January 1948, an action that was soon being lauded as saving the city from destruction. He ceased to be a war criminal and became respectable. There was face all round.

Leaders of the taking-over-Beijing group threw a Chinese New Year Party on the previous night, 28 January, in the Summer Palace, behind which we were now living. It was held in the restaurant next to the marble boat which the Empress

Dowager, with wry humour, ordered built with a tiny portion of the money squeezed out to build a Chinese navy but which she squandered on creating the Summer Palace itself.

A long side table was loaded with bottles of *Wu Xin* (Five Star) beer, a good Pilsner type and the first beer I had seen since Shenyang. As I was busy with this, a pleasant American voice said from behind, 'Leave a drop for me, brother.'

It was Dr George Hatem – better known as Ma Haide – of whom I had heard a lot but never met. George was an American medical man who had long ago decided to spend the rest of his life with the Chinese Communists. As his name suggests, his origins were in the Levant and this was borne out by his large black eyes and indeed his whole appearance. He was on familiar terms with all the top people in the Chinese Communist Party and had been very useful to them during the Marshall talks. George was married to a lovely former film actress named Zhou Sufei and as far as I can recall was a dual American and Chinese citizen.

That night in the Summer Palace – which was plastered with great advertisements for American goods, especially Coca-Cola – was a celebration which had been earned. Ma and I and some of the leading take-over people groped our way up Longevity Hill to the Precious Cloud Pavillon, much favoured by the Empress Dowager and carried on the party. I recall dancing a demonstration tango with Ma on the Empress Dowager's bed and falling off.

General Ye Jianying, full of *baigan* and happiness, kept making speeches which were all the same. The common people were never able to see this place, he said. Even since the downfall of the Ching dynasty, the price of entry had been so high that only the well-to-do were able to visit it. Now people in padded uniforms were holding their own functions there.

Then he added, 'We told Fu Cuoyi, "Stop pretending that you are giving up peacefully to help the people. After your record. In fact, it is because you cannot fight. But still you can set a good example to others. You can tell General Chiang Kaishek by name that he betrayed the Chinese revolution in 1927. You can publicly repent. Your own acts will determine whether your name can come off the list of war criminals."'

*

But I had to fight my own way into Beijing.

We were to march in on 21 January. On the previous day Peng Zehn sent an aide to tell me that I would not be allowed to go in with the troops. He said the officer commanding would not guarantee my safety.

I blew up, talking to the air, as is my practice, I said that down at headquarters, Mao, Chu, Liu and Zhou had all agreed that I should and could go in, and now there was a subordinate scared of risking the responsibility and passing the buck to one of his own underlings like a typical petty-bourgeois. All war correspondents had to run physical risks. Part of the job. And so on.

This set the bells ringing. Peng Zhen lived round the corner and sent for me. His sharpish nose was redder than usual and twitching with rage. Had I called him a typical subordinate petty-bourgeois? It was a typical Chinese situation where everyone had to try to find a way to maintain face.

Absolutely not, I replied. An unhappy misunderstanding due to my miserable inability to master the Chinese language. What I had meant was simply that such a change should have been discussed with me and referred to the comrades at headquarters. Of course, he was finally responsible for my care and I was grateful, but there were occasions when risks must be taken. After all, I might have broken my neck falling off the Empress Dowager's divan last night. This seemed to tickle him.

At that time I was sleeping in the boarded-up window of an empty shop. In the middle of the night, I had to get out of my sleeping bag and be measured for a suit by candlelight. It was ready next morning, a well-fitting padded uniform, buttoning up on the calves to fit into my Japanese cavalry officer's felt boots. Wearing this, with an ear-flapped hat and a white cotton face-mask, I was indistinguishable from a Chinese high officer, having brown eyes, too. But the order that I could not go in with the first troops still stood.

I was invited to breakfast with Peng Zhen and Ye Jianying. Peng Zhan was now very friendly and said he had talked to the responsible military people – himself, I suspected. Would I be willing to enter in an armoured vehicle? Would I, indeed! Everyone's face saved.

In the event, the liberation of Beijing, the high point of the

Chinese revolution, was an anti-climax.

Not an egg was thrown.

The citizens, fed on flying hearsay, had no belief that America's favourite general would give up the city, and were taken by surprise as the PLA approached the unique wall – biggest in the world. I saw the West Gate looming and we went into its dark curves and out to the light again along Xi Zhi Men Nei Da Jie. Behind us the cavalrymen pranced on Mongolian ponies and behind them the infantry marched sprucely, no longer hung with pots and pans but clean and smart and superbly in step. Behind them came miles of captured American vehicles and weapons.

At first people going about their affairs stared without realising what was happening. Then a street vendor, selling soya milk and gaping at our column overfilled the bowl he was pouring for a customer as he yelled, *'Ba Lu lai lo!'* ('The Eighth Route Army is here!')

In moments the street was full of shouting, laughing, cheering people, crowding in, slowing the column to little more than marking time.

In contrast to what can happen when supporters of rival football teams clash, there was not a single incident between the PLA soldiers and nearly 300,000 Kuomintang troops still in the city who were not even confined to barracks.

Weeks of preparing, with our people filtering into and out of the city disguised as peasants, had not been wasted. The PLA forces seemed to vanish. In an office of the take-over headquarters all had been arranged by Liu Chengzheng who guided the officers to their first duties and billets.

He was a jolly little man who had joined the Communist Party at the age of sixteen in 1926. His family arranged a marriage for him to a small-foot peasant girl and he would have refused but he had to placate the family in order to continue his secret political work.

'It turned out well, though,' he smiled. 'She unbound her feet and joined the Communist Party. Being young, her feet grew half-way normal again. We have seven children and are considered a model couple.'

He described his wedding night – his bride sitting in the lotus position on the *kang* to display her tiny, embroidered shoes. There was a cup of wine before each. 'We had never seen each other before. She was beautiful, so I think.'

There was no antipathy between the soldiers. They were all peasants and the main difference was that Fu Cuoyi's troops had been press-ganged. Now they were given the choice of being reorganised into the PLA with their former rank or handing in their weapons and going home with a free railway pass and three months' pay.

Fu's officers, as soon as Sun Zi's precept had been realised – 'to subdue the enemy without fighting' – had three aims: to ingratiate themselves with their conquerors, recover the bribe they had paid for their rank and preserve the squeeze they had made from being an officer – what was usually defined as 'feeding dead mouths'.

Kuomintang secret agents in Beijing, paid torturers and assassins with no ideological motivation, queued up to comply when given the chance to wipe the slate clean by handing in weapons and radios and identifying themselves. Very commonly they left their equipment in the streets at night and disappeared.

There was not even a curfew. I used to walk alone without being challenged from the former Nazi embassy in the Legation Quarter, where Ye Jianying had his headquarters and I lived, to the old German Hotel near Hatamen where Ma Haide was a member of Peng Zhen's staff.

Mostly I drove about in a beautiful white Studebaker that I had found, former property of some Kuomintang big-shot. Jia Yulin preferred to sleep and I preferred to let him.

Jack Rosenfeld, being with the military, was in the Beijing Hotel, which gave me the run of the cellars. He had got to Beijing in time and now his ambition was to see Vienna again. He died there of a coronary attack a few weeks later.

In Beijing the PLA men were billeted on the citizens. There was no other way and the people were at first understandably unhappy about that, having experienced the Kuomintang. But even the disdainful Beijingese found that they had no cause to complain. PLA men, when offered space on the family brick bed, preferred to sleep under the broad eaves. They swept the courtyards, fetched water, carried night soil, made coal balls, asked for nothing, accepted nothing, sang, taught the children the Yangko dance, drank no alcohol, treated women with respect, held meetings and studied.

This immaculate conduct should be recalled to correct false conclusions drawn from what happened later in China and indeed in this same city. It has precedents. The perceptive Sun Zi said that it occurs when that moral force exists 'which causes the people to be in harmony with their leaders'. He might have said: when the leaders are fulfilling the desires of the people.

It occurred during the English Revolution which was regarded by many as the reconquest of England by the English people. Describing the integrity of Cromwell's Ironsides then, Macauley wrote, 'In that singular camp, no oath was heard; no drunkenness or gambling was seen and, during the long dominion of the soldiery, the property of the peaceful citizen and the honour of women were held sacred.'

As the Beijing garrison was progressively reduced, its hosts could be heard regretting its departure as though they were losing their own children.

Those were days when anyone who wore the badge and uniform of the PLA was more than a friend: when soldiers and young women with face were evidence enough of historic change.

Expert predictions were upset by the impetuous reconquest of China by the Chinese people and Old China Hands were driven into a tight spot by the sudden occurrence of the impossible. They hopefully put it down to Chiang Kaishek's follies rather than a revolution under able Communist leadership and hopefully gave out, as self-evident truth, that the Communists, even less than Chiang, would be able to steer the unmanageable Chinese junk through the stormy waters into which it had been blown.

With the exception of Chen Yun, and he was nothing but a Shanghai compositor, they were a rabble of peasant guerrillas without any other experience. China was bankrupt, inflation was galloping and if the Communists managed to hang on they would have to put the country in pawn.

The Russians, even if they wanted to, could not help. China had no capital, no technicians, no industry. It would bleed to death on corruption, famines, secret societies, squeeze and opium. Especially corruption: the universal lubricant without which nothing in China moved, however slowly.

Observers of this kind were judging the Chinese from sitting in rickshawks and talking to officials. Never meeting the Chinese poor, they could not know that the average Chinese person had always been honest, even puritanical, rather than corrupt; crushed rather than dumbly humble; civilised even though illiterate and desired above all, apart from food, 'face' and national pride.

Those things upset the calculations that the Communists would soon find the whole thing unmanageable and China would again become a Tom Tiddler's ground – a state of affairs to America's advantage, whose Western rivals and Japan had gone under in China during the war.

What actually happened was that honesty became a matter of pride.

While the PLA was still sweeping the Kuomintang off the mainland, I went back to Britain briefly to collect some additional British Communists to work in Beijing, and so became the first foreign Red to travel by boat from Tianjin to Hongkong after the revolution.

After the Chinese threatened to put me on board under a military escort if the manager persisted in requiring me first to see the British consul, who was accredited to the Kuomintang government, I got a berth on a Jardine Matheson boat.

It was a typical 3,000 ton tramp with only one other passenger, a Chinese. Every eye was on me as I lurched to the captain's table for my first meal. He stood up, shook hands, introduced me to the officers. Was I a Communist? Had I been with the Chinese Reds? How long? Would I tell them all about it?

'By God! Who would have believed it?' he went on. 'On the China coast, a port without squeeze! We docked in Tianjin, ready with the usual "presents" – money and the rest. First time since your lot took over. What happened? Nobody would even accept a cigarette. No money, no percentage, nothing. There was one soldier and some civilians. In a Chinese port! Brother, as far as China is concerned, the Communists have got my vote.'

When I got back to China with my new colleagues shortly

after, probity had established itself in the country that had been held up as the world's most corrupt. You could not tip a waiter or even offer him a cigarette.

Red China was not about to collapse. Instead, having pushed the Kuomintang off the mainland the Communists were preparing to clear them from Taiwan and so complete the revolution.

Two courses remained for Washington: accept the situation and improve relations with Beijing's new rulers or continue to support the rump government on Taiwan and presumably try to restore America's protege to power in Beijing.

In those days an American statesman could not be objective about the Chinese revolution without being suspected of having a Communist Party membership card in his pocket. Officially China had come under a 'foreign yoke'. The Chinese Communist Party was simply a 'Soviet tool'. Laughable indeed.

A frontal assault could not be launched by the Kuomintang against the mainland but, looking at the globe, there were South Korea, Taiwan, the Philippines, Indo-China and Japan forming an immense Pacific arc from which the Communists in China could be contained and rolled back.

As usual, the arguments of the China lobby became common talk: since a new war between the Americans and the Russians was inevitable, it would be folly to allow the Russians to recover from their wounds and catch up with the US in nuclear weapons. Also, the Chinese Communists were consolidating their new rule and time lost would discourage the anti-Communists in China. The situation could only get worse.

That was how things stood in June 1950.

9

War and Massacre in Korea

A day will probably come when documentary evidence will prove who began the Korean War. Until then we shall have to be satisfied with the circumstantial evidence.

In June 1950, I was a guest at a small informal supper with Mao Zedong, Zhou Enlai, Chu De and Liu Shaoqi at the Chung Nan Hai, a section of the old imperial palace used by party leaders. It was a very jolly evening for things were indeed going well. Best of all, inflation had been slowed and plans were in hand to reshuffle grain so that famine could not recur, China actually being a grain-surplus country, and famines due to bad distribution and speculation.

Mao Zedong had proposed to the recent Central Committee meeting that the PLA should be drastically reduced, retaining only enough troops for action to take over Taiwan and Tibet. Much the same had been said by Liu Shaoqi in his May Day speech. That night the talk was all about land reform and industrial construction.

These demobilisation plans were abandoned five days later, on 25 June, when the Korean war broke out across the 38th Parallel.

Within days I was crossing that Parallel as correspondent for the *Daily Worker* and the Xinhua News Agency, with the immediate aim of catching up the Korean People's Army which was driving the South Korean Army down the peninsula.

In those few days, Western reaction had been fast and drastic. America took over the protection of Taiwan from the impending assault of the Chinese PLA and, in Russia's absence from the United Nations, pushed through a ready-prepared resolution making the war a 'UN Police Action'. US General MacArthur was appointed 'Commander-in-Chief, United Nations Forces', to which Britain and others, without quibble, gave 'token' forces. The Communists, in general, who were supposed to have started the whole thing, appeared taken by surprise.

Whether the North Koreans went over to the offensive after being attacked by the South, as they said and I believe, or themselves attacked the South without provocation as the Western powers claimed, one thing is indisputable – only the anti-Communists gained.

Before I left for the front, my Chinese friends openly deplored the war and hoped for its early end. For one thing, they could not finish their own civil war by taking Taiwan, without coming into direct military conflict with the United States Navy, with all that must follow.

Japanese bomber bases so conveniently near Vladivostock were to be retained by the US.

America's hated puppet Syngman Rhee was saved from his electoral debacle in the May elections and in consequence of the war, the impending peaceful re-unification of Korea was prevented.

Far East post-war rehabilitation was destabilised when both China and Russia needed peace and, as a bonus, America's enormous and profitable arms industry got the go-ahead.

Most important of all, the US-Soviet disparity in nuclear weapons was a standing invitation to the American hawks to find a way to use them before parity robbed the Pentagon of the chance. And as *The Times* later admitted, General MacArthur was determined to go down in history as the man who brought a *Pax Americana* to the Pacific. His plans, according to US General Matthew B. Ridgway, in his book *The Korean War*, included 'preventive war' against China regardless of 'the very considerable risk of igniting World War III'.

Being a new war it had no time to develop its own rules, which all wars do depending on terrain and weapons. My train from the China border to Pyongyang was the last in daylight. Probably the next one was attacked. I never heard.

On the ground it seemed absurd to suppose that the North Koreans had begun the war. They had no planes for self-defence and all supplies had to run the gauntlet at night down the single dirt road.

Breakfast with Mao

Life in Pyongyang was still staggering on. A few trams ran without windows. One hotel stood, blacked out and damaged. My huge, carpeted room stank of bugs and I typed my first sweaty story sitting in my underpants on a towel, being bitten.

My bed-sheets were smeared with the blood of former victims. As soon as I put out the light, the bed seethed. While I murdered a few, the rest got away. The red plush sofa was very short and the insect concentration as high.

I shook out my sheet, spread it on the carpet, ran US Army insect-repellent round the edges and lay in the middle naked but sweating. A not too distant bomb blew in the black-out blanket so that I could not put on the light again. But now there was relative peace, except for the tiny rare sound of a bug which had parachuted itself from the ceiling. When next I saw Pyongyang the United States Air Force had disposed of the hotel, the bugs and Pyongyang city.

It took a few days to find an old Russian Pobeda car, a driver and an escort with whom I could communicate in pidgin Chinese, and by that time the air war was being set in the pattern of a heavyweight boxer fighting a child.

B29 Superfortresses worked on the 'blanket bombing' of towns; Sabrejets flew missions needing speed against defended targets – bridges, tunnels and junctions; slower propeller fighter-bombers strafed and napalmed villages and refugees; B26s were used for night bombing of the road. US air power grew daily and the North Koreans had nothing to put against it.

I got my Pobeda because no one wanted a saloon car. We had to keep our heads outside all the time looking for planes between acacia branches used as camouflage.

Not far south of Pyongyang, I had my first taste of what kind of war this was going to be. North of Sariwon the road ran dead straight for ten kilometres. At the beginning, we hid the car and sat under a tree to eat our cold boiled rice and pickled *tolaji*. A brook was tinkling, cicadas plaintively shrilling, peasants were feeding their cabbages with diluted night soil.

Along the road there were groups of refugees: women with long billowing skirts, big bundles on their heads and children on their backs. The few men were old with white trousers tied in at the ankle.

A vibration in the air became a hum and a black shape grew quickly. A Mustang, flying very low, swerved to line up the road and opened up its multiple guns. I flung myself down, was pressed into the ground by the turbulence and the din went away.

It left screams, moans, babies' cries, calls for help, death, tears, blood, bereavement and life disfigurement. The pilot knew what was in his gunsights and his gun camera would have recorded it. This was policy. If refugees had also to move at night they would hamper military traffic.

Next day just after dawn I was the cause of such a road-sweeping pilot's death. We were going along one of those banked roads, empty but for our inappropriate saloon car when I saw a group of planes coming in at hill-top level and screamed 'Stop', the word for which is the same in Korean. One plane was peeling off opening up his cannons as we fell from the moving car and rolled into a rice paddy. A second later there was an earth-shaking bang as the pilot, out of control, hit a nearby hillside. We kept our distance until the ammunition had stopped exploding and we were pretty sure no more napalm was on board. We found the pilot had been hurled out of the plane. His boots were torn off and his toes scorched and curling in the heat. He was dead. Papers from his pockets lay all around including photographs of a woman with two young children and letters from his wife urging him not to take risks but to think of her and the children.

There was also an official military document, printed in English, Korean and Chinese, offering free conduct through the lines and a big money reward to anyone who would help the bearer, Chuck Duffy. But Chuck, a few feet away, would no longer need such help. If it is still of any interest, the plane was a Marine fighter, No. AD4 Navy 123844.

Not long after we drove round the Pine Tree Peak, over the 38th Parallel, through Kaesong and Panmunjom – names soon to be household words – and into the burning bomb-damage of Seoul, the South Korean capital.

My Chinese-speaking escort found his way through the rubble to a luxurious American-built underground bunker which the Korean People's Army (KPA) was using as its headquarters. Koreans are sticklers for dress so the high brass here were dressed as for parade. Their brains were obviously saying to them: English comrade? Why English? They welcomed me politely and in a preoccupied manner introduced me to a pallid civilian who then addressed me in a familiar-sounding language. It was in fact English.

The brass had called in the man in charge of industry, one Choi Tai Ryong, because he knew English. He was pallid after twelve years in Seoul's ghastly West Gate Gaol, having been gaoled by the Japanese as a Communist, kept there under the Americans for the same reason, and rescued in the nick of time by the KPA's quick advance south.

Choi had learned English in gaol from bits of newspaper, without the benefit of hearing its pronunciation, rhythm or accentuation. His written English was good; his spoken English had to be learned.

What could they do to help? These smartly dressed officers looked at me worriedly, wanting to get on with their map work.

Choi and I went into a corner. I knew what I wanted. Once again I had landed in the journalist's favourite position: I was where events were shaping history and I was there alone. I had to get to where the action was and ensure sustenance and communications. Without communications it would be better to stay at home; for it is a sad thing to go through shot, shell, bombs and snipers, sleepless nights, blistered feet, hunger, dysentery and the breath of death on your cheek only to realise that there is no way to send your priceless information to where it must go.

I asked for the lot: authority to go wherever the KPA went, an interpreter, transport, food and authority to send my reports to Beijing by any available route.

They looked at each other. One said, suddenly inspired, 'Comrade Choi really has no industry to manage at present. He could arrange these things for Comrade Ah Lan.'

In two days I had become a going concern with three jeeps, an escort of a captain and eight soldiers, Choi and a manager, Pak Bong Min, who had been freed from the same cell as Choi in West Gate Gaol. We had rice, dried fish, red pepper, salt and bourbon.

It was dawn and already much too light when we set off on a

journey which soon led to the British Labour Cabinet debating whether to hang the *Daily Worker*'s editor and myself, if available, for treason. At that moment I was concerned with avoiding US aircraft and did not give a thought to the gallows.

Choi had made a date for us to meet people in Suwon, twenty-five miles south. I tried to persuade him to wait till dusk but I could not risk appearing nervous. My escort regarded the whole thing as a great lark. Off we went, as to a picnic, driving much too close together and leaving a dust column visible for miles.

Someone started to sing a sweet old Korean song, 'Ariran', in the inevitable waltz time, 'If you cross Ariran mountain without me, you'll break a leg before you go ten *ri*.'

Even for Korea, the Land of Morning Calm, it was a day of splendour. Cicadas were sawing crescendo in the acacia trees. Peasants waved, saw me and their mouths dropped open. Old men squatted under deep eaves of straw smoking long pipes. Groups of women at streams with babies on their backs banged washing on smooth rocks. Others carried water pots on their heads wiping away sparkling drops. Inside cottages staccato batons rang like xylophones, flattening clothes. The world was drowsy and full of peace.

People suddenly ran from under their bundles. We scrambled from our jeeps. A Mustang, dark and crushing, blazed over at tree-top height, multiple guns firing, leaving its din behind with the havoc it had caused.

We had not even gone ten *ri*, five kilometres, and had lost one man with a broken leg, another man to take him back to Seoul on a cart and one jeep riddled with bullets.

Nobody argued now about travelling after dark; trying to sleep as we filtered through military traffic jams and groups of refugees while bullets from dispersed enemy snipers whizzed past. By day the driver tried to sleep, Pak foraged, we went on foot investigating and I wrote reports while supper cooked. We were never free from the stink of burning army gear and putrid roasting corpses.

At Taejon, where US General Dean's 24th Division had been smashed a week before, we overtook reports we had been hearing of 'a very big slaughter' of thousands of political prisoners somewhere not far from Taejon.

Taejon itself lay in flames, a total ruin but still being bombed daily to deny its use as a road junction. We holed up two miles out of town in the empty house of a rich landlord where peaches and nectarines grew.

Pak came back from foraging with some vegetables and some hard news about the massacre. It had taken place in San Nai county, about eighteen or twenty *ri* from Taejon on the road to Yongdong and Taegu. We walked round the burning town and down the road, taking cover from fighter planes slowly combing the area until we came to a village, actually a few ruined cottages under feathery purplish ash of their burned thatch.

It was called Rangwul. Villagers who had stayed with their land in makeshift shelters had all been witnesses of the massacre. They had been forced to dig great pits in a nearby valley and shovel earth back on the dead and dying victims. They showed us the way but stayed outside the flat-bottomed valley between low mountains.

It needed an effort to move into that charnel-house stench. We could walk safely in the middle of the valley though our shoes rolled on American cartridge cases. Otherwise the floor of the valley was largely a thin crust of rain-washed soil covering the rotting corpses of at least 7,000 men and women. Through the fissures could be seen among the stinking mass of flesh and bone, hands, legs, grinning skulls half stripped to the bone, heads burst open by bullets, wrists wired together.

For days I could taste the smell and see the waxy flesh and limbs thrust through the light soil covering by rigor mortis. One of the escort looking back as we went, sank up to his thigh in the hideous mess below. I grabbed him and he stood staring at his leg and suddenly vomited.

They had all been political prisoners, suspected opponents of the Syngman Rhee rule thrust on them by Washington, taken from gaols around Taejon and concentrated here for slaughter. Rangwul villagers reckoned them to number over seven thousand. American military advisers had been present but had not done the killing.

I paced out the pits, took photographs, made notes, collected US M1 and carbine cartridge cases and Lucky Strike cigarette packets.

We walked back slowly to the Taejon-Yongdon road, unable to speak or meet each others eyes. Miles up, a flight of B29s slowly droned over and loosed their bombs on Taejon.

A silent group of villagers had stayed near the road, among them an old woman, and Pak had sat with her on a grassy bank with his arm round her, comforting her as she wept. Her son lay somewhere among that stinking flesh. Pak too was weeping. So was Choi. They had been saved from that fate in Seoul.

Choi whispered to me, 'Pak's wife was in Taejon prison. And now ...' He nodded into the valley.

In August 1950 I radioed a 12,000-word roundup of my first impressions of the Korean War and the *Daily Worker* published it as a pamphlet. It included full details of Rangwul's death pits, with photographs.

By the time it came out, the 'UN' forces had retaken Taejon and Rangwul. The British, lending colour to Washington's 'UN Police Action' myth, had officers, troops and journalists attached to MacArthur's command and could have disproved my report if it had been a lie. Since I was the only European journalist with the KPA and working for a Communist paper, this chance would never have been passed up if it had existed.

Apparently not a single British or American journalist paid a visit to Ranwul to investigate what would have been a world scoop if they uncovered it as a 'Commie' lie. The British did not ask any of their advisors in Korea to look into it. The Labour Cabinet even concealed that they had discussed it, by recording their discussion in a secret Cabinet paper not to be made public till thirty years later when they would all be dead or in the House of Lords.

The Attlee Cabinet began by endorsing the opinion presented by Sir Hartley Shawcross that my pamphlet – *I Saw the Truth in Korea* – constituted treason because it 'made grave allegations against South Korean and American soldiers and airmen and attacked the United Kingdom government for their support of United Nations action in Korea,' so bringing 'Aid and comfort to the King's enemies'. Treason has only one penalty – death.

Nobody in the Cabinet mentioned the possibility that these 'grave allegations' might be true or suggested they be checked, or that there was no declaration of war, or that the King was not King of the United Nations. It was at the height of the Cold War and casting doubts on the US was rather worse than treason if it came to that and should merit death by the slicing process rather than hanging.

For Attlee, Bevin, Shawcross and Chuter Ede it was rather a matter of sweeping the thing under the carpet. This was understandable if you can understand the poltroonery of those Labour leaders.

I was not in the jurisdiction. Their reluctance to drag Johnny Campbell out of the editorial chair at the *Daily Worker* to face a charge of treason was also understandable. Campbell was not a man to go quietly. He was after all the man who had been indirectly responsible for the collapse of the first Labour government, and why give him the chance to double his score?

Such a man would certainly have subpoenaed the peasants who had dug those death pits, demanded an impartial inquiry and an examination of that dreadful valley – five years after Belsen and not even a decade since the Home Office had been forced to lift the ban on the *Daily Worker*.

Everyone present at that Cabinet Meeting knew that the Korean War was not accepted by the British public or the British soldiers who had been sent willy-nilly to face death to lend a 'UN' fig-leaf to American intervention in the Korean civil war.

At that meeting in No. 10 Downing Street, the belatedly released Cabinet record shows, there was more opportunism than righteous indignation. The ministers' discussion was very self-revealing.

They noted that:

> other newspapers had published information about alleged atrocities by South Koreans ... It would therefore be said that the author and publishers of this pamphlet were being prosecuted because of its political bias. There was also a risk that a jury, knowing that the penalty was death, would refuse to convict. Even if a conviction was obtained, this would be regarded as a government prosecution and it might be thought anomalous that the Home Secretary should thereafter advise the King to commute the only sentence which the court could impose.

War and Massacre in Korea

This was the first of many occasions during the Korean War when the British or US governments confirmed my reports by failing to disprove them when it would obviously have been possible if they had been untrue.

And if Katyn is still news for some, why not Rangwul?

10
Chinese Strategy and American Fire-power

To be captured by the Americans was no part of my intention or wish, but I could not tell Choi, much less the others of my escort why I had decided that I – and therefore they – must return to Seoul and probably further north.

They argued bitterly against going back. We were installed in a comfortable house whose owner had fled. It was the season of fruit and day followed balmy day untroubled by aircraft as we listened to the distant rumble of guns on the Taegu front. Their greatest hope was to be present when Taegu fell and the last American soldier was driven into the sea. They drew maps in the sand. The KPA now controlled nine-tenths of South Korea. There was only the other tenth – the Pusan beach-head – to be cleared to 'rid Korea of the American imperialist'. Only!

But I did not believe that Taegu would fall. Since leaving Seoul I had become daily more worried about the KPA's almost unhindered advance south.

Travelling at night filtering through the military traffic it was obvious that every kilometre we advanced added to our troubles and played into MacArthur's hands. That thin thread of unsurfaced north-south road, without air cover, could not maintain reinforcements much less bring up the increased supplies needed to smash the shortened and strengthened American front at Taegu.

Formally it was the KPA's right to drive the Americans into the sea but I did not believe that they could. And to exercise this right they must leave out other considerations.

Looking at the Pacific situation as a whole, pushing the Pusan beachhead into the sea would put Truman's back to the wall politically. From the start it was an ill-conceived idea. The bitterness of such a defeat at the hands of badly equipped Asians would enhance MacArthur's prospects of getting a free hand to broaden the war, which he made little effort to hide was his aim.

At or before Seoul was where the North Koreans in my view should have paused, with their army intact and shorter supply lines, to talk politics from a position of vantage.

As things stood MacArthur seemed to be holding the KPA in a clinch at Taegu while he prepared to open a second beach-head further north. Sitting it out on a static front was inviting capture or worse when the trap closed. And journalistically there was nothing to do till Taegu fell, which I was prepared to gamble it would not.

We loaded the jeeps and drove north.

Back in the capital, the Seoul Hotel was still standing and little more damage had been done to the city since I had left. I met a Chinese military officer I knew, in civilian dress, there to observe the scene, and asked his opinion on my own ideas.

He touched his finger-tip to his nose and said in that Chinese way, 'Some think (by which he meant at the very least that he personally thought) that the military strategy has been wrong. We cannot judge that and as friends we cannot suggest it. Our Korean friends have their main forces in the south, at Taegu. If their possibility to manoeuvre were reduced or even cut, it would present a problem.'

'I have noticed,' I said in the same style, 'that this city has been spared heavy bombing.'

'Do you intend to return to the south?' he asked.

'No. Do you?'

'I have seen all I need there. Here or further north are more interesting for me.'

A few days later, on 15 September, MacArthur made his predictable landing at Inchon, on the west coast of South Korea about twenty miles from Seoul, with some 300 US and British warships, 500 aircraft and 75,000 men.

This force began to smash its way toward Seoul taking an extremely long time to do it. This was because the advance, against very light resistance, was done in the new style of warfare based on overwhelming firepower used to save the lives of nervous, ill-trained and undisciplined soldiers. It was a political matter back in the States.

America's tremendous weaponry was used to ensure that as far as possible, the foot soldiers never met the enemy. Their task was to follow behind tanks in the swathes of undefended devastation cleared for them by massed long-range artillery and air-strikes. Behind the extreme prodigality needed for this keeping-out-of-reach war technique was a vast industrial and political machine hungry for war contracts and votes and anxious that casualties could lead to anti-war movements.

First came the artillery; then, as the barrage lifted, a nervous tank advance with jittery over-use of automatic small arms fire, usually without an opponent in sight. At any sign of opposition, a halt was called to tanks and infantry, artillery moved up and close-support air-strikes were radioed in, with dive-bombing, multiple machine-gunning and napalm. Then another hesitant advance into the rubble.

The method worked magnificently when MacArthur's forces pulverised their way from Inchon to Seoul against an enemy armed with little but small-arms, mortars and grenades – all hand-to-hand weapons – without aircraft or artillery and hampered by the proximity of their own civilian countrymen.

Victory came when there was no cover left among the rubble and nothing moving to shoot at. It all took time and there was no evidence that it saved any of the lives of the road-bound Americans.

Certain it was that civilian men, women and children were killed and maimed in Seoul without discrimination in their thousands and all their poor belongings of a lifetime destroyed. These were the people whom the Americans and others who were lending their support such as the British, were supposedly rescuing from their fellow countrymen in the north.

It did not matter for they were only 'Gooks'. With this word they took away humanity from the men, women, children, wives and husbands of their own purported allies, on whose behalf they claimed the right to be in Korea. Later it would be 'Cong' but now it was 'Gook' with which they turned people of another nation into a subspecies. A dead Korean, regardless of sex, age or place of domicile was a 'good Gook'. It made a person's life simpler. And what does it mean, this word that acted as a pall covering dead human beings whom one is licensed to kill? Country. That is all. I am a *Yungguk saram* if my memory serves me and the GIs were *Meiguk sarami*.

American soldiers in Korea were beweaponed delinquents and at the same time the most pampered soldiers in history. Not for them a pound or two of parched grain-meal in a cloth roll on which a Korean or a Chinese fighting man could survive with no more than water. American combat rations then ran to meats, poultry, hamburgers, vegetables, fruits, biscuits, coffee, sugar, milk, vitamins, confectionery, packaged to attract the eye of a supermarket customer and made (profitably) by the same firms who would be selling the same things in peacetime. Wherever the troops passed there was a litter of empty or wasted packages. They had clothes in absurd variety, mostly unsuited to the terrain they faced but providing nice profits and free advertising. It was the same story of war contracts and votes.

Irresistible metal, explosive and flame carried the 'UN' forces slowly forward. Outnumbered twenty to one, shelled, dive-bombed, strafed and napalmed, the KPA retreated street by street, exacting some 14,000 casualties from MacArthur's assault force. Then they disappeared like wisps of smoke into the surrounding mountains.

When the Americans formally entered Seoul, it was almost completely devastated but for the Capitol which they had carefully avoided demolishing.

An American sergeant clambered up the building and ripped down the North Korean flag. He fixed in its place – not the flag of the United Nations under which MacArthur was supposed to hold his command, not the flag of South Korea, but Old Glory itself – the Stars and Stripes. A fine photo for the folks back home.

Both sides were now back to where the war had begun and the question was: what next?

Neither the Chinese nor the Russians had intervened in the three-month-old dispute and had made it unmistakably evident that they wanted it localised and ended, and wanted no foreign troops on their border. China whose border with Korea was a long one had said that it would not tolerate the invasion of a neighbour. This could only mean that it would not tolerate 'UN' forces north of the 38th Parallel. A ceasefire and peace were being offered.

For Truman, peace would complicate various things which had been simplified by the war. Peace would remove the pretext for the presence of the American Seventh Fleet to protect Taiwan. How then could Communist China be kept out of the United Nations? America would have difficulty in maintaining Syngman Rhee in power. How would the pace of rearmament be maintained? To take a single example: the price of the light tanks littering the Korean landscape had gone up from $39,600 to $126,000 each during these few months.

President Truman appeared to dither. Indeed he needed very little make-up to play the part of a small-town haberdasher uneasily trying to damp down the aggressiveness of the military. And while he equivocated, the soldier-darling of Congress, General MacArthur, with his casual dress and corn-cob pipe, perfect for the role of the great soldier impatient of political fuddy-duddies, ordered his troops across the 38th Parallel into North Korea – China's neighbour. He also demanded the unconditional surrender of the North Koreans and 'accidentally' bombed Chinese territory.

Once these things had been done, Washington naturally had to support them though anyone familiar with Truman's political record tended to regard it all as playing patball over the net.

MacArthur's assurances that there was no intention of crossing the Yalu River, China's border, or maybe accidentally bombing the Soviet Union, lacked credibility because of similar assurances given and broken about the 38th Parallel and China. But the real point was that neither power could tolerate having the Americans – even under the flag of the United Nations – advance to their borders.

MacArthur's advance was threatening the series of power stations along the Yalu River supplying current to North Korea, China and the Soviet Union.

A task force of Chinese military crossed the Yalu River into North Korea and took up positions to protect the dams, stop the American advance – which was actually spearheaded by British troops – and provide time for second thoughts. They came through the mountains silently on soft-soled shoes, lightly armed with small arms and mortars, and delivered a terrific lesson in mountain warfare to the road-bound forces of MacArthur. In spite of continuous US air reconnaisance they achieved total surprise.

MacArthur's careless dash for the Yalu River collapsed at a single blow, delivered by men armed with not much more than hand-guns. They pushed the 'UN' and South Korean troops back across the Chongchon River and then on 6 November, as silently as they had come, they disappeared. MacArthur's press corps called it a 'surprise manoeuvre'.

Actually it was China emphasising its warnings and its desire for peace.

MacArthur's reply came on 8 November – 79 B29 Superfortresses and 300 fighter planes attacked Sinuiju on the Korean side of the river border with China. They dropped 630 tons of bombs and 85,000 incendiaries, including napalm, destroying 90 per cent of the city.

A delegation from Beijing, scheduled to go to the United Nations on 15 November was therefore postponed till 24 November. On that day MacArthur launched his 'Home by Christmas' offensive.

A month to win a war on that front, where a terrible defeat had just been suffered!

It was neatly calculated. If MacArthur's new offensive took off well, the Chinese, in showing an interest in peace would appear as supplicants and lose face. If the Americans were pushed back, Truman would run grave political risk by talking peace. Also, to give MacArthur his due, he had not said which Christmas.

The 'Home by Christmas' offensive nonetheless forced the Chinese to send back the Chinese People's Volunteers – CPV – (volunteers in international law). There was some fighting, lasting a week or so, and then MacArthur's forces began withdrawing rather quickly and without apparent reason. Nor did the CPV seem in a hurry to catch them up.

To judge from the handouts, the US Eighth Army was in headlong flight before a powerful enemy. Actually there was no contact on the ground. It was bizarre. *The Times* military correspondent wrote of the Chinese, 'It seems manifest that their one object was to shepherd it (the enemy) south of the 38th Parallel without further fighting and, if that was so, they succeeded.'

He was not the only one. Peter Fleming, military expert of the *Spectator* said that the CPV had a no 'more exacting role than that of sheep dogs'. The British 29th Brigade covering this strange retreat, said, according to the *Daily Mail*, 'None of them has yet seen a Chinese Communist.'

Korea has no shortage of natural and man-made caves which make very comfortable bomb-proof homes. Extra rooms can usually be added at will by cutting into the granular but firm sandstone. Some of my friends commanding the Chinese People's Volunteers lived in one through which a little stream tinkled into an ice-cold pool. They sat there informally in the evenings relaxed and sipping a little white fire with their supper while from outside came the throbbing of a generator, the sharp barks of guards and occasionally a thrumming as an American night-bomber prowled.

Among them was the choleric friend of Chu De, General Peng Dehuai, Commander-in-Chief of the CPV and waging a much different kind of war than that he had fought so long against Chiang Kaishek. He was remarkably like Chu De in appearance and ruggedness, but taciturn. That he had been chosen for this difficult military and political task said all that was necessary about his quality.

In that comfortable cave with its floor of warm drifted sand the CPV leaders were not discussing how to drive the Americans into the sea but how to bring them to a standstill and force them to negotiate a ceasefire; how to prevent the Korean war from spreading and engulfing the Far East and possibly the world.

This was the actual explanation for the leisurely Chinese dawdle behind the apparently precipitate flight of the Americans. If the 'UN' forces left Korea they must make it obvious that they were not being pushed.

Most of the CPV remained in North Korea, making occasional patrols in strength over the 38th Parallel, while

General MacArthur's press office and his favourite agency journalists fought their imaginary battles in the vacant landscape.

On 4 January 1951, the Americans quite unnecessarily abandoned Seoul again. To explain this retreat, MacArthur's press office summoned into existence 'Red Chinese hordes, estimated at 1,250,000 fighting men'.

Nobody could find these men. The US Air Force admitted finding no trace of them. Selkirk Panton of the *Daily Express* wrote: 'There has been no sign of any Communist "hordes" in the front-line fighting.' Nor was there any front-line fighting, or any fighting at all. US patrols went almost to Seoul and found no enemy troops. Towns that MacArthur's press staff described as centres of fierce battles were actually silent and empty.

At one conference, a journalist, Michael Davidson, asked the briefing colonel: 'Will you tell us how many Chinese battalions go to a horde, or vice versa?' Later his accreditation was withdrawn.

Handouts from MacArthur's headquarters told of fierce battles which I knew were not happening. On the other hand the American retreat was so fast and careless that they appeared to be bent on getting out of Korea while elaborately staging a pretence of being overwhelmed by sheer numbers; drowned by 'human waves' against which civilised people with regard for human life – the Americans – could not prevail.

It looked as though MacArthur had again taken over the wheel to avert the danger of peace breaking out, as he had by crossing the 38th Parallel. But what could be the reason for staging the spurious rout of his own forces? A fake defeat might be a means to rally his jibbing allies, especially the British, and suppress their cowardly squeaks against the General's rough handling of the war. But if the correspondents of *The Times, Spectator* and others, including even the *Daily Mail* could see that there was no real war going on – and say so certainly America's allies could see it too.

MacArthur's aim could certainly not be to abandon Korea and accept humiliating military defeat. But that is what appeared to be happening. Why? What could be the aim of the apparent attempt to be driven out of Korea by overwhelming manpower? The answer seemed to lie in Truman's threat to use atomic weapons. America was then still superior to the Soviet Union in nuclear weapons and this was a standing temptation, much talked of.

Suppose there were a South Korean 'Republican' government-in-exile on, say Cheju Island similar to the Chinese 'Nationalist' one on Taiwan; suppose all 'UN' forces were safely 'driven' out of Korea; would not President Truman's threat to use atomic weapons – impractical while the 'UN' troops were in Korea – move into the realm of the practicably possible?

A pre-emptive nuclear war based on the Philippines, Taiwan, Japan, Indo-China and Cheju and the Soviet Union's evanescent disparity in nuclear weapons, could vaporise resistance in Asia and settle the world's fate under American mastery.

There were minds thinking and acting on such premises and, given MacArthur's record, he would certainly be among them. His place in history would be assured and America, through his genius, enabled to rectify its error in failing to press ahead after Hiroshima and Nagasaki.

At this point, President Truman threatened to use the atomic bomb and declared a state of emergency and total mobilisation of the USA for war. He set up the economic mobilisation machinery which had twice heralded American entry into world wars.

Attlee flew to Washington and was promised that there would be no evacuation of Korea unless 'UN' forces were actually pushed into the sea. But on the atomic bomb itself he only got a vague assurance that Britain would be 'consulted' before its use.

That much came to light at the time but what was kept dark was that the British Cabinet secretly wrote to Washington accepting the risk of world war by supporting the US in bombing targets inside China. This was only revealed thirty years later, under the thirty-year secrecy rule. On 8 May 1951 Foreign Secretary Herbert Morrison wrote to his US opposite number, Dean Acheson, saying that an attack on Chinese bases 'will involve serious risks of an extension of the war, perhaps even into a global conflict, but the consequences will have to be faced and shared by all of us'.

By mid-January, nobody could any longer believe in MacArthur's great retreat which was so palpably leading to nuclear disaster. Under British pressure, 'UN' troops received orders to go into reverse and fight. When they did so, they found emptiness, 'Where are the Chinese in Korea?' asked the correspondent of the *Daily Mail*. 'UN forces today pushed forward to answer the question – and found nothing. They re-entered Osan without a fight, another Allied column reached Kumyangjang, and a third is advancing west of the Seoul-Osan road.'

When they were located, the Chinese forces with their Korean allies had quietly dug in and had been paying no attention to MacArthur's enticements to advance. Quite simply they had made it impossible for the Americans to evacuate Korea. Peng Dehuai had selected a defensive line athwart the 38th Parallel and dug deeply into Korea's friable sandstone, creating a system of caves, tunnels and trenches that virtually could not be turned. On the map, what I called the Peng Dehuai Line, was as though the parallel itself had been swung five or so degrees anti-clockwise on an axis in the centre, leaving as much territory south of the 38th Parallel to the west as north of it to the east.

This line, chosen with military skill, produced stalemate. Every assault on it was repelled. The heaviest bombing had no effect. Day by day it was improved. Once inside its maze of convolutions you could sleep through any attack. It was possible to walk from coast to coast in safety. There the Chinese and Korean forces waited for the Korean War to be drawn to truce talks by the military facts.

They came, but not before General MacArthur, having mistaken the illusion of grandeur for the actuality of power, had been made to take at least part of the responsibility for the catastrophic campaign in Korea. He was sacked, feeling victimised, by Truman, who in a showdown could out-politick MacArthur with one hand.

One of the endearing customs of Ho Chi Minh was to drop in for breakfast with guests in Hanoi, practising some of his languages and drinking half a cup of strong coffee while he smoked thin cigarettes rolled from makings in a battered tin box. On one such occasion when the Americans were trying 'to bomb Vietnam back into the stone age,' as US General Lemay put it, I asked President Ho what he thought was the main weakness of the American forces in Vietnam.

He laughed and answered, 'They don't understand bamboo and that is what we have.'

I said it had been like that in Korea. They hadn't understood mountains and that was what Korea had.

When the CPV crossed the Yalu River for the second time in late 1950 General Peng Dehuai's secret orders had been to push the Americans back to the 38th Parallel and keep them there. Pushing was not necessary. Following them down the peninsular he had to take two important facts into account: that the 38th Parallel was a political or geographical concept and not merely useless from a military viewpoint but a positive incitement to cross it. Secondly, the Americans would never agree to a truce which cost them real estate and therefore face.

Korea's unusual terrain gave the answer and the Peng Dehuai line was the result. They could be held there as long as necessary.

I had jeeped through Kaesong several times in the dark, dodging random bombing, but in July 1951 I first saw it by day – a lovely little traditional walled city surrounded by low hills and almost the only place in Korea with some houses undamaged. Under pressure from America's allies, talks were starting a stone's throw south of the 38th Parallel in Kaesong, which had been declared neutral.

I guessed that the talks might take a month but they took a month of months for I saw the moon wax and wane over Kaesong thirty-one times and what happened in the first days was a reliable guide to the following two-and-a-half years.

Now I had the company of some Chinese and Korean journalists and of Wilfred Burchett, an Australian journalist doing a stint for the Paris *Ce Soir*, and glad I was, for accredited to the 'UN' negotiators was a horde – certainly a crowd – of assorted English-speaking press people, and we were the only two on the northern side.

We were a sensation and they crowded round like South Sea Islanders meeting Captain Cook, almost feeling our clothes. 'Two White Commies' one agency man wrote on his clipboard. At first we were excitedly mistaken for Burgess and Maclean, two British diplomats who had gone missing just before. After all: Burgess – Burchett; Maclean – Alan.

The American ('UN') military delegates demanded that hostilities must continue till all truce issues were settled. They made clear their distaste for having to talk to people they called, among themselves, 'Gooks' and 'Chinks'.

The chief Korean delegate, General Nam Il, proposed to Admiral Charles Turner Joy, his 'UN' opposite number, that the two sides should cease fire at the 38th Parallel where the fighting had begun, exchange prisoners and withdraw all non-Korean forces from Korea.

Admiral Joy disagreed. There were three battle lines, he said, land, sea and air. As the Koreans and Chinese had no navy and no air force, they must offer something in lieu. This must be 12,000 square kilometres of Korean 'real estate' – the words he used – north of the battleline.

Burchett and I had access to the speeches and documents of both sides and sent these facts to our papers. The 'UN' correspondents were briefed by a US Airforce Brigadier General, William P. Nuckols.

Tuning in that night to the Voice of America to check what the opposition was doing, we stared at each other in disbelief. Nuckols had briefed the 'UN' journalists that Admiral Joy had proposed a ceasefire at the 38th Parallel and the 'Communists' had flatly refused to discuss it. And that was the story most of the world got and swallowed.

Burchett and I got the speeches verbatim and passed them on to the 'UN' correspondents who were being deceived by Nuckols that the Korean-Chinese negotiators refused to talk about a ceasefire at the Parallel. After all, we were Communists and therefore not to be believed. Some of the correspondents possibly sent reports that we seemed to have authentic information that Admiral Joy was demanding a large slice of North Korea as the price of peace and it was actually the Commies who wanted a ceasefire at the parallel, but if they did, these reports never got through the head-office filters.

At last INS (International News Service, later merged with United Press to become UPI) seemed to decide that if necessary they must sacrifice their man on the spot and set off the firework.

On 3 August INS sent out a story which contained the following words:

... and Winnington declared that a 'perfectly reliable authority' has informed him that the UN is pressing for a line considerably north of the present battleline.

The 'UN' briefing officer, Nuckols, came under heavy cross-questioning. General Matthew B. Ridgway, successor to MacArthur, gained a few days by breaking off the talks three times on minor issues but each time the Korea-Chinese delegates deliberately gave way to save the talks.

Ridgway's press office gave the comforting impression that peace was only one or two meetings away. This was suspicious because actually the talks were frozen and the Americans had intensified their bombing of the north, although 'there were no more targets in Korea', according to General O'Donnell, Commander of the Far Eastern Bomber Command. Most sinister of all, Korean-Chinese intelligence, which was very good, reported the Americans as preparing a major ground offensive.

Time passed, public worry mounted that the truce talks seemed to be petering out amid such headlines as 'Ridgway Warns of Red Trickery' in *US News* on 17 August. In spite of the build-up what came next was a surprise.

At 10.20 pm on 22 August I was enjoying the summer night at the press camp near the Korean-Chinese headquarters below Pine Tree Peak when I heard a low-flying bomber – an unmistakeable B26. I yelled to Burchett, reading under his mosquito net, 'Put that bloody light out,' and hit the ground as I heard the familiar whistle and whip-crack of near bombs. The plane droned round and came back with machine-guns firing and flew away dropping some napalm bombs as it went.

The 'UN' liaison officers came, headed by US Air Force Colonel Andrew Kinney, but broke off the investigation on the ground that journalists, including myself, were with the Korean-Chinese liaison team. Kinney promised to return next day bringing 'UN' journalists but next day there were reports on all Western radios that the Korean-Chinese side had 'fabricated' an incident and 'broken off the cease-fire talks ...'

How far up the line did this bombing incident go? That was often the question when dealing with the US Air Force. Someone had briefed that B26, filled its tanks, loaded its guns, anti-personnel bombs and napalm. That had to be the Air Force. Nuckols was an Air Force Brigadier, Kinney was an Air Force Colonel. It keyed in with the obstructions in the talks and the new American offensive which had been launched.

Kaesong's neutrality could not now be relied on and it would very likely be blown off the map like every other Korean town.

Our contact man with the Korean-Chinese delegation, Shen Jiantu, solemnly told us that bad and dangerous as the situation was, 'we shall never break off the talks.' The delegations had moved and 'we too must move today. Keep only what you can carry. We may have to walk out. In any case, keep moving. Secret agents have been sent into the neutral zone and are armed. Be ready for any hardship – any danger.'

Burchett, myself and Ju Jiping of the Chinese Da Gong Bao were allowed to stay in Kaesong. During the next two months the liaison officers kept the door formally open. We lived with them.

Day and night at half-hourly intervals two Korean girl radio operators talked to their American opposite numbers: 'Hallo, Addition. Hallo, Addition; This is Festival. I have no repeat no communication for you. Have you any communication for me? Thank you. Over and out.'

To those of us left in Kaesong, watching gun-flashes outlining the hills on a 'front aflame from end to end' as a lyrical American journalist wrote, it was obvious that if the talks were ever to start again, we should have to wait till Ridgway's offensive had burned out.

We moved around that lovely little city like bad tenants, with well-informed US aircraft dropping bombs and firing .50 calibre machine-guns never far behind. Kaesong being neutral under the agreement which only we were observing, and also only a couple of rifle shots from the military line of contact, had spies the way a hedgehog has fleas. Among the constant breaches of agreement, sometimes the 'UN' liaison officers agreed to a meeting to which we went in trepidation because they knew where and when it would be.

But even in no man's land, Korea is always beautiful and never more than in autumn. We stole away from our bodyguards to picnic dance-parties in peach orchards and barbecued pheasants while we learned Korean from tall girls who floated rather than walked in their flowing dress. Amazingly, we discovered that they made Calvados in Liaoning. We watched the hills turn every colour from pale brown to scarlet.

'Addition' and 'Festival' stayed in touch, but the actual contact was along Peng Dehuai's do-it-yourself Maginot Line against which two full-scale offensives were smashed in two months.

Inside those honeycombed mountains were tunnels, artillery emplacements going deep into the ground, a maze of trenches, underground arteries for bringing in stores, mess halls, baths, toilets, recreation and lecture rooms. Ridgway's technical superiority meant little to the men playing cards inside those hills. While the shells and bombs were bursting they stayed there. Some mountains were ankle-deep in rock dust. When the barrages lifted, the 'UN' forces assaulted uphill at a disadvantage. They had little stomach for it and who could blame them with peace talks supposedly going on. Burned-out American tanks and 'UN' bodies littered the gorges.

Between US onslaughts, the military seemed more interested in getting back to the war than to the negotiating table. General Van Fleet, the Eighth Army commander, said on 12 September, 'The enemy is badly hurt. We will hurt him much more before the winter is over and then he will want peace.'

But even before the winter had begun Van Fleet's next offensive had gone the way of the last and he was looking for some face-saving headlines. A 'Caucasian division' was in action in the north. 'Russian Artillerymen Believed Responsible for Recent Accurate Communist Shooting.' 'Pilots in Chinese Planes Heard Talking Russian.' Better be beaten by Russians than Asians. But no Soviet POWs; no Soviet bodies. Associated Press reported that an offensive to encircle Kaesong had failed.

On 4 October General Bradley declared 'there is a chance of winning a military decision in Korea.' But on 16 October Ridgway acknowledged 'the situation from some standpoints could be readily construed as a military stalemate. It all depends on how you look at it.'

Having had to swallow a lot of words, the Americans

diverted attention by refusing to return to Kaesong for the talks which now were to start up again. Not wanting to meet in a Korean-Chinese neutral town was understandable though it later emerged that actually they wanted their hands free to capture it. Eventually a desolate village eight kilometres from Kaesong was chosen – the now well-known Panmunjom.

That day I went to have a look at it and hearing planes, took cover. They were F-80 jets and as I watched, they sprayed the road with .50 calibre, killing a little boy Kang Yong Dong and wounding his two year old brother, the only living things on the road. The US Air Force had served notice that nothing had really changed.

The truce talks resumed 63 days and several offensives after they were broken off.

11
The Inn With the Wooden Door

Pan Mun Jom – The Inn With the Wooden Door – was as small as a village can well be. There was no inn, there were no villagers, only three crumbling wattle-and-daub hovels and a romantic name. Marquees were pitched on high ground facing the desolate cottages. On the dirt road between, scores of 'UN' journalists mingled with the few journalists from the north.

The US Air Force had lost control of the daytime air and Admiral Joy had to drop his claim to North Korean 'real estate' in compensation. Talk about the truce line began again.

In the two months interval the Americans had worked hard to convince everyone that the cease-fire line, for this, that and many other reasons, must and could only be along the line of battle contact – 'with adjustments'.

The Korean-Chinese side had equally insisted that the war must end where it began – on the 38th Parallel. This was believed by the Americans to involve politics or face or some inscrutability fathomable only to Orientals, but in any case inviolable.

Now almost strangers to each other after sixty-three days, the chief delegates entered the tent, Admiral Joy taking his seat at the green baize table with his portfolio full of prepared texts, and facing General Nam Il.

In one Marx brothers film, I think it was Chico Marx who is seen leaning against a house wall on his outstretched arm. He has to flee, takes his arm away and the house falls down.

At this point the Korean-Chinese delegation took away its arm. 'We agree,' they said, 'to the (American) proposal to a ceasefire along the line of battle contact – with adjustments.

Now let us proceed to the next agenda item.'

In a moment, Joy's prepared speeches became useless. The Americans packed them together, proposed an adjournment and hurried from the tent. Moments later their helicopters took off, jeep tyres squealed as Nuckols herded 'his' journalists away before they could get briefed by the Red correspondents. That night he did not tell them of the dramatic change. Only Radio Beijing, the *Daily Worker* and *Ce Soir* had the news and were ignored by the western world.

Next day in Panmunjom, we found that Nuckols had convinced the 'UN' journalists that there was nothing new in the 'Communists' vague and unclear suggestion'.

Confident in their water-tight news blockade the now-recovered American negotiators laid their adjustments on the table – a total of 1,000 square kilometres of territory extra, including Kaesong. During the next month they bargained for Kaesong in the tent and fought for it outside.

Within sight and sound of Panmunjom, they tried to take our battered home from home by force. Day and night the heavy shells whined in, machine-guns chattered and men fought and died trying to by-pass Kaesong to the north-east. Peng Dehuai's line could not be moved.

One day the Korean-Chinese delegates charged the Americans with faking the line of battle contact to show hundreds of square kilometres they did not hold as being in their lines and offering to exchange these areas for Kaesong. I was chatting or arguing with Cecil Brownlow of INS (now the 'I' of UPI) when he told me that Nuckols had hung a map in the 'UN' press-tent showing the front-line situation and he (Brownlow) could see that the American standpoint was absolutely fair.

'Without seeing that map,' I said, 'I will bet two bottles of Ginseng liquor against one of Remy Martin cognac that it's been doctored.'

Brownlow was a short-tempered redneck from the Deep South, an America-believer who even wore a square-topped rebel army cap in Panmunjom. He stalked angrily down the road, brought the map and Nuckols version of the American proposals for adjustments and challenged me take them back to Kaesong and tell me next day what was wrong with them. At that moment I saw Nuckols hurrying toward us and took off in my jeep with his map.

Next day was filled with radio and television interviews demonstrating that map and a corrected version, under Nuckols' bitter eye, and as a bonus, the American military chose that morning to shell, dive-bomb and napalm nearby hills which on their map were shown as within their own lines.

This incident was the beginning of a turn. Pressure went on from their head offices. United Press sent out the following typical item date-lined Panmunjom, 10 November 1951:

> Radio Peking broadcast a dispatch from Communist newsman Alan Winnington at Panmunjom Saturday night which said, 'If the Americans give up their demand for Kaesong a settlement can be reached in a matter of hours.'
>
> Winnington claimed that the UNC (United Nations Command – AW) had published 'red herrings and plain falsehoods' about the 7 November Communist demarcation line proposal. He listed three 'falsehoods':
> 1. Nuckols said this side wants an unalterable demarcation line before the discussions are completed. This is not true.
> 2. Nuckols said this side wants to be able to veto any adjustment. This is not true.
> 3. Nuckols said this side wants a de facto ceasefire. This is not true.
>
> Winnington said the Allies tried to tie up the agenda in order to encircle Kaesong by military force. He said: 'Kaesong remains the crucial issue ...'

Kaesong now disappeared from the Americans' demands but war was declared on the Red correspondents. There was a growth in the number of photographers not attached to any known news services but smelling strongly of CIA, who took photos of 'UN' journalists when they talked to us. Some journalists who had good relations with us were assigned elsewhere. Top agency men arrived to clean things up. Our photographs were posted up in the front-line units as 'Wanted' and to be seized on sight, though the real purpose was to frighten the 'UN' correspondents away from having contact.

When anything big was on at Panmunjom, the journalists flocked to us and then fled like sparrows. One minute we were surrounded and then alone on the empty road. A craps school began in their press tent and rarely a brave spirit came to the mud huts to drink and eat Yunnan ham with the Reds.

We had the facts straight from the baize table but if they finished up in the *People's Daily, Daily Worker* and *Ce Soir*, they would not effectively expose the devices being used by the US military to drag out and enlarge the war. Already the facts we had given our 'UN' colleagues had affected the course of the talks. Somehow we had to get the whip out of Nuckols' hand.

One of the best-kept secrets of Kaesong was that directing the Korean-Chinese delegation behind the scenes, was Qiao Guanhua, one of Zhou Enlai's closest collaborators. I often used to meet him casually strolling in Kaesong for fresh air. 'The Thin Man', as we called him, was widely travelled, spoke excellent English and German and knew that there was a world outside the Central Kingdom. I several times discussed our journalistic problems with him usefully – he was among other things, chief of the Chinese International Information Department. I put it down to his sophistication that we were able to do battle with Nuckols in our own way as journalists. I first met Qiao Guanhua in a tenement room in Hong Kong where he was doing extremely dangerous work for the Chinese Communist Party. He went on to become an Assistant Foreign Minister and, after Zhou Enlai's death, Foreign Minister, and had become anti-Soviet by that time. What happened to him after the Cultural Revolution is not yet clear, but he was superseded by Huang Hua, another Kaesong graduate.

The ostracism of the Red correspondents had reached the limit when suddenly, in its clubfooted way, the US Army decided to get into the propaganda business. One reason, probably the main one, was that army morale had skidded too low to be longer disguised.

George Barrett of the *New York Times* reported that the men in the field were convinced that 'their own commanders, for reasons unknown to the troops, are throwing up blocks against an (armistice) agreement'. The American delegation, he said, had created the impression 'that it switches its stand whenever the Communists indicate they might go along with it'.

'This was the state of affairs when the issue of Communist atrocities was suddenly injected into the situation,' the *New*

York Times commented.

This issue – the new block against an armistice – was a handout that 6,270 American captives had been 'butchered' at the Yalu River prisoner camps. Its promoter was Colonel Hanley, Judge Advocate General of the Eighth Army. General Ridgway put the disclosure down to God's 'inscrutable way' of exposing the Communists, but James Reston, also of the *New York Times*, impiously suggested that the world might see it as the US 'purposely trying to avoid a ceasefire in Korea'.

By chance, up in Number 5 prisoner camp on the Yalu River, at Pyoktong, was a veteran Associated Press photographer – Frank 'Pappy' Noel – captured during the 'Home-by-Christmas' campaign a year previously and waiting in the wings to step into a lead part.

Occasionally but without hope, three AP men – Bob Eunson, Bob Tuckman and Bob Schutz, a photographer – had whispered enquiries about smuggling a camera to Noel so that he could photograph the American POWs and send the results via us. On each occasion the Korean-Chinese delegation had rejected this idea. Discussing Hanley's new move with Qiao Guanhua I raised the idea again and he said, 'Ah. Go ahead and quickly.'

Bob Schutz barely contained his ecstasy next day at Panmunjom. He only had a Speedgraphic and his usual day's film supply. 'Oh, my God,' he kept whispering. 'Oh, Jeez. I'll bring more tomorrow.' We smuggled the stuff into my jeep.

AP ran splendidly to form. Having now the incredible luck to have their own man in the camps, the first thing AP head office did was to tell their people in Korea to pull out of the 'pool' which made all photos taken by the American agencies mutually available. By withdrawing, they of course wrecked it. But Bob Schutz said, 'I would do murder for this. It's the scoop of the century.'

It was indeed a scoop. Frank Noel, undistinguished personally, was a Pulitzer Prize Winner. It was too much for AP to have it all alone. Civil war would have broken out among the agencies and would have encouraged the army to stop Noel's photos. But we could not force AP to share and as a result, their own isolation and greed might ruin the whole action.

The Inn With the Wooden Door

To break AP's monopoly, another camera went up by a young Xinhua photographer, Xiang Yi, with the job of shooting a mass of photographs of the prisoners to hand over to the other agencies and press. Noel's photographs were handed to AP: well-fed young Americans and other prisoners in CPV quilted uniforms, guaranteed to bring joy to wives and mothers and obviously not faked.

It was sensational. I don't think I ever saw such concentrated jealousy on one hand and smug gloating on the other. But it was short-lived. We gave out the photos taken by our Chinese photographer, Xiang Yi, except to United Press, whose chief man there, Dibble, had been among the leading anti-Reds. But UP was the second largest agency and to exclude it would have been a foolish act of revenge which would also endanger the whole project.

On his way down from the Yalu River, Xiang Yi had taken time to shoot a roll of film of General Dean, commander of the US 24th Infantry Division which had been wiped out at Taejon. Other than getting captured, Dean had little to his credit but since he had been rumoured dead he had become a hero and was now manifestly alive. As a scoop, those twelve Rollei pictures rivalled AP's. After he had sweated for an hour, I passed them to Dibble, whispering what they were.

He took them with shaking hands, hardly able to believe it. Next day they appeared as a centre-spread in – of all papers – *Stars and Stripes*, the official US army newspaper – under the banner 'General Dean Happy and Well in Communist Prison Camp'. After this, photos of the prisoners playing volleyball and football and skating on the Yalu River appeared regularly in the Western press. Noel was awarded the photographers' prize of the year.

The demand was enormous. The larger agencies wanted to put things on a commercial basis, partly to evade the charge of collaborating with the enemy. AP said to me, 'Let us open a banking account, anywhere in the world. Name the sum and we'll pay it in. No obligations. Let us at least buy you a house in London or somewhere.' Not to appear toffee-nosed we accepted an occasional case of liquor, tobacco, razor blades and chocolates for the Kaesong girls we knew.

Peter Gruening of UP took me for a walk up the dirt road

— 139 —

and told me he had bribed a pilot to drop him at night behind our lines. Did I have enough pull to make sure that if he told me the exact time and place, he would not be shot at? This was a courageous idea and I was sorry that it could not be arranged. It indicates the Panmunjom atmosphere at that time.

General Ridgway now issued a ban on contact between 'UN' and 'Communist' journalists. His edict referred sorrowfully to 'excessively social consorting, including the drinking of alcoholic beverages with Communist journalists ... fraternising and trafficking with them' to the danger of military security. All the military secrets possessed by the journalists of both sides would not have bought Mata Hari a lipstick.

Starved of news, battered with lies, made into fools by the military, the journalists revolted. When I arrived in my jeep next morning, the air crackled with the tension. An unusually large number of 'UN' press people were herded together expectantly. They seemed to be waiting for some lead.

It came from Dwight Martin, head of the *Time* magazine Far Eastern Bureau and one of the most experienced of them all. He stepped out of the group and came straight up to me on the road. Loudly enough for Brigadier Nuckols to hear from his point of vantage on the embankment, he said, 'How about a stroll, Alan?' Watched by all eyes we walked a hundred paces or so and came back. Dwight brought out a fat flask, unstoppered it and handed it to me. I drank, wiped the top on my sleeve and then he drank. He said, loud and clear, 'That's to us and fuck the military!'

It broke the Ridgway veto before it got launched.

Martin wrote in the next issue of *Time* (18 February 1952):

> Since summer UN newsmen have been faced with a dilemma. They have found that Communist newsmen whom they see every day at Panmunjom, are often a better source of truce-talk news than the sparse briefings by UN's own information officers. From such men as Alan Winnington of the London *Daily Worker* and Wilfred Burchett of Paris' pro-Communist *Ce Soir*, UN correspondents have extracted Red reaction to UN proposals even before the UN negotiators announced that the proposals had been made. And high-ranking UN officers have

frequently asked correspondents what the Red reaction seemed to be ...

The *New York Times* (16 February 1952) wrote:

The Communists (journalists) know everything that is said at Panmunjom. The Allied ('UN') viewpoint, however, is that the U.N. Correspondents cannot be allowed to send the same information for publication ...
 The Peiping (Beijing) radio did not neglect to chuckle at the situation. It gave prominence yesterday to a dispatch by Alan Winnington, London *Daily Worker* correspondent, in which he posed the question: 'Who's Got the Iron Curtain Now?'

George and Ruth Barrett, reviewing the truce negotiations in *Reporter*, the New York fortnightly, wrote:

As one Associated Press reporter, a veteran of the Panmunjom beat, said recently: 'I hate to think of the half-baked stories we would all have written if Alan Winnington (the London *Daily Worker* correspondent) hadn't been around.'

Associated Press correspondent Bill Barnard wrote defending himself in *Stars and Stripes* (10 February 1952):

Now all Allied newsmen know what kind of guys the Communist correspondents are. They are tough babies from the word go and communism is the only creed they know. But many's the time they have given hot news stories on what is happening in the armistice tents to Allied correspondents and the stories have turned out to be correct. A few months ago, the United Nations Command announced that there would be no further briefings to Allied correspondents while the sub-delegate armistice sessions were in progress. But the Communist journalists got briefings and, in turn, 'briefed' the Allied newsmen. For days that was the only armistice news the newspapers of the free world got. The Army doesn't like it because the pictures of Allied prisoners in North Korean camps show the prisoners looking well-fed and comfortable. No adult American would expect a picture from Communist territory to show anything else ... But the recognisable faces of the UN guys, published in the newspapers must have meant a great deal to the folk back home. Communist propaganda? Sure, that's what the Reds intended the photos for ... Nobody does any bargaining with the Red newspapermen. Pictures and stories from those boys are absolutely free ...

But he left out that it was his own agency, AP, that took the initiative to send a camera to Noel and started the entire photograph affair which he then described as Red propaganda.

War correspondents such as Martin and the Barretts risked losing their accreditation by reporting what went on when they could only get that information from the 'Communist correspondents'. But they worked for influential papers and could rely on their support – up to a point. Lesser breeds preferred to react to call-backs from their offices to confirm reports emanating from their less vulnerable colleagues.

However all, in differing degrees, entered into a conspiracy with the man they all regarded as their enemy – Brigadier Nuckols.

Intelligent correspondents must have realised why the US briefers tried to prevent 'their' press knowing what they were doing in the tent, and tried to fudge them off with 'Admiral Joy raised an eyebrow and tapped with his pencil on the baize,' and 'Nam Il snorted angrily.' Human interest.

Since the Koreans and Chinese knew; since Winnington knew, the aim of Nuckols' secrecy and lies was unmistakably clear and went all the way up to the Pentagon and White House – to bamboozle the readers of the 'newspapers of the free world'. What about? That was the dangerous line they must not cross. Barrett and James Reston might hint at it but there would be no forgiveness for saying it out loud.

They were trying to bamboozle the Western world into believing that they were negotiating a truce when actually they were doing no such thing. They were stalling the talks by making impossible demands or flatly rejecting reasonable proposals, thus preventing a truce while they squandered men and materials trying to smash through Peng Dehuai's uncrackable line. In conversation, Barrett, one of the most thoughtful of all the Panmunjom regulars, always angrily defended the American negotiators against the charge of deliberate stalling, obvious as it was.

Some escaped their own consciences by asserting – perhaps even believing – that it was 'just the army again'.

I hesitate to write something that sounds so guileless, even priggish, but simple as it must seem, truth was the strongest weapon of the Korean-Chinese side. I was in a position to judge this, for I lived with the Chinese liaison officers led by Colonel Quai Chengwen in some Korean cottages near the bombed-out Kaesong hospital, ate with them at the same table when they were discussing the truce talks (I speak Chinese) and never found them lying. I also read the full texts of both sides' speeches and arguments in the negotiating tent.

It took time for the truth to assemble enough force to break through the smoke-screen laid down by Nuckols into the Western news media. The 'UN' correspondents came to expect the truth from me and I was often able to pass them full texts of speeches being made by the American chief delegates while they were getting a different, often opposite version from Nuckols.

'Red newsmen said' became inner-office code for 'these are the facts' though head-offices did not or could not always use them. They watched each other to prevent their competitors gaining headway, leaking out the facts in penny numbers when forced to.

The truth had a rough ride in Panmunjom and the talks followed the same pattern right through – jolting from one contrived delay, and its exposure, to the next delaying device, each manoeuvre being used as an opportunity to launch fresh US offensives in the hope of winning military victory over Asians, who should have been defeated by the vast military forces launched against them.

British coverage of the talks was scandalous. Much of the time Reuters was represented by Americans or even by South Koreans and Kuomintang Chinese newsmen who were without exception agents. *The Times* covered the talks from New York. Other British media turned up occasionally when someone decided a feature article would fill a space.

Only one British paper had access to the truth in Panmunjom and printed it, the *Daily Worker*.

The British did not even have a negotiator in the talks. They left it all to the Americans, including the fate of British soldiers and prisoners, with the result that the war lasted almost two years longer than necessary after the talks began. Whitehall was equally responsible for every British casualty from July 1951 to July 1953.

To the normal arrogance of the American military was added a contempt for the 'UN' correspondents and photographers deriving from their power to break media representatives who got out of line. The hatred I earned from American officials comforted me in boring, fascinating, uncomfortable and occasionally dangerous times. Minor discomforts were a small price to pay for a front seat at those vital talks; for playing a part in frustrating US tricks and in mobilising opposition to the war.

There were a few fairly obvious CIA narks sprinkled among the 'UN' media people. Otherwise the Panmunjom regulars from both sides mostly maintained good relations. It was, curiously enough, silently but generally accepted that the Chinese and Korean negotiators were under instructions to get a ceasefire. 'UN' journalists pretended to believe that this was true of the American military but that was often hard.

Some of them were clever and well-informed and it was possible to have serious discussions with them. Indeed there was nothing else to do while the talks were on in the tent than exchange opinions and drinks, and it was no secret that both delegations made use of the pressmen to test the possibilities. There were three levels: delegations, liaison officers, press, all coming into play and moving out at different times. Friendships developed and confidences were almost always kept.

One sad exception was Reuters – that down at heels, underpaid, unacknowledged bastard child of the British Foreign Office. It seemed that every British Reuters man (they were often represented by low-paid foreign stringers) had been personally briefed to stay clear of Winnington. They did not really need to be so instructed. Being British, they felt in any case superior to the American journalists, with whom I spent most of my time. As for me, a through-to-the-bone Englishman, letting the side down, hob-nobbing with Americans and, even worse, Asians, and being denounced every week or two in Parliament as a traitor ... It was like having one's dipsomaniac Cockney uncle turn up at one's marriage to a teetotal employer's daughter: something of a let-down.

On one or two occasions I was able to point out to the Reuters men that I was not letting the side down at all; I was not on that side. I was on the side – Communist admittedly – which wanted a truce; they were on the side that was finding endless reasons for keeping the war going and getting British soldiers killed. I argued that Whitehall had committed treason by sending thousands of British conscripts unconstitutionally to fight in an undeclared war under the command of Americans who had purloined the United Nations flag. 'Tokens' they called these men in Whitehall, but they were not dying token deaths in the Korean hills and were often killed because their American allies left them with their flanks exposed or bombed them due to carelessness or rotten navigation.

Moreover, I said in one of these rare discussions with a Reuters man, they were being captured too but neither Whitehall nor Reuters took any interest in their fate as captives except on one occasion and then they showed the white feather half-way.

That was when the great flurry was on over the first pictures of POWs from the camps. There were also photos of British POWs. Noticing the Reuters man hovering, I said, 'Useless suggesting you send these to London, of course?'

Amazingly Reuters (Tokyo) dropped their supercilious attitude and agreed to take over London distribution on my terms, ensuring no payment by the *Daily Worker*. Reuters could make what they liked out of it otherwise. Their man in Tokyo, McSwann, said London was keen on the deal and wanted as many photos as possible. I handed over a large batch of negatives.

A day or so later, another Reuters man, Zalsberg, an American, came to me while I was speaking to a group of journalists in Panmunjom, handed me back the negatives and said loudly, with intent to have witnesses: 'My company doesn't want your pictures.'

I took them and turned my back.

Bob Tuckman of AP said, 'I'll take them for London if you like, Alan – seeing who took them.' (They were from Noel.)

Someone at Reuters head office had blundered no doubt and just been saved from doing business with a traitor. It was a pity, although AP's service was better. When later I took photographs of all the British POWs in Number Five Camp in Pyoktong – some five hundred of them – and sent them to their relatives in Britain, Reuters led the field in denouncing me for using the POWs for propaganda. Curious thinking that letting relatives know that their sons and husbands were well was harmful. They were certainly harmful to US atrocity inventions which were keeping the POWs from going home.

'UN' journalists had to tread a wary track. They had to rely on the Communists to avoid the pitfalls dug by Nuckols. But they had to try to steer away from the charge of being labeled pro-Communist themselves. When caught between a rock and something hard, some of them misquoted.

As the talks went on, the Chinese delegation developed an excellent monitoring service and provided a daily sheaf of reports from the Western agencies, stories radioed by 'UN' correspondents to their head-offices, service instructions and such information that could be picked up from open morse. This monitoring service was housed in a cluster of Korean cottages and to protect them from the US Air Force the legend was fostered that it was inside a mountain.

Exactly on the 38th Parallel, leaning over Kaesong and visible from Panmunjom, was a dramatic wedge of rock about three hundred metres high, known as Pine Tree Peak – Song Ak San. The B26 that attacked our headquarters just after the talks began had used it to line up his bomb-run.

The legend of Pine Tree Peak began one frosty morning when I said to a United Press man, in the presence of a dozen assorted journalists, 'Mac, you misquoted me in your story last night. You know what I told you and here is what you wrote.'

I unfolded a sheet of monitored copy and handed it to him. It was his report, sent out from Munsan, the 'UN' press camp just south of no man's land, a few hours before. 'If I get misquoted,' I went on, 'people on this side may get chary of talking to me and that's going to be bad for us all.'

They looked at that piece of paper fascinated, passing it

round. It took them some time to think of anything to say. In the end Mac broke the silence and what he said was, 'Shit! Where did you get this?'

It was taking them time to work out how awkward this could be – realising that service messages, inner-office instructions, etc. – came on the same waves. Oh, dear!

So I told them that Song Ak San was riddled with caves and lined with radio receivers manned by radio operators monitoring everything germane to the talks.

They were shocked and did not want to say anything until they had all had a chance to talk. Except one and it had to be Reuters; a man I had known in Fleet Street. What he said was breath-taking.

'What a rotten, low-down thing to do, Winnington. Eavesdropping. But what else could you expect from a Communist?'

As we stood there in cold sunshine, US shells were bracketing a village not more than four kilometres to the south; inside the tent the 'UN' negotiators had concocted another stumbling-block to a ceasefire; all over Korea people were being killed by bombs and napalm; on the hills Ridgway's men, including the British 'tokens', were still dying for the sake of the military victory the Americans wanted; Mac had lied for the sake of his job and cheated the great American public, not for the first time. But I had broken the great public-school code. Gentlemen don't eavesdrop.

Mac said, 'I owe you an apology, Alan.'

Of the US so-called wire-services there was little to distinguish AP and UP with INS a short way behind. In these days of rampant cheque-book journalism there are few people left who think of journalists generally as men and women gathering the facts and forwarding them to the public. Then, even the clipboard and ballpoint, rat-race newsmen were less corrupt than today – but they were learning. Hence the chagrin at knowing that their service messages were being monitored.

I collected many samples showing how the agencies manipulated their employees to deceive the American – and Western – public about the true state of affairs. It was quite simple.

When the sick and wounded POWs were being exchanged,

doctors examining those from North Korea said, as Reuter reported correctly, 'It is surprising to see the men so physically solid.'

On the day before, our monitors intercepted an inner-office service-message from UP New York to UP Tokyo, Number 24202, marked Urgent and signed Payette, 'Need only limited coverage on returning POWs except for tales of atrocities and sensations.'

For those agency men covering the world's biggest story of the day, indeed for a long time, that radio message meant: At all costs get atrocity stories. From that moment the rat-race was on for the most tear-jerking atrocity tale that could be fed into bewildered POWs' mouths and taken out again.

This was going rather far, considering that UP had been making a lot of money out of photographs showing the 'UN' prisoners in good shape and for once I reported this internal message. This brought the following reaction:

> UP Service Message April 28 URGENT ATTENTION TOKYO – Hoberecht: Undoubtedly Winnington has his own reasons for circulating distorted interpretations of our service messages. But I would be surprised to hear him being taken seriously outside his own group. Payette 24202 was a normal message. Naturally the Commies resent publication of their brutalities.

It is often the main, sometimes the only, role of 'journalists' in the field to provide a local dateline for some invention that suits their head offices' politics. As:

> UP TOKYO TAIPEH COLON NEED REPORT TAIPEH NATIONALISTS REPORTING FROM UNDERGROUND SOURCES CHINESE COMMUNISTS PLANNING TO SEIZE ANTI-COMMUNIST PRISONERS.

Headlines are what is needed to manipulate public opinion.

12

Germ Warfare

It never became clear what crimes I had committed in Korea, which led to my exile from Britain for almost twenty years. They varied according to what was happening in the war and the truce talks. It was not known at first that within weeks of the war beginning I had been classified as a traitor. This charge, carrying the death penalty, was never pursued nor was any other ever seriously made.

I always supposed that I had committed no crime at all in law and my bruited criminality was part of the propaganda to disguise the illegality of Whitehall's own entry into the Korean civil war in any capacity.

High on my charge-sheet for some time was my reporting of the Americans' use of bacteriological warfare, beginning in the winter of 1951-52. Forecastably my reports encountered disbelief, indignation, ridicule coupled with the charge that it was a 'Communist propaganda campaign' of which I was a dupe or, as some said, the initiator.

Whitehall had no means of substantiating its vehemently expressed disgust at the bare notion of its ally and patron America stooping to use such a diabolical weapon. Britain did not count. Its part in the 'UN' force – supplying some unfortunate 'token' soldiers – was entirely cosmetic. The United Nations itself had no command relations with the motley force which had usurped its flag. Much less did London have any voice in the matter or any means of knowing what the Americans did in its name in Korea. And the Americans had done quite a lot of stooping so why not this? They had not left one brick standing on another in North Korea and not many bricks in the South. Personally, having seen the effect of napalm on non-combatants, especially growing children, I would always – given the choice – opt for cholera which is not always fatal and kills relatively humanely.

There were excellent reasons why the 'United Nations Command' – in a word the Pentagon – would call in the germs. Nobody could be accused of undue cynicism for suggesting that the Americans, apart from global and economic considerations, might also be spinning out the war because of its unique value as a testing ground for weapons and techniques and for training men.

But there were also urgent military reasons of a different kind. General Van Fleet's obscenely named 'Operation Killer' had mainly killed civilians and had quite failed to break the battleline or move it north. No greater success could be recorded for 'Operation Strangler' – sadistically named no doubt by the same gun-toting, middle-aged adolescent – which was supposed to cut the supply line from the North. And it failed in this task regardless of having complete air supremacy at the time.

Hanson Baldwin, of the *New York Times*, a confidant of the Pentagon, wrote (28 November 1951), 'Operation Strangler has not strangled, and the ground battlefront is virtually stabilised.' Later he added,

> There is no such thing as real isolation or interdiction of any continental battlefield by airpower. The enemy's supply lines can be cut finally and irretrievably only when ground forces are firmly astride them.

We on the ground were aware of that. A narrow dirt road carried everything to the front, kept open by courage and ingenuity. It was probably the most severely attacked road of all time.

In daytime thousands of tubular steel handcarts were pushed by Chinese volunteers and Korean peasants. They were piled with stores and covered with leafy camouflage. When planes were heard the carts were pushed to the sides of the road and stopped – invisible and more or less invulnerable to air attack. It was a device of staggering simplicity.

In the dark lorries ran with headlights full on, protected by an equally simple warning system. All down the road, at every kilometre, was a rough shelter and a guard who blew a whistle ever time a lorry passed. Suddenly from the distance out on a hill came the sound of a shot, then another. In a moment every headlamp was out, lorries eased their pace and steered clear of each other by tiny lamps on their left mudguards, invisible from above. The next guards did not blow their whistles. Then in front, headlamps began to go on again and the next guard blew his whistle and our lights went on.

So simple. The men out on the hills could not hear the road traffic but could hear planes and vice versa. A few men and a few rounds of ammunition to each kilometre made the US Air Force blind.

River crossings, always a problem in wartime, were convincingly disguised in unexpected ways, making use of the Americans contempt for Asians' intelligence. A bomb might knock out a bridge section. For weeks air photos would continue to show it knocked out until it dawned on someone that it was being replaced at night and removed before dawn. A detour, camouflaged by day, might lead to a ford. Imitation bridges and approaches were provided to keep the pilots busy. Bridges were constructed under the superstructure of damaged ones. Hundreds of ways were found to deceive pilots making daytime strikes.

And all the time the balance of airpower was slowly changing and with it changes in the mode of travel. At first I had to drive everywhere by night. Later, when MiGs grew in numbers, day traffic was normal north of Pyongyang. Later I could drive anywhere in safety by day after what US Air Chief of Staff Hoyt S. Vandenberg described as a 'sinister change' had taken place.

It was a change in quality; sinister for the USAF and the 'UN' forces, welcome to us in the north and, most important, removing any remnant of credibility from Operation Strangler.

On 23 October eight Super fortresses (B29s), escorted by 100 F86 Sabrejets, raided Namsi airstrip in North Korea, a jet-fighter base under construction. They were jumped by 150 Russian-built MiG-15 jet fighters flown by Chinese. Three of the B29s were shot down, the other five were ditched or cracked up on landing.

Eight out of eight. All hope of using the B29 to deliver nuclear bombs was finished. The role of the subsonic bomber was finished.

Finished too was the cocky certainty of the Americans that the Russians were supplying the Chinese and Koreans with do-it-yourself jet aircraft powered by converted vacuum cleaners or knicker-elastic. Or that dog-fighting against the best American pilots at the speed of sound was beyond the abilities of 'gooks' and 'chinks'.

MiG-15s were powered by Soviet redesigned Rolls-Royce engines, but what the Soviet specialists had done to those engines took the West by surprise. The *Manchester Guardian* asked, 'How had the Russians used such an engine to fly at the speed of sound?' And the *American Aviation Week* of 17 December mourned the passing away of the Sabrejet's control of the North Korean air and explained,

> MiGs coming downhill can't be headed off even if the Sabre pilots see them at maximum visibility. By the time the Sabres turn 90 degrees to meet the attack the MiGs pass and are on the bombers.

For me personally it meant that I could take off at any time in my jeep and drive through the Land of Morning Calm in all its sunlit splendour. It meant the same for military transport. Civilians – men, women and children – could walk without fear.

Clinging to the Strangler straw, in January 1952, Brigadier General Nuckols was put under growing pressure by 'his' journalists to explain the huge numbers of lorries which he said had been destroyed by USAF night-fighter planes. Exaggerating wildly as briefing officers tend to when driven into untenable places, he made the incredible less credible by saying that pilots' debriefing figures of lorries destroyed were divided by ten before being issued officially. On being asked by astonished journalists to repeat this, he did so.

It had recently been claimed that 800 lorries had been knocked out in the previous twenty-four hours. Multiplied by ten this makes 8,000 claimed by pilots. But to keep to the official figure, it still means about one lorry knocked out per kilometre.

I travelled that road on the next day and all that I saw from

Kaesong to the Yalu River was the familiar handful of rusting cannibalised truck carcases that had become landmarks. There were no new ones. Operation Strangler was a sadistically misnamed flop.

After the Battle of Namsi the Americans either had to accept stalemate and sign a truce agreement or come up with something new. They came up with new offensives and germ war.

Incredulity and horror at my reports that the Americans were using Germ Warfare with Mao in Korea were predictable then. There would be fewer sceptics today. Actually, the Pentagon began secretly testing bacteriological weapons against its own American population only three months after the Korean War began. The first known germ war victim was not a Korean but a US citizen, Edward Nevins, a San Francisco pipe-fitter, whose relatives sued the US Army for eleven million dollars.

Between 20 and 26 September 1950, a US Navy ship, sponsored by the US Army, blanketed San Francisco with smog laden with the bacteria of *serratia*, an often fatal type of pneumonia, and Nevis was one of the victims. This was reported by the *Herald Tribune* on 18 September 1979, citing declassified Defence Department documents.

It is more or less impossible for lay people to prove the deployment of bacteriological weapons, which is one of the advantages put forward by advocates of their use and established in the San Francisco case. I saw enough evidence on the ground during the first part of 1952, as well as the universal and vigorous counter-measures taken by the North Korean authorities, to convince me that Operation Strangler was being replaced by Operation Insect, but a photograph of a plague-carrying flea proves nothing.

It was a relief to me when in mid-1952 an 'International Scientific Commission for the Investigation of the Facts Concerning Bacteriological Warfare in Korea and China' arrived. Among its members was the British biochemist, Professor Joseph Needham, former Counsellor (Scientific) of the British Embassy in Chungking, former Director of the Department of Natural Sciences, UNESCO, an internationally respected scientist and Sinologist. The Commission included famous experts in bacteriology, microbiology, parasitology, anatomy, veterinary sciences and others.

Their findings produced a 665-page report of which only two paragraphs are needed here:

> The peoples of Korea and China have indeed been the objective of bacteriological weapons. These have been employed by units of the USA armed forces, using a great variety of different methods for the purpose, some of which seem to be developments of those applied by the Japanese army during the second world war.
>
> The Commission reached these conclusions, passing from one logical step to another. It did so reluctantly because its members had not been disposed to believe that such an inhuman technique could have been put into execution in the face of its universal condemnation of the peoples of the nations.

Almost two decades later, in response to a query, Professor Needham, since become the Master of Conville and Caius College, Cambridge University, said, 'I have in no way changed my opinion since the (Commission's) report was issued. Nor, so far as I know, has any other member of the International Scientific Commission expressed any doubts about the findings.'

America and her satellites in Korea dismissed this array of world-known experts as Communist stooges and suppressed the findings of the report.

Germ war brought some relief to Nuckols. His 'UN' newsmen, constrained to join in the general chorus of disgust and disbelief at our reports, shunned Burchett and myself and made the most of the chance to demonstrate their 100 per cent anti-Communism.

Secrecy about germ warfare was strictly kept down every link in the chain of command. Even the personnel loading the bacterial weapons onto aircraft did not know what they were loading, but there the secrecy had to stop. The aircrews became the last and weakest link in the chain of concealment.

We on the ground knew that a very large proportion of US bomber pilots – they were now only night pilots – dumped their bomb-loads blind not far north of the battleline, flew around to waste time, avoiding anti-aircraft emplacements, and flew back for drinks and debriefing, leaving Nuckols to divide their 'truck count' by ten.

This would not do with bacteria. They might blow back and spread pestilence among their own forces if they failed to drop them far to the north. To ensure this, a minimum of information had to be given about what they were carrying, with threats about secrecy under the Articles of War.

Articles of War meant little to these pilots when they were brought down and captured. They had already been convinced by their superiors that if they fell into 'Communist' hands they could expect death by torture in the tradition of Fu Manchu. Almost as soon as they hit the ground they were hastening to admit what they had been ordered to do in the hope that torture would not be found necessary.

They were isolated, interrogated and their stories cross-checked for falsities aimed at deceiving their captors and not falling foul of the Pentagon if ever there were a truce. Enough pilots' stories tallied to provide evidence that the USAF was waging systematic bacteriological warfare concentrated in north-west Korea. Most captives gave the reason that the war was deadlocked on the ground and that Operation Strangler had failed.

When the pilots themselves broadcast these facts the Pentagon had its answer ready – these poor brave airmen had been forced by tortures beyond human endurance to make statements confirming the Communists' germ-war propaganda.

This was good headline stuff and, as a *Daily Express* correspondent once said to me after he had wired a fictional account of the capture of Quemoy Island when he desperately needed a story: who reads denials? Long after the war the Pentagon admitted that no American prisoner had been tortured and their haste to collaborate with their captors had been mainly due to the misfiring of US torture propaganda.

This does not rule out that in some cases these germ war pilots were genuinely conscience-stricken as they all claimed to be.

But they were small fry and Nuckols had a splendid time dismissing their confessions as the result of brainwashing.

And then, by one of those marvels that tempts one to believe in providence and which would not be acceptable in fiction, the highest-ranking bacteriological warfare officer stationed in Korea, and his Ordnance Officer were captured and spilled the whole story.

Colonel Frank H. Schwable was Chief of Staff, First Marine Aircraft Wing and his Ordnance Officer was Major Roy H. Bley. Both were deeply involved in the detailed organisation of bacteriological warfare directly under General Ridgway, Supreme Commander of the 'UN' forces, including the British.

Schwable and Bley were on their way back to base for cocktails having been on a flight to 'top up' their required flying time when they mistook their position and were shot down by ground fire north of the battlefront. They were captured at once and isolated from each other and from other pilots and interrogated separately.

It was most careless of the highest-ranking germ-war officer in Korea to have been flying so close to the battlefront with, of all people, his ordnance officer, especially because it provided their captors with an infallible cross-check on what they said. What they needed apart from flying hours was more navigation training or maybe fewer Martinis.

In separate statements they said that in October 1951 the US Joint Chiefs of Staff sent a directive by hand to General Ridgway, Commanding General Far East Command to prepare to start bacteriological warfare. Cholera was the main agent but the opportunity was being used to test a wide range of other diseases.

A belt of disease was to be established across North Korea at its narrow 'waist' above Pyongyang and the Marines had the task of contaminating the left or west flank of this area, including the cities of Sinanju and Junuri. The centre would be handled by the Air Force and the east flank by the Navy. The purpose was to stop enemy supplies reaching the front lines since Operation Strangler had not succeeded in this.

Long detailed statements of the two men, given separately, matched each other down to minute detail – dates of high-level meetings, who were present, what they said, details of germ weapons, how they were handled, means of securing secrecy. While the Korean and Chinese military experts were checking the details I drove up to the Yalu River to interview them.

Everything fitted and only one thing worried me. It was just possible that they had been planted, sent across the battle line primed with a story that could then be proved false. Unlikely but it had to be tested.

I spent a lot of time with them in their little Korean style rooms with heated floors, went for walks with them. I spent evenings analysing the statements written by pilots captured before Schwable and Bley. Details in these also matched exactly and took away my last doubts. The two men themselves were not of the type who could carry through such a complicated deception. Schwable and Bley were not lying.

During this time I became very familiar with these two men. They were out of their depth – family men, desk officers with high status but low cultural level. They dreamed of going home in the evening to cocktails before dinner with their wives dressed and made up. Neither had read Twain, Sinclair, Dreiser, Melville or Lewis until they borrowed them in the camp library.

The *Daily Worker* splashed my interviews with these two men in the biggest possible way and sent copies to all United Nations delegations to show them what the American military were doing in Korea under the United Nations flag.

All this detailed and dovetailed evidence was brushed aside by the Americans as having been extorted by the 'mind-annihilating methods of the Communists' and Whitehall, wrinkling its nose at Washington's lack of finesse, made the best of it. It promoted my germ-war reports to the top of the pile of my activities which, in Anthony Eden's words, were 'prejudicial to the national interest'.

Correspondents accredited to the 'UN' did nothing to follow up my reports on Schwable and Bley, though any journalist south of the battlefront could have raised questions. When I asked about this in Panmunjom their escape was that the whole thing was a Communist propaganda exercise and to investigate it would give it undeserved status.

But those journalists were among the most experienced available, otherwise they would not have been on such an assignment and as such they knew that if a single fact could have been proved false in the Schwable and Bley statements, if any person mentioned had not been where and when and of the rank he was stated to have been, or any aircraft wrongly defined and sited, the journalist who produced this negation could have written his own cheque.

No such attempt was made, itself evidence that the journalists themselves believed that Schwable and Bley had told the truth. And they went on denouncing Winnington for having 'brainwashed' these two officers as an acceptable excuse for not prying further and risking worse than mind-annihilation at the hands of the CIA Directorate of Operations – the Dirty Tricks Department.

A good occasion for Schwable and Bley to stand up and recant, confirming American assertions that their admissions resulted from inhuman treatment, would have been when they were returned to their own side during the prisoner exchanges. It did not hapen. Colonel Schwable was brought before a Marine Corps Court of Enquiry but I believe only for having made his revelations not for having made false statements, and the full findings were never published. The two men were neither praised for their courage nor reprimanded for their cowardice. They disappeared from the public eye into the hazy realm of desk jobs and Martinis.

Germ warfare failed in its object in Korea for the reasons given by Hanson Baldwin – it did not cut the supply line. Relatively few people were infected and still fewer died. My own opinion was that it failed because of the stringent counter-measures of the Korean authorities; the weather; that the types and strains used were inadequately developed or failed to adjust from laboratory to natural conditions or both. In spite of American denials, the shock and scepticism in the Western world were too high a price to pay for negligible results. Bacteriological warfare was halted. I hope that I played a small part in bringing that about.

13

The British Prisoners

Of the four and a half thousand British soldiers sent to fight for America in the Korean War 749 were killed, 159 were listed missing believed killed and 2,556 were wounded.

The rest, 978, were taken prisoner and lived on the south bank of the Yalu River in Chinese-run village-style settlements. These men were totally ignored by the British government although its duty was to ensure that they were treated according to the Geneva Convention. However, the Americans, who had not ratified this Convention, treated the prisoners as a means of bargaining and delay in the truce negotiations and the British avoided conflict with the 'UN' (American) command by doing nothing about their own men.

How much 'UN' there was in this force could be judged by the facts that the real United Nations never sent a single instruction to the American commanders of the 'UN' forces and nor did Whitehall, who handed thousands of British soldiers to the US Army and washed their hands of them. From this arose the question whether I should go up to the camps, especially Number 5 Camp at Pyoktong, where most of the British were, to see how they were getting on.

I hesitated long. I was the only Englishman at large in North Korea, correspondent for the British Communist Party's newspaper but out of reach of British law. My paper, the *Daily Worker*, was not.

As the talks bogged down, families of the prisoners who got no response from Whitehall began sending me letters through various channels and prisoners' committees sent messages urging me to go north.

I had to refuse. I had already cabled the *Daily Worker*

proposing to visit the British POWs and send some stories about how they were living.

At once came the answer: 'Don't visit the lads.'

'The lads!' It did not need signing.

Since I had left London four years before Bill Rust had died and his chair had been taken by Johnnie Campbell. When he read my cable his long Scottish face must have reflected a wry and jaundiced train of thought.

Now he was editor, the fall guy. His correspondent in Korea was – *in absentia* – unhangable. Neither he nor I knew then about the Cabinet discussion over whether to try us for treason. But Johnnie was not a man who needed to have it shouted in his ear.

As I saw the law, probably wrongly, by visiting the 'lads' I might be committing sedition. But the *Daily Worker* would only be seditious if it printed my reports and then it only needed a few soldiers to be volunteered to say that they had been seduced by them from the strait path of blinkered loyalty and Johnnie would be in trouble. So why go? I stayed away from the lads then and was taunted in Panmunjom for being kept out of the camps because the POWs were hostile.

Some months later, the Americans announced that they would detain most of the Korean and Chinese captives after an armistice because 'they had become disillusioned with Communism'. About 80,000 of these POWs held on Koje Island, South Korea, revolted. They took Brigadier General Dodd, the American Camp Commandant, hostage and demanded the right to go home after the war.

Stupidly, on the verbal promise to meet this demand they let Dodd go and the US Army went in with tanks, machine-guns and flame-throwers. Another scandal ran round the world and there was speculation that reprisals would be taken on the POWs in Korean-Chinese hands, including the British.

This was no time for Jesuitry. The *Daily Worker* could only get into difficulties for what it printed not what I wrote and the truce talks were again in the doldrums because of Koje Island. I got into my jeep and drove north through the lovely hills and rice-paddy landscape to the Yalu River.

Pyoktong, centre of the POW camp system, was open. Prisoners wandered around at will. Sometimes they ran away out of boredom, knowing that a non-Asian would not get far. It made a change. They did this seldom because their whole group could be penalised in some way. Their own-built adobe houses were just like ordinary Korean cottages, with underfloor heating. There were libraries, meeting halls, all kinds of sports grounds, skating on the Yalu River and more food than I could eat. Most of the British, varying from five to six hundred, and many Americans were housed in Pyoktong.

English was the main language and the Chinese contacts and interpreters were civilian functionaries – *ganbu* – temporarily wearing khaki in place of the usual blue cotton. Since they could read and write in Chinese and English they were intellectuals from well-to-do families caught up by the revolution and being used for these skills. An entire historical epoch separated the prisoners, reared in capitalism, from the *ganbu* with their feudal background.

A *ganbu* said to me in wonder, 'Where there are three British prisoners there is a committee.' The POWs especially the British, formed committees for every purpose, some to ensure better living and some to take on tasks which their captors wanted done and kick them about till they were lost, as with Royal Commissions.

Their political mentors were usually somewhat owlish, as Chinese intellectuals tend to be, and very naïve. Prisoners who among themselves would naturally identify themselves as working class, good-naturedly pulled the legs of the *ganbu* who enlarged on the class struggle in Marxist-sounding gobbledegook. They were more familiar with 'Them' and 'Us' than with 'bourgeoisie' and 'proletariat'.

Compulsory classes had been dropped before I reached the camp area. Some of the sessions must have been hilarious as prisoners asked and answered questions in Cockney, Scottish, Scouse, Geordie, Welsh and Somerset, explaining that these were the languages of British national minorities. It was all done very straight-faced.

One incident at Camp 5 went into POW lore when a *ganbu* asked a group of British prisoners, 'What is the highest form of class struggle?' to which the proper answer in the study notes was 'Revolution'. A POW held up his hand and said with a frown of concentration, 'Travelling first class with a third class ticket, Comrade.'

The Chinese quickly learned that they were being chaffed and soon the companies were allowed to arrange their own programmes through Discussion Committees.

Toward POWs in Korea the Chinese – who took charge of most of the 'UN' captives – applied what they defined as 'the lenient policy'. As the description implies the captive was guilty of something – imperialist aggression. However, being proletarians, they had been misled or forced to take part in the Korean War by their capitalist-imperialist masters. It would therefore be politically incorrect to punish them for something that did not stem from their own criminal initiative.

On the contrary, they would be well-treated and given every chance to learn the truth. Lectures and study would enable them to correct their false notions about the war which was killing their comrades and had nearly killed them. They would then want to join the struggle for peace and progress. One way was to broadcast to their comrades who were still fighting, urging them to help to bring about a ceasefire in Korea.

Simple indeed and not hard for the Chinese to believe. Chiang Kaishek's army of starving peasants, roped together and dragged off to fight, had been happy to change sides. Half the 'Communist' troops besieging Beijing had been fighting against the 'Communists' two months earlier. Since the true, proletarian-internationalist interest of the world working people were identical with those of the Chinese and Korean peoples it made good sense to awaken the captives to the fact and enlist them as allies in ending the war.

Most of the British-POWs in the early nineteen-fifties were depression children raised in radical, Labour and trade union traditions. Class politics were normal and many of them knew Communists personally. In Britain, the Communist Party was part of the political palette and would have been the electoral choice of many but for the British system whereby a vote for a Communist might let in the Tory.

Indeed the writer failed on five recounts by two or three votes in 1947 to be elected standing as a Communist to the Essex County Council in a three-cornered contest for Walthamstow East which was regarded as a safe Tory ward.

The British Prisoners

'Leniency' toward the POWs was not a phrase but a policy based on regarding them as potential allies in speeding up the truce negotiations. This precluded ill-treatment. (Years later the Pentagon admitted this for its own reasons.) Prisoners were treated with respect, food was good, clothing was as for the troops, there were self-management, libraries, a wide variety of sports and on one occasion an inter-camp Olympics – all things which I reported then and for which I was denounced.

But I believed and still do that it was a humane and sensible policy which benefited everyone concerned and could have been far more effective but for the separation between the CPV command and the *ganbu*.

Naturally I spent most time with the British. They pulled the legs of the Chinese *ganbu* but believed that their desire to get a ceasefire was sincere and that it was the Americans who were stalling the talks at Panmunjom. With few exceptions, they had no objection to saying this on the radio and off it.

In that, the Chinese had in their hands a very sharp weapon which they themselves blunted. The POWs showed me some of the talks they had written for broadcasting to their comrades at the front. They were artless talks in plain soldiers' language by ordinary men who had been flung into what they reckoned was the wrong war and the wrong side. They told of the good treatment and desire for peace and denounced the Americans' delaying tactics.

These were translated into Chinese by the *ganbu* whose English was far from colloquial, so that the higher-ups could read them before they went on the air. They criticised the POWs' talks as not being sufficiently political. There should be less chat and more about exploitation, capitalist reactionaries and imperialism. The POWs wanted to get on the air. They were less concerned with what was said than that broadcasting was a certain way of letting their relatives back home know that they were alive and well. They collaborated with the *ganbu* in making the speeches more 'political'. Between them the Chinese officials played into the wrong hands. As well as rendering the broadcasts less convincing they gave the Western powers the opening to claim that the use of such stilted non-working-class language showed that the broadcasts were written by others and made under duress.

If there had been time, this would have been a unique chance to live with and study almost a thousand fellow countrymen who had become prisoners of the 'Communists'. But Panmunjom had to be given priority. Down at the battlefront people were dying. On the Yalu River they were suffering nothing worse than boredom and lack of female company.

In the short time that my paper would spare me from the truce talks there was plenty to do. Taking mail; although there was official mail exchange, the POWs did not trust it but preferred me to send it via Tokyo or Beijing. There were constant demands to speak at camp meetings. I had chances to arrange marriages by proxy so that girl friends at home could draw some pay. One day I got some cine-stock to feed into my 35 mm camera and took photographs of all five hundred or so Britons in Number 5 Camp to send to their next of kin. On a brief visit to Beijing I brought skates, footballs and playing cards, of which they never had enough.

As a group, they were irrepressible and full of fun. I ate with them, went skating on the river with them and smoked my first marijuana with them. It grew wild on the nearby hills and they planted it round their cottages. The artless *ganbu* congratulated them on beautifying their homes. They had plenty of local tobacco but were only supplied alcohol on holidays. Some brewed or distilled their own and dug caches inside their huts. I was having a sample of this white fire with some men of the Fifth Company when a *ganbu* came looking for me. He sniffed and stared at our enamel mugs. 'Ah, come in, Comrade Liao,' one said coolly. 'Mr Winnington brought us a drop of *shao jiu*. Will you join us in a drink?' He did not but after that I had a plentiful supply of millet liquor for entertaining POW guests.

There was sometimes trouble caused by 'hardcases' who ganged up and produced dangerous situations. One problem was homosexual rape caused by a gang known as the 'bum bandits'. Revenge would be taken for that and for raids on hidden liquor. It was a matter of pride for those who formed the POW committees that they should handle all these difficulties without resort to the camp officials.

All in all they acted collectively and with humour. They were people to go into battle with – certainly into a prisoner camp with. They were quite admirable and I am glad to possess so many letters from them and that they still, decades later, meet me for drinks when I am in Britain.

That I would be denounced was obvious. But without visiting them I could not have challenged the propaganda. Whatever I did would have been wrong so I did what I thought and still think to have been right.

Almost exactly two years after the truce talks had begun, the US negotiators appeared to have run out of presentable reasons for further futile offensives. Washington's allies were exerting pressure, pushed by mass unrest at home over the prodigal waste of life. By the middle of June, the third anniversary of the war, an overall agreement was ready for signing. Peace could break out in fact at any moment and the Pentagon's situation was desperate.

There was still an unplayed card. Washington's vassal, Syngman Rhee, nominal ruler of South Korea though scarcely able to speak the language, came on stage in the role of a wayward puppet – a device later to be repeated in Israel with Menachem Begin – and threatened to wreck all efforts made so far to get peace.

Rhee's troops, passively watched by US prison camp guards, drove 27,000 North Korean war prisoners out of their compounds at rifle point. Rhee announced that they would be incorporated into his South Korean forces and vowed that he would go it alone.

This was judged by the commanders of the North Korean and Chinese forces to be no longer a case for dallying. They struck hard, putting four Syngman Rhee divisions out of action in twenty-four hours. In two weeks they wiped out 123,000 'UN' troops of which over 100,000 were Rhee's.

At this point, Canada, as we learned later, threatened to withdraw if hostilities were continued, which would have exposed the whole farce. (In itself it proved that it was the Northern side which really wanted peace). The US Command had no alternative but to give assurances that it would bring its puppet Rhee to heel.

This was the end of the line for the Pentagon's Korean plans, for the great Pacific roll-back, for Chiang Kaishek's restoration, for *Pax Americana* on a world scale.

Signing the Armistice Agreement, American General Mark Clark, who had taken over the 'UN' Command from Ridgway, commented, 'I cannot find it in me to exult at this hour.' Exult: American officers tend to use words they do not understand. He assured his subordinates, 'This does not mean an immediate or even an early withdrawal from Korea. The conflict will not be over.'

In a sharply contrasting order of the day the North Korean and Chinese commanders required strict observance of the Armistice Agreement which 'has made all peace-loving people in the world rejoice'.

Peace had won. The three mud-and-wattle huts with their torn paper windows, which had given Panmunjom its name; where the journalists had argued, co-operated, eaten and drunk, were bulldozed flat to be replaced by the Peace Pavilion and huts for prisoner exchange. Our bewildered swallows flitted along the dirt road searching for their nests.

Ten o'clock on 27 July 1953 came and went and an incredible quiet fell over no man's land.

In the three years since I caught that last train to Pyongyang, the Americans and their chorus of fifteen 'UN' satellites had destroyed the whole country but been forced by poorly-armed Asians to a stalemate which they regarded as defeat.

Revenge is a compliment paid to an opponent to sweeten the sourness of discomfiture. I hardly needed to be told, when the British authorities confiscated my passport at the end of the Korean War, that American rancour was behind this petulant act – which had only happened once before in this century.

Anthony Eden, the British Foreign Secretary, was not very clear what my sins had been. He said only that 'Mr Winnington's activities abroad have been prejudicial to the national interest.'

Johnnie Campbell, still *Daily Worker* editor and thus responsible for publishing all those prejudicial things, replied at once to him that 'Winnington's work has been of the utmost value to the British people.' He continued:

> As is well known the American press has been calling upon the British government to impound Mr Winnington's passport. We can only conclude that the present act of the Foreign Office is a

servile response to American pressure.

Mr Winnington wanted his passport renewed in order to go to Geneva to report the conference on Korea and Indo-China.

Your decisions prevents us from using the man who in our opinion is the best available correspondent for this purpose.

Up to that point my contacts with the British POWs in Korea and my various activities on their behalf had not come into the picture.

Whitehall had reasons for wanting that aspect of the Korean War forgotten. When they were handed over at the war's end to British Army representatives, the British prisoners had only good to say of their Chinese captors but harsh words for the British authorities who had abandoned them as bargaining counters for the American negotiators, whom the POWs regarded as responsible for dragging out the talks and therefore their own period of captivity.

Also, the evidence of their good treatment by their captors was on the record.

Colonel McCannar, Assistant Chief of the Medical Services for the British Forces in Korea said during the prisoner exchange, 'It is obvious that the men have been treated with reasonable care and given decent medical attention, including dentures where necessary.'

Major General J.M. McFie, of the Royal Army Medical Corps, who was interviewed at the quayside at Southampton when the troopships *Asturias* docked with 530 prisoners from Korea on board said, 'They are all in very good form indeed. They are very cheerful and not a grouse of any kind. They all seem agreed that the Chinese medical services were pretty reasonable.'

Mr Nigel Birch, Parliamentary Secretary to the Ministry of Defence told Mr Hamilton, MP on 18 November 1953, after the prisoners had returned to Britain, 'Questioning (of returned prisoners) is almost complete ... few appear to have been involved in anything that could be called an atrocity.'

In the same month the Attorney-General in reply to a leading question from John McGovern, the pro-American and bitterly anti-Communist Labour MP, stated, 'there is no evidence that he (Winnington) took part in the interrogation of British prisoners.'

This was obviously the Limeys screwing things up as usual. Everyone knew the prisoners had been maltreated beyond endurance. The Brits should have left it all to the Pentagon, where they knew that their fine American boys must have been subject to terrible suffering to make them collaborate with their oriental captors; must have been subjected to a modern *melange* of ancient Chinese torment, unspeakable mental anguish, modern brain-bending chemicals and experimental rays.

Moreover, the Americans had handled things better at the exchange point. Each GI had been through the screen. The price of a speedy return to the United States was an atrocity story. US journalists had been primed by service messages to pose the right questions: had maltreatment included beating, solitary confinement, starvation or worse? If worse, what? They kept getting the right answers.

Before the end of the POW exchanges, the American press was demanding to know how come Winnington was still at large with a British passport. Then came the Geneva Conference; my passport had expired and I applied for its renewal at the British legation in Beijing.

Anthony Eden's hastily improvised reason for impounding my passport was obviously not likely to satisfy people concerned with civil liberties. After meeting me in Beijing, Mr Desmond Donnelly, MP, wrote to Mr Anthony Nutting, Minister of State in the Foreign Office, asking for more details about my supposedly prejudicial activities and in a reply in July 1954, it was evident that the British Cabinet had decided to adapt to Washington's policy about prisoners.

Since the Korean War was a civil war in which the Americans, British and others intervened, and called it a 'United Nations Police Action', the question of what to call the person taken into custody has never been satisfactorily answered. 'Arrested policemen' on one side? And on the other? War was never declared by Britain, so how can the writer be described as a traitor, as he often was? A traitor to the United Nations? One dotty MP tried to get a Bill through Parliament creating this new offence, and was squelched.

Mr Nutting now claimed that Winnington had 'interrogated British prisoners of war on behalf of the Chinese in Korea'.

The British Prisoners

Lonely like that, that was thin stuff since not one returning prisoner had made such a charge. But it is evident that at the same time the Cabinet took a decision (not yet published) to have a Ministry of Defence Blue Book prepared outlining atrocities said to have been committed on British prisoners in Korea.

When this appeared, a few months later, the British prisoners who had previously had 'not a grouse of any kind' had subsequently become victims of atrocities which would have left most of them crippled or dead. They also had the advantage of having no names. They were 'one private of the Gloucesters', 'one British prisoner', 'another was made to ...', 'prisoners were often'.

A single quotation will be enough:

> In winter opportunities for torture increased, and prisoners are known to have been marched barefooted on to the frozen Yalu River where water was poured over their feet. With temperatures well below 20 degrees of frost the water froze immediately, and prisoners were left for hours with their feet frozen into the ice to 'reflect' on their crimes.

No frostbite, no gangrene and not a grouse of any kind. I was not named as pouring the water. No prisoner was named. It was all implicit. But to get the full flavour one has to imagine the British Cabinet taking a solemn decision to turn the previously announced facts upside down and giving the job of fleshing it out to some ignoramus who had never heard about frostbite.

Shortly after the British government had issued this humiliating invention, the Pentagon rubbed it in by declaring that there had never been any atrocities at all against the 'UN' prisoners. Far from being ill-treated, the GI prisoners had been so unexpectedly well-treated that they had willingly collaborated with the Koreans and Chinese.

There had been no brainwashing, no torturing, no cruelty, no killing. There was no factual basis for the whole chamber of horrors which had been concocted during and after the Panmunjom talks. The purpose – to hinder and if possible prevent a cease-fire – was now tacitly confirmed.

But as the atrocity lies were pulled aside, the fact emerged with greater clarity that the US Army's morale was even worse than was already known. At the end of the Korean War the US military wanted to find out why one-third of the American prisoners had collaborated with their Korean-Chinese captors and why 2,730 of them out of 7,190 had died in captivity ·38 per cent.

Atrocity tales were good enough for the newspaper-reading public but the top military were worried. The history of each former prisoner in Korea was closely examined. This produced over two million pages of statements housed in 210 feet of top-secret lockers.

Unprecedented facilities for studying that official material were given to Eugene Kinkead, one of the *New Yorker*'s editors. The book he wrote, *Why They Collaborated* had the approval of the Pentagon and it turned the British Blue Book on its head.

'Severity could not have been used in dealing with the men,' the US Army confirmed, 'without arousing resentment and even rebellion among them, which was exactly what the Chinese policy aimed at avoiding.' Captured GIs, indoctrinated by their own officers, had expected to be tortured. Instead 'the Chinese to our great bewilderment would greet each captive with a smile, a cigarette and a handshake.' This 'confused our men'.

Then there was food. In the first period of the war things were bad in North Korea. American bombing had a good deal to do with that. I lost about twenty pounds, living on boiled millet, sweet potatoes (when lucky), and *kimchi* – Korean pickled cabbage. But it was enough to sustain life. American prisoners tended not to believe that. They had been through a lot of mental conditioning – vitamins, milk, roughage, protein, calcium, calories, snap, crackle and pop …

American prisoners died – 1,500 in five months – while in the same conditions other nationalities survived. They developed a strange psychosomatic disorder for which the US Army adopted the name I had given it in the earliest days of the war – 'give-up-itis'. I met my first case in Seoul in July 1950 in a school being used as a POW transit centre. Nobody knew what was wrong with the man.

According to the US Army, and the description is accurate, the symptoms of 'give-up-itis' were:

The British Prisoners

the sufferer first became despondent; then he lay down or covered his head with a blanket; then he wanted ice-water with his food; next no food, only water ... You could actually predict how long it would take such a man to die.

'Men afflicted with it seem to will themselves to die,' Kinkead wrote. But he did not explain this phenomenon of the mass death-wish.

He described what we all observed who were in Korea all through the war. Badly wounded American prisoners were treated brutally, but not by their captors. Their GI fellow-prisoners tried to abandon them and had to be ordered by their captors to help them along. 'The strong regularly took food from the weak.' Helpless dysentery cases 'whose clothes stank from their own excreta were rolled outside the huts by their comrades and left to die in the cold'.

Kinkead found no answer to the Pentagon's questions. They were the wrong questions. The British prisoners lived because they were co-operative and organised; they set up democratic bodies to share out food and drugs, sacrificed their rations for sick comrades, maintained strict hygiene and above all were optimistic. They had a background of trade unionism and solidarity. Those fine American boys died because, through none of their own fault maybe, they carried into battle and captivity the traditions of free enterprise and devil-take-the-hindmost.

With the truce safely in the bag, I was able to fly back to Beijung on a rickety old Dakota for a holiday and to get married. Not before time, since our first son was already two months old.

14

Ideological Reform and Old Beijing

In the first years Beijing changed slowly. Camels, mostly carrying coal, plonked along Shit Street as we called Parliament Street. It was used by the 'honey-carts' taking the city's night soil out to the farmers. Old gentlemen in long grey gowns, with black skull-caps took their cage-birds out for walks; the famous whistling pigeons flew with tiny whistles fixed to their tails; countless family street-side stalls sold cheap, delicious snacks of a thousand varieties in mouth-watering sauces; hawkers cried their goods; mangy pye-dogs lay suppurating; bare-bottomed children romped in the dust and left steaming snacks for scavenging pigs. Beijing, keeping itself intact within the world's most splendid city wall, retained its imperial dignity and ancient pride.

Under the trees and in sprawling courtyards which had housed the first parliament and the Emperor's elephants, my own institution, the New China News Agency, quickly inflated by hundreds more staff, was in the torments of *si-xiang-gai-zao* – translated as 'thought reform' or 'ideological remoulding'. Groups of underemployed staff in blue cotton uniforms squatted on their heels or tiny portable stools each with a big mug of weak tea or hot water. They talked at great length about their own and others' attitudes to the revolution while leading office people took notes.

Dawdling, I caught snatches of talk. 'If Li Lienmei is happy in the new society, why does she feel that the future does not belong to her?' 'She should re-examine her thinking about the old society and the new.' 'On Wednesday she told us that she had a friend who worked in the secret service of the Americans.' 'Why did he show her his Chiang Kaishek medal?'

Ideological Reform and Old Beijing

They were all men and women from families well enough off to provide their children with literacy, the key to becoming members of the intellectual élite. And as well as being able to read and write in Chinese, they possessed in varying degrees some knowledge of a foreign language, usually English. They were my colleagues in Xinhua where I would resume my work as adviser when the Korean War was over.

China's vast size and lack of communication would supposedly have provided a near impossible task of ruling but in fact, for more than a thousand years, it was largely self-governing by a system of village and family supervision (*bao jia*) which made household and village heads responsible for their members. Higher control was exercised by scholar-bureaucrats sent out from the capital. Imperial examinations, ostensibly open to all, were in fact the narrow stair by which the sons of feudal landowners entered and monopolised politics.

That upper stratum, holding the monopoly of literacy, formed the indispensable administrators for the dynastic rulers. Kingdoms waxed and waned, dynasties rose and were overthrown, barbarians conquered, always the literati resurfaced by means of the scholarly monopoly vested in the unique Chinese script.

What began as pictographs had developed into complex characters not depending on pronunciation to convey their meaning. Inhabitants of Beijing, Guangdong and Shanghai who cannot talk to each other possess the same written language. This cultural unity has always overcome political break-up.

The scholars, the literati, guardians of traditions and the written records, played a part out of proportion to their number, which remained small. A moderately literate person must memorise some ten thousand of these complicated symbols which are also capable of various meanings according to context. A personal example gives some idea of the nature of the problem. The five sounds of my name as usually written – Ah Lan Wei Ning Dun – require 82 strokes, and these must be written in their correct order.

To be literate needs long application. It is of little use to learn a few characters each day. Even if you know the spoken

— 173 —

language, the characters are of no practical use until you know enough. You learn ten and forget eleven. Concentrated study is needed, two or so years doing nothing else. This alone kept it safely in the hands of the landowning class. Dynasties could come and go but the basic allegiance of the literati was always to the same feudal class. Now with a socialist revolution and land reform, other questions arose.

My Xinhua colleagues were fairly literate in their own language, I gathered, semi-literate in English and far from educated in either. Being able to read and write in two languages was good stock-in-trade and they hurried to find some place in the new dynasty – the Chinese People's Republic.

This is not intended to suggest that they were unsympathetic to the new regime. Imperial powers had long humbled China and now China had become great again. Face had been restored. Life had been hard under Chiang Kaishek and the Japanese and could scarcely be much worse under the Communists. Taken as a whole, and if they lasted, things might be better.

They quickly mastered the new jargon about exploitation, socialism, feudalism, imperialism, relying on their literacy to ride the waves made by others. The vast illiterate masses remained the *lao bai xing* – old hundred names – and not the *renmin* – people. It was better to be a *ganbu* – cadre.

The *ganbu* had their worries. Mostly they had well-to-do backgrounds they preferred not to talk about at present. Nothing really, but they had worked for Chiang and before that, maybe, the Japanese. It was worrying when MacArthur's forces had neared the Yalu River. Suppose Chiang Kaishek were restored and there they were working in the Communist apparatus? America was strong and pledged to restore Chiang Kaishek. Hadn't they perhaps not only thrown away their chance of a good job with the Americans but run themselves into trouble working for the Communists? But suppose the Communists did hang on: they would not be likely to forgive those who hung back.

Then the truce talks began and a tremor ran along the fence on which the *ganbu* had been balancing. Then came the 22 August bombing incident and the talks were broken off. The

Ideological Reform and Old Beijing

Communist Party launched a 'Truth and Loyalty Movement' described as a 'serious political struggle to distinguish between enemies and friends'. I had walked accidentally into the Xinhua part of it on a brief visit to Beijing for dental treatment.

Ideologically, Xinhua was vital. It handled what went into the media and out to the world. No less a person than Fan Changjiang, director of the *People's Daily*, central paper of the Communist Party, was sent to soften up the cool, elusive *ganbu* in the English section of Xinhua.

I was still in Beijing and heard his long talk. An impressive effort, made entirely without notes, pacing behind a table with only a single gesture, a slicing motion with his open hand. It went on for hours – a mixture of cajolery and threat, emphasising guilt by class background and the need for each person to get rid of the evil remnants of the old regime, the ideological poisons carried over from a corrupt society. They must become new people in a new society.

'Some comrades,' said Fan, 'have not made their history clear. This causes tension. There are those who say: "I am a nobody, only a translator, leave me alone." There are those who are not agents but try to hide their former links with the Kuomintang. This makes them uncomfortable. They would prefer to speak out. They even talk in their sleep.

'Most comrades are good but many have things they try to hide. Now is the time for those who did bad things to repent openly. We are not working in the dark. Secret agents have surrendered, others have been captured. They have confessed. We have documents, names. Isn't it better to tell the truth now than be caught in a lie?

'If you take only the English Department of Xinhua and only a few comrades: we know that Jang Pihua concealed that her father worked for Wang Chingwei (who headed the puppet South China government for the Japanese). Li Pinghong hid the rape case against his father and his father's ties with the American imperialist, Leighton Stuart. Ye Zhou hid the fact that he was kidnapped, not wanting us to know that his father was rich.

'We all come from the old corrupt society, bringing rotten morals. Do we want to carry them over into our new China? We must try to be bright new people.'

Fan continually stressed that the Chinese People's Volunteers in Korea had stopped the Americans. 'Expectations, hopes, fears that the Kuomintang might return have disappeared.'

It was the first 'ideological reform' meeting that I had attended. Fan's talk lasted several hours and seemed to me naïve. Later I realised that I had underestimated the astuteness of the Chinese Communists in the psychological sphere as I had also overestimated the support they seemed to enjoy among the intellectuals.

'Thought reform' is a skilled method of psychotherapy drawing much of its effectiveness from the *bao jia* system of family and group responsibility. It begins with light and friendly open discussion, encouraging warm group feeling. At a moment decided by leading office personnel guiding the activity a specific individual is subjected to intense questioning, accusation and pressure by his own peers to lay bare his 'evil remnants', recant and swear selfless service to the people (government) in future.

In this phase, the target individual is made to feel guilt, shame, loss of face, lonelines and despair. Real or pretended surrender is the only way to avoid becoming an outcast; of being under threat of a 'struggle meeting' before hundreds, maybe thousands of colleagues; of reform through labour. Ultimately, only the state can provide work for an intellectual.

The evils charged are for the most part unprovable. They play on the common inherent feelings of inadequacy, insecurity and nameless guilt. 'Arrogance, liberalism, lack of faith in the masses, contempt for physical work, erroneous political thinking' – all derived from past ruling-class influence, of course, and only serious if unavowed. Admission brings relief. More than relief, the positive sense of belonging.

In a society where face, filial respect and family loyalty mean so much, it seemed staggeringly daring of Fan Changjiang to challenge the Xinhua *ganbu* directly to denounce their fathers' political, social and economic wrong doings – to lose so much face as the sole means of keeping some. This especially is an emotional leap, hardest to make, leading to depression, tears, crisis and often suicide. Once through the torment, they can

Ideological Reform and Old Beijing

take others through the same process.

At one such meeting, I heard Zhu Muzhi later head of Xinhua say, 'A person who has committed errors and been criticised usually becomes very careful. Those with no mistakes get conceited.' So, not to make mistakes was also a mistake. Which shows the actual purpose of the whole operation.

In the course of the movements, people willing to question official absurdities dwindled away until when father said turn they all turned.

I tuned in as usual to the BBC one day in April 1955 and it took a few moments for my stomach to resume its normal place. A time-bomb had been planted in the All India Airlines charter plane *Kashmir Princess* flying from Hong Kong to Indonesia for the Bandung Conference of African and Asian countries which gave birth to the non-aligned movement. All the journalists on board were killed including such close friends of mine as Li Pinghong, Shen Jiantu and Fritz Jensen, the Austrian writer. Only two Indian crewmen survived.

I should have been on that plane but the *Daily Worker* had stopped me at the last moment because I had no passport. Anthony Eden had saved my life.

This kind of escape I find far more unnerving than the closest kind of shave with death when the adrenalin is running. I have that feeling when I recall debating with my brother Dick as we left the Clachan, which used to shut at nine, whether to go to a pub off the Strand for a final beer. We did not go and as we turned from Fetter Lane into Holborn, we heard and felt the buzz-bomb which wiped out that pub just as we would have been saying 'Cheers'. Virtue disproportionately rewarded.

My luck was compounded because I was free to conduct Harry Pollitt on his first trip round China. In London, Pollitt was a man you were most likely to meet on a Number 11 bus or having a quiet pint in a tucked-away pub. In China he had a special train and in between we stayed at the guest houses used by General Marshall. At night, Harry used to strip to his vest and wash one of his two nylon shirts with toilet soap, braces dangling, while we drank Tianjin brandy and lemonade and I briefed him on China.

The first half of the fifties were the 'golden years', still so called *sotto voce* by many of my Chinese friends who experienced them with me. The Communists rode on a wave of success: currency stabilised; famine ended; railways restored; industry booming; coal, steel and power leap-frogging. We found workers already at lathes while building workers were finishing the factories. Everyone was better off – very little better off but in China that could make the difference between life and death. All was going its proper way and now half the world was creating socialism and the little children in China were calling after us '*Sulian lao da ge*' – 'Soviet elder brother'.

Pollitt was overwhelmed. Even in translation, his enthusiasm swept Chinese audiences to their feet as he spoke of the combined power of the Soviet Union, China and the other socialist countries guaranteeing world peace.

This was my first chance to talk about my passport. Pollitt, D.N. Pritt, QC and Jack Gaster, a well-known Communist lawyer, were all in Beijing together. Everyone agreed that I had done no more than my duty and broken no law but should stay out of England till my passport was returned.

Pollitt said, 'You've hurt Whitehall where it hurts most, in Washington. Keep out of their reach. We've got other things to do than run unsuccessful "Don't-Hang-Winnington" campaigns. Reckon yourself lucky. You've survived the Korean War and now you're living through the Chinese revolution instead of being stuck in our King Street rabbit-warren. But that's up to you. If you want to go and live in some other socialist country let me know and I'll fix it.'

I decided to stay in China where the possibilities were vast, where I could speak the language, knew the situation and liked the people, with reservations about the *ganbu*. After my nearly four years in Korea, where I worked for both the *Daily Worker* and Xinhua, I had been told that I could write my own ticket from the Gobi Desert to Hong Kong and Mount Everest to East Siberia.

Knowing the transience of such splendid promises I made the most of them. In two years I had driven along the unbelievable new roads across Tibet to Lhasa, Shigatse and the Indian border; lived in the Burmese border jungles with the Wa head-hunters; studied the Norsu slave society on the Cool Mountains, one of the last in the world, and visited many other places where anthropological rarities were still briefly to be studied. I was the first British person to travel across Tibet since the Chinese revolution, and out of that came the biggest series of illustrated articles the *Daily Worker* ever published, as well as a book – *Tibet*. The other material was published in *The Slaves of the Cool Mountains*.

Another of Mr Anthony Eden's unintended bonuses was that I could attend the Eighth Congress of the Chinese Communist Party, which was a watershed though we did not know that till later. My wife, Esther Cheo Ying, myself and our two sons went to the airport to welcome Harry Pollitt. Liu Shaoqi was doing a stint shaking the arriving VIPs' hands. He patted the head of our two-year-old, Di Di, and asked in that soppy way grown-ups have, 'And what did you have for breakfast?' Di Di gave him a beady stare and answered in perfect Beijing nursery language, '*Za pi-er*' (fried arseholes). Liu's mouth twitched. His wife, Wang Guangmei, who showed such bravery a decade later defending her husband from the Red Guards, failed to suppress a giggle.

Pollitt had been at the Twentieth Congress of the Soviet Communist Party, at which Khruschev had denounced Stalin. He groaned every time the subject came up, angry that delegates from other Communist parties had been kept out of the private session and 'left floundering'.

The Stalin disclosures shocked him as deeply emotionally as politically but he had no sympathy for those who tried to write off Stalin's positive qualities and belittle his part in building the Soviet state that had been able to defeat the Nazis. Deeply hurt, he never lost his sense of humour. 'Where do you reckon I was when Comrade K. made that speech?' he asked me rhetorically. 'I was being conducted round a French-letter factory. At my age, I suppose that was a compliment.'

In the controversy that arose from Nikita Khrushchev's seemingly ill-considered denunciation of Stalin, I took the same position as the Chinese Communist Party and still do. that despite his errors which were terrible, and the cult of his person which he encouraged, Stalin had 'creatively applied and developed Marxism', as the Chinese put it. He had also had the good sense and independence of mind to have spiked the guns of Chamberlain and Daladier by signing the Non-Aggression

Pact with the Nazis in 1939. It was, after all, the Red Army that had marched into Berlin.

Perfection does not seem to be anything we have the right to demand or expect of revolutionary leaders. We should regard a credit balance as welcome and this could hardly be denied in the case of Stalin. But it became simple and fashionable for European Communist parties, when not doing too well themselves, to off-load a good measure of responsibility for this on to the leadership of the Soviet state in its most difficult years – without which one has to wonder what and where Europe would be now.

At the same time it would be interesting to find out why a far less critical attitude is taken in the case of China and toward the far graver, gratuitous and even infantile wrongs committed by Mao after he openly turned anti-Soviet.

Most of the 'golden years' I was in Korea and when I came back to Beijing I was amazed at how swiftly the Communists had swept away corruption and made way for the honest, cheerful, friendly Chinese to flourish. Beijing was vivid, kaleidescopic, optimistic. If you went into the clay-walled *hutungs* where its real life pulsed, the city's ordinary activity was an exciting pageant, bright with the genius by which the Chinese can make the simplest everyday things attractive.

Makers of everything, sellers of everything announced their presence and their wares and services: the taps of second-hand dealers, the clash of knife grinders, trumpet calls, and whistles were all part of the daily scene. Moslem priests went round to slaughter sheep in the ordained manner. Falcons sat hooded on their owners' wrists. Women gossiped as they stitched shoes, spun noodles, cooked wonderful simple meals on home-made clay stoves in a single pan. At every corner there was something delectable to eat, costing pennies. Life had vastly improved since those days when we had marched in as liberators.

In the summer, there was boating, swimming and picnicking at the Summer Palace of the Empress Dowager; in winter there was skating on the Bei Hai, just round the corner from the house which Xinhua had bought for me – at my request – so that I could live among the Chinese and also have greater professional freedom than was possible living in a Xinhua dormitory off Parliament Street.

In the mornings a dozen little stalls had always appeared outside my door at 17 Yong Xiang Li (Eternal Fragrance Mile) near the back door of Bei Hair Park. One made soya 'milk' on a hand quern, another fried salty dough-sticks and another buckwheat crêpes to wrap them in; there were fruits and ice lollies in seasons and the sweet and sour turnips that the Chinese love. Cyclists on the way to work paused for a bowl of hot 'milk' and then rode on eating as they went. That was all swept away. One of Beijing's delights was the countless tiny eating stalls – usually a trestle-table and backless benches on the wide pavements – specialising in hand-pulled noodles, *wuntun* (meat dumplings), deep-fried eggs, bean-curd 'brain' and delectable mixtures of pig's-guts gently simmering in sauces you could smell a mile away. All were now conglomerated into garishly lit shops to ensure that they did not use their charcoal griddles and tiny querns to establish capitalism.

Just outside my garden door under the shade of a large tree a stall built of matting sold 'Hundred-Year' eggs, sunflower seeds, liquor and many other necessities. Up the road, the last emperor of China, Pu Yi who had been emperor of the Japanese puppet state Manchukuo, lived in a tiny house, working now as a gardener. Next to him in a still smaller courtyard the three wives of a former landlord continued to live with him though the new marriage law allowed men only one wife. But no one bothered, they had got used to living together with their numerous children. The difficulty was that his unearned income had been cut off. They still had a sewing machine and set up a sewing co-operative. Now the former landlord shopped, scrubbed, cooked and looked after the children while his wives earned their living. Not far away, behind the huge new swimming pools, was the famous Kao Jou Chi, the grilled mutton restaurant. North a little was a new school for rehabilitating prostitutes who, in China, were mostly girls who had been sold by starving parents.

Brothels, strip-tease joints, night clubs and taxi-dance halls had been shut and their clientele left uncatered for in the puritannical aftermath of the revolution. Extra-marital sex was almost unknown. Even married couples had no easy task to find privacy – always a problem for the mass of the Chinese. Sexual license was the prerogative of the rich and powerful male from ancient times and now heavily punished if it came to light. There was said to be an official brothel south of the Forward Gate for diplomats and foreign businessmen. It is hard to prove a negative but I would bet my right hand to tuppence that no such place existed. Foreign representatives had to solve such problems within the limits of the diplomatic and trade circle. Rare exceptions resulted in scandals, expulsions, punishment and recall.

For foreigners and a few select Chinese *ganbu* the International Club was the centre of public social life. It had a library which was kept locked, billiards, tennis-courts which in winter became an ice-rink, a swimming-pool, ten-pin bowling, three bars and a restaurant with first-class Sichuan cooking and a dance on Saturday nights. Imaginably competition was fierce among the men for the favours of the few foreign women and overseas Chinese.

On summer evenings it was more pleasant to sit in the darkness outside in the street, chatting with the shopkeepers and pedicab men, sipping tea, drinking *baigan* the rough moonshine made from millet, and cracking melon seeds. Mixing with the ordinary Chinese was something few foreigners could do and was one reward for my ruthless insistence on moving out of the Xinhua buildings. Another gain was the stream of visitors, foreigners and Chinese who would never have battered their way into my old guarded quarters.

Sometimes on Saturdays we would make up a party to eat 'on the street' at some of the miles of little stalls with their age-old specialities and to drink *baigan*. Some stall-holders cheerfully claimed that their sauces had been simmering without pause for a hundred years.

When foreign visitors came, it was the done thing to eat Peking Duck at the famous Quan Ju De (Meeting of All Virtues), now wiped out, where hundreds of identical force-fed ducks hung in long rows, and waiters shouted the amount of the tip throughout the whole ancient building as guests departed, or at the Clay Saucepan, which served only pork from the tip of the tail to the grunt and is said to have originated Di Di's expression fried arseholes. On the way home there might be theatre groups of tumblers or conjurers practising in the cool tree-scented darkness.

I have often wondered whether it was so or have I seen those days through rose-tinted glasses, but even Chinese still call them the golden years. And one of the reasons was that foreigners then were all reckoned to be Russians and therefore friends and helpers, not like the toffee-nosed colonialists they had known. You could chat to anyone.

My wife was a *ban-ban* – Eurasian – half-Chinese and half-Jewish born in Shanghai and brought up in England till she was seventeen. Esther (her Chinese name was Cheo Ying) returned to China in 1949 and was working in the Xinhua Radio set-up as it was then. Being a Chinese citizen she had to get permission to marry a foreigner.

This was easy. For one thing she had become pregnant during one of my visits to Beijing from Korea and for another, much more telling, she was half-foreign. In general the Chinese strongly oppose mixed marriages but, though they may be Chinese in law, Eurasians are regarded with as much or more disdain than foreigners as a whole. No difficulties were made to our marriage, but it would have offended theoretical principles to give the real reason and her superiors said with much embarrassment that we were both *li-hai* (hot-tempered) and could wear each other out. This was intended as a laboured joke but was actually the usual xenophobia.

Being married to a foreign friend, on loan from a brother Party, former officer in the Eighth Route Army and the Chinese People's Volunteers, adviser to Xinhua, lecturer at Beijing University and correspondent to a 'brother' paper, lent her considerable protection from the earlier movements. The most her colleagues could get away with was harassment at work where she had the English habit of giving as good as she got.

The two boys went off each morning to the street nursery in a tiny eight seater 'bus' drawn by a pedicab driver, Uncle Li. Di Di, the younger, was spoiled by the *baomu* (nursery workers) because of his fair peach complexion, which the Chinese consider beautiful. Joe, a year older and looking more oriental, was called by them in his presence the dark one and preferred the company of westerners, who found him more beautiful.

Outside our front door was our pub and local shop, made of matting and selling a range of necessities such as sesame paste, soy, peanuts, noodles, fruit, moon cakes, dates, red pepper, spirits and, after our advent, Five Star Beer. We became part of the local scene which was a rare thing for foreigners, and my affection for the common Chinese folk – the *lao bai xing* – waxed as steadily as my feelings for the officials declined.

And the more I travelled through China the more was this confirmed. Even in the remotest village the Chinese peasant has an ingrained, self-confident civility quite different from the cautious politeness of the *ganbu*. These were the real Chinese like my friend and bodyguard Shen Liantang, a former miner who was with me through most of my Korean years and afterwards in Beijing for a time. He was a model of calm self-control in danger, steadfastness, modesty and self-sacrifice. He had too a great sense of humour.

General (Vinegar Joe) Stilwell, who knew the Chinese very intimately and spoke excellent Chinese, wrote on this subject, 'I have faith in the Chinese soldiers and Chinese people: fundamentally great, democratic, misgoverned. No bars of caste or religion ... honest, frugal, industrious, cheerful, independent, tolerant, friendly, courteous.' He had nothing good to say for the officials, the literati.

Unlike Vinegar Joe, most foreigners never meet the basic Chinese and that is not only because of the language problem. The ones they meet and fall for are the educated ones and they are adept at conning foreigners. This sounds harsh but they are deliberately persuasive and charming in a way that a European accepts because they are oriental but would find nauseous in his own countrymen.

What Mao feared but tackled in the wrong way came to pass – the literati resurfaced.

15

One Hundred Flowers

The Eighth Congress of the Chinese Communist Party in August 1956 – the first since the revolution – provided no such shocks as Khrushchev had produced the previous February.

But there was also no sign of the bitter hidden fight in the Chinese Central Committee which had led Liu Shaoqi to make the kind of political report that he did. On the surface it seemed that the influence of the Twentieth Congress of the CPSU had been entirely welcome and beneficial.

Liu Shaoqi attacked errors that existed in the Chinese Party – specifically 'leftism' in 'demanding that socialism be achieved overnight and not step by step' – but he did not name any individuals. Deng Xiaoping attacked the 'cult of the individual' saying that the Soviet Twentieth Congress 'showed us what serious consequences can follow from the deification of the individual'. He reminded the Party that on the eve of victory, in 1949, decisions had been taken to prevent the adulation of individuals.

Mao Zedong made only a brief opening statement referring to the Twentieth Congress criticisms of 'shortcomings which were found in the (Soviet) Party' and ambiguously predicted 'very big developments' as a result but not whether they would be positive or negative.

In the general post-revolutionary successes there seemed to be unity at the Congress, and it was very cheering to Pollitt after his uphill work to surmount political setbacks in Britain following the Stalin disclosures. Here was a great, victorious, monolithic party, settling its affairs democratically, learning from its own and others' errors, setting its face especially against the glorification of individuals, basing its policies on Sino-Soviet friendship.

And so, too, it seemed to me.

Leaving China, Harry Pollitt sent me a note: 'You will see it happen all over the world.'

But actually that was the end of the 'golden years'.

My disenchantment with the Chinese Communists began six months after the Congress when, according to them, my 'bourgeois tail' started to wag and I became a 'lagging-behind element'. Since the Eighth Congress nothing had changed at the Gate of Heavenly Peace – Tian An Men. Giant portraits of Marx, Engels, Lenin and Stalin hung there facing north but on the gate itself, the wall of honour, despite the congress decision against the cult, the motherly visage of Mao, four times as large as the others, stared complacently at them, mole and all. The message was clear. Stalin was dead and Mao Zedong had inherited the leadership of the world Communist movement. On the other hand it could be argued that he was the CPC Chairman.

But what started me really thinking was Mao's controversial speech 'On Contradictions' (In full: 'On the Correct Handling of Contradictions Among the People'). This sweet-sour collection of home-spun homilies, sprinkled with Marxist terminology, was made 'off the cuff' in February 1957 but there was no printed text until four months later and by that time it had been greatly altered and many things had happened.

I heard the speech several times on tape and had the opinion that it challenged the policies agreed at the recent congress. To others also who studied 'On Contradictions' with care, it seemed as though the party – if Mao was speaking for the party – was backtracking. Having publicly agreed an array of praiseworthy policies it appeared to be quietly opening the door to their reversal.

'On Contradictions' landed in the midst of what had been cautiously welcomed as a moderate, even friendly, campaign to help the Communist Party to improve its working style and its attitude to the people and to win over the intellectuals, under the slogan 'Let one hundred flowers bloom together and one hundred schools of thought contend', usually known as the 'Hundred Flowers Policy'.

The ranks of the intellectuals had been swelled as, in the general euphoria, thousands of highly-trained overseas Chinese had come to the mainland to put their skills at the service of the New China. The Communist Party and press solicited open criticism, urging the people to speak out boldly and turn the spotlight on Party shortcomings.

Rather quickly, the tentative breeze of comment was fanned into a hurricane which, because it was criticism that was demanded, became one of seeming hostility to the Communist Party. Leaders of institutions like Xinhua drove the *ganbu* to write first ten, then twenty, fifty 'big character posters' giving their views of what was wrong in society. Red and white posters grew on walls, up the stairwells, inches thick, all being noted down. There was no question of non-participation. Silence was assessed as guilt. Guilt of what? A hectic atmosphere developed as though cattle were being prodded to the slaughter. *Ganbu* became confused and reckless, writing criticism they did not feel.

But a common criticism, reflecting a widely held anxiety, was that there should be a proper legal system as promised by the Party Congress instead of 'rectification campaigns'.

Then the gears clashed into reverse and a campaign was begun against the people who had been pressed to give their opinions for having had the temerity to give them. Speaking, as it said, for the Central Committee, the *People's Daily* gloated that 'now the reactionary class enemies have fallen into the trap ...' Now, it said, 'the people will destroy all this scum with their own hands.' The Anti-Rightists Rectification began.

It seemed not merely perfidious but mad to drive a wedge deliberately between the party and the intelligentsia, to scrap the congress decision to formulate civil and criminal codes of law and instead to launch at once a campaign of ideological repression. But there was not then any means of knowing that the whole action was Mao's well thought-out opening skirmish in an as yet undeclared war against his own Communist Party colleagues who had damaged his self-esteem in the run-up to the congress.

Obsession with keeping secrets, especially from foreigners, is a universal feature of Chinese life, taken over from the old imperial contempt for everything outside the Central Kingdom, and now vested in the general custody of the Communist Party. Most such secrets are not worth keeping from a non-Chinese viewpoint. A nationwide briefing system ensures that information, in forms regarded as suitable for each stratum, goes down from above, through *ganbu*, to the populace who are told it is better that foreigners learn as little as possible. Consequently although almost everyone in China had heard 'On Contradictions' in various versions, it remained a 'secret' for four months till it was printed, though nobody ever said so. It was *nei*, internal.

I was drawn into discussing it because as a Xinhua adviser I was privileged, being almost as good as a Chinese and in the need-to-know class. My views could have no bearing on the matter; I had ceased to be a member of the Chinese Communist Party and of the PLA at the time of the foundation of the republic. But I said, in response to a request for my opinion, that 'On Contradictions' appeared to be a hastily knocked together hotch-potch of Marxist-sounding hedgerow philosophy which was no doubt at this moment causing Marx, Engels, Lenin and Stalin considerable discomfort in the shades.

However, all kinds of hearsay versions of the speech had got out via embassies and so on, and were being published in the West, so I cabled two reports to the *Daily Worker* giving a relatively accurate idea of what Mao had said before his speech had been published, after considerable doctoring by Chen Pota, Mao's theoretical filter.

There was certain to be trouble. One day I was told that Wu Lengxi, the director of Xinhua, hoped that I would be at my desk at eight that evening to discuss some problems. At eight exactly, the director of my department, Chen Long (Ancient Dragon) a round-shaped overseas Chinese with a bottle-brush haircut put his head in and asked if I was ready. The long corridor had doors every few yards and as we went along they opened right and left and people fell in behind us. It was perfectly timed.

Wu Lengxi's office was big and carpeted and used for conferences. Chen Long and I reached it at the head of twenty or so solemn *ganbu*. It should have been impressive. I was intended to feel the seriousness of the moment; the gravity of my offence. But I could only think of all those directors, sub-directors, people in charge of this and that, who had been waiting behind their doors listening for the exact moment when they should emerge to play their part.

Forecastably it was a silly meeting, everyone present being concerned only to go on record with a sharp word or more criticising my bourgeois journalistic methods. Somewhere up the line my reports about Mao's speech had set the bells jangling and the Xinhua leaders had the job of taking me to task.

I rejected any idea of having done something improper. I had a duty to the British Communist Party and the *Daily Worker* to report on a matter of common knowledge. If Chairman Mao chose to put out a revised version of a speech made and remodelled several times it did not change what had happened and so on. At this point Chen Long said hotly, '*Ta shi womendi Mao Chuxi*' (He is our Chairman Mao).

So I thanked them for having drawn my attention to our difference of view and said I would give it careful thought.

From this time trying to combine work for Xinhua and the *Daily Worker* became more difficult. Journalists in general do not like information imparted in confidence. It shuts their mouths. Things in any case were destined to become worse.

In the movements for ideological reform there was a contradiction: too many opponents would present a picture of unpopularity; too few would cause the question to be asked whether it was not much ado about very little. At the outset of the Anti-Rightist movement it was said that most intellectuals were well-intentioned toward the new society and in general no more than five per cent were class enemies in the new Mao sense. All the same, it was a time for the literati to keep their heads between their shoulders.

In the Xinhua English section at that time I had one hundred Chinese colleagues exactly. Of these, five were judged to be Rightists. And if that did not establish how accurately the people at the top had estimated the situation, then what could? Five per cent exactly.

Xinhua's sacrificial Rightists were put up at meetings, forced to stand in unbearable positions or to kneel. They were spat at, screamed at, made to write confessions which were never acceptable until finally they went off to labour or gaol.

The hocus-pocus of the entire Hundreds Flowers and Anti-Rightist movements is demonstrated by the sort of guidelines put out for judging people who were forced into writing criticisms often against their will – people who had mostly been accepted as loyal to the new social order in previous and possibly necessary movements. A gem from the CCP's central organ, the *People's Daily* of 12 June 1957, read:

> Well-intentioned criticism is not necessarily all correct. Pay attention to what is reasonable and correct in criticism. Sharp criticism may not be entirely correct; mild criticism may not be entirely wrong!
>
> So long as it is basically well-intentioned, accept the correct part and help the critics overcome their one-sidedness. We should bravely accept correct criticism.

Personally I had no success in trying to discover what was well-intentioned, correct, sharp, mild or wrong.

That summer I met a friend who had shared some dangers with me in Korea, a Hui as the Hans call Chinese Moslems. He was in charge of National Minority affairs in Yunnan Province, which contained at that time among its many minority peoples several which had never been visited by any foreigners or even by Hans – among them the Norsu slaveowners and the Kawa headhunters.

My Moslem friend said that for old times' sake he would risk fixing me travel facilities in relative safety. I consulted no one in Beijing, where they would most certainly have refused permission. During my respite from the disheartening witch-hunt in the capital on this rewarding anthropological study the Russians put the first satellite into orbit.

At this time, conforming to the Congress decisions, the CPC was trying to improve the lives of the ethnic minorities by economic aid and peaceful discussion. It was made difficult by the hatred which the minorities bore toward the Hans due to centuries of oppression.

The Norsu (Black Bone) nobility of the Cool Mountains

(Liang Shan) lived in a fastness that the Hans had not dared to penetrate. In the early part of this century two British officers had attempted to survey the area and had been killed in the attempt. Where their maps were marked 'Unsurveyed, Lolo' remained an isolated slave society of some 3,000 hereditary 'nobles' ruling and owning about 53,000 commoners – half bondsmen, half slaves.

My Hui friend gave me an escort of soldiers, an interpreter and food. After leaving the ancient chain bridge over the Upper Yangtse, at the foot of Twelve Barrier Mountain I had a week's journey on foot and horse, through passes 'narrower than a bird's flight' into Norsu country.

When I got to the heart of the Norsu areas after more than a week of walking over mountains north of the great bend in the Golden Sand River, this was the fulfilment of a long-held hope. Norsu society was a true slave society whose highland clans had protected it from encroachment by the hated lowland Hans right down to 1956. It was a unique place of living history.

The Norsu slaveowning ruling class – a highland branch of the Yi minority – had for long raided the surrounding lowlands and carried off Hans to freshen their stock of slaves and I was able to meet and talk to slaves who had been captured when very young and also to first generation 'Norsu' slaves. They proudly regarded themselves as Norsu and would sooner be Norsu slaves than freed Hans.

The abolition of slavery by peaceful means met with difficulties at every point. Slaveowners feared revenge, slaves feared freedom. A slaveowner could not envisage a life without slaves; slaves could think of themselves only within the frame of what they knew – slavery. Freedom had no meaning. If a slave day-dreamed it was of being a slaveowner. Norsu society seemed natural and immutable. If slavery were abolished, how could anyone survive. To be a Norsu slave was in any case superior to being a *Swor* – pejorative term for Han, equivalent to *Lolo* which was a Han term for minorities in that area.

But the Communist work teams persisted and were having considerable success as I reported in great detail in my book *The Slaves of the Cool Mountains*. That was in 1957 when the impatience of the Great Leap sponsors had not overthrown the decisions of the Eighth Congress as they did later, bringing misery and oppression back to the ethnic minorities.

Unlike previous visitors, I left the Cool Mountains alive. In any case, nobody would have been much tempted to make me a slave. An aristocratic slaveowner named Buyu Heipo reckoned my market value at £7.50 'as a curiosity'. Surveying me appraisingly he said, 'Ordinarily a slave of your age, not broken-in even, would fetch no more than one ingot (£1.50).'

'Foreign friends' flocked to post-revolutionary China and were employed in Xinhua, the radio and other institutions which needed people with foreign languages – mainly English. China had everything, a vast exotic country, wonderful food, a revolution, a high standard of living for 'experts', and deliberately charming people – the *ganbu*. It was impossible anyway for foreign experts to meet the *lao bei xing* as I could. They were self-programmed to succumb to the pervading air of ideological manipulation and they reformed themselves and others fervently.

From what they said, their desire was to learn from, be like and become integrated with the Chinese. Which Chinese was not too clear, for the actual Chinese had then as now an extremely low standard of living, including the relatively well-off *ganbu*.

The greatest ambition of these voluntary exiles was to take part, just like the Chinese, in their office thought-reform movements, not even seeming to know that there was nothing airy about a manner of 'debate' which could result for a Chinese in something rather worse than hard labour. Their appeals were politely turned down by the Chinese Communists who, for their own reasons, encouraged them to hold ideological seances among themselves.

Among them were the starry-eyed do-gooders who did their harm by ignorance and played into the hands of petty intriguers who did their harm with the purpose of ingratiating themselves with the Chinese and becoming leaders of the *émigrés*. They were the ones who later landed in gaol. In my days in Xinhua, we who avoided the movements called them the '300 per centers'. One in particular, an East Londoner, was called 'Holier than Mao' by a woman veteran of the

International Brigade and 'The Blivet' by an American doctor. A Blivet, he explained, being 'two pounds of shit in a one pound bag'.

The Blivet was a first rate intriguer, partly no doubt for the pure love of it, partly to hit back at the many people who did not hide their feelings about him. At least an unprepossessing person, he entered into thought reform with a rare unction and lack of humour, organising the foreign friends to cleanse their souls, spinning little threads of fact into character assassination, filling notebooks with what others said and solemnly retailing it, his pale eyes emptied of their slyness along with everything else.

I think it was Max Beerbohm who said that envy was assuaged by the thought that its object would come to a bad end. He might have added that the next obvious step was to ensure that this happened. Understandably the other Xinhua advisers, of whom The Blivet was one, were extremely envious of my rewarding field journey in Yunnan coming soon after several months travelling along the Himalaya, although it was not their business. But when I came back from Yunnan I found that the foreign advisers in Xinhua, under the leadership of The Blivet, had classified me as a Rightist. This was typical of the kind of ganging up that went on in the movements. If I had been a Chinese I could have been in serious trouble.

At the first advisers' meeting after my return, unusually Chen Long, the Ancient Dragon, who had crossed blades with me over Mao's speech, was in the chair. It was announced as a criticism and self-criticism meeting and I waited for it to unfurl. The Blivet offered to start the ball rolling by criticising himself. I said that if he wanted to bare his breast and beat it, well and good, I would wait and see. Chen Long looked uncomfortable and I wondered whether this meeting had the sanction of Xinhua's leading people.

The Blivet began his confession with regrets for his occasional lateness and crimes of similar gravity for which he promised to make amends and to correct. But! The weakness which had him lying awake at night biting the corners of his sheets was – Liberalism. Yes. Liberalism. The besetting petty-bourgeois sin. He quoted Mao, '*Dang mian bu shuo, bei hou luan shuo.*' ('Saying nothing to one's face, talking wildly behind one's back.')

His primary weakness was his failure – knowing better – to prevent others from doing wrong. In particular, of course, Comrade Winnington. There I was, throwing frequent parties at which I and others drank too much; playing western music, even rock and roll, having lent a Bill Haley record for others to copy; hob nobbing with bourgeois journalists and diplomats and, giving the Chinese people a bad impression of British Communists. And he, to his shame, through his liberalism, trying to avoid strife, failing to lay the comradely hand on the erring shoulder, failing in his duty because of his own weaknesses.

He had failed to do battle with Winnington over his expressed contempt for Mao Zedong's great work 'On Contradictions', his support for criticisms made by Rightists favouring a code of law instead of revolutionary movements, his harsh words against the Hundred Flowers and other campaigns.

Comrade Winnington had even given a big party at which Professor J.D. Bernal had learned to jive, the ginger-beer had been laced with vodka, causing Sydney Rittenberg and other abstainers to get tipsy and a large painting in the Chinese style bore the derisive title: The Hundred and First Flower – Rock and Roll.

At about this point, according to my notes, I stood up and said I did not intend to enter a clique war. If the Xinhua directors had any comments about my work they should tell me directly and privately.

A private meeting was arranged, indicating that the Xinhua leaders were behind the concerted advisers' attack in which I had refused to play a part. This time it was indeed private, only the director Wu Lengxi and myself being present.

It is sometimes observed that 'China is a sea that makes salty all the rivers which discharge into it.' Our private talk was a determined effort to make me salty.

The contretemps over Mao's speech showed that if I remained a foreign correspondent and worked as such, I would be an alien body in Xinhua, like a transfusion of the wrong blood-group. Xinhua obviously would not tolerate differences that went much further than grammar. And if I conformed to the requirements of Xinhua I could not do my work for my own paper and the British shop steward whom I always had to keep in mind as my audience. Neither of us raised these basic matters.

It was suggested to me that I should not have parties at which Chinese and foreigners met or in which 'reactionary' journalists and diplomats mixed, danced, ate and drank and made noise. Come to that, I should have less to do with bourgeois journalists anyway, owing to the confidential nature of my work for Xinhua.

I insisted that what I did in my own home was my own affair; that I would invite whom I liked and whether they came or not was their affair. A broad palette of contacts was essential for me in my journalistic work. This was something Xinhua could not grasp at all.

Although Xinhua made such a fuss about the confidential nature of my work, actually my contacts with 'bourgeois' diplomats were more, though not much more rewarding. These perhaps worried Xinhua, I imagine, not because I might leak secrets I did not possess but might learn facts they did not want me to know.

As to such vital questions as why the Hundred Flowers and Anti-Rightist movement had come immediately after the party had set its face against movements, I could get no answer from Xinhua except 'it's in the documents', which it was not. On two occasions mention was made of 'high leading people who took the Rightist road', but no names were to be had.

From diplomatic sources and others I gathered a generally correct but unclear picture of the personalities involved in the still unhealed split in the Chinese Communist leadership, which had led to Mao being voted down on the decisive issues which Liu Shaoqi and Deng Xiaoping had stressed at the 1956 Congress.

Liu had said plainly, and the Congress had endorsed, 'We must enlist the services of the bourgeois and petty-bourgeois intellectuals in building socialism, and learn from them.' Among other things, Congress had endorsed Liu's proposal to end movements in favour of a legal code. Deng's attack on the deification of individuals had clearly been using the criticisms of Stalin to attack Mao obliquely.

Mao had needed only a year to reverse these decisions in practice.

What we, on the spot, found so misleading was that no split in the leadership ever showed. Rather Liu Shaoqi, Peng Dehuai, Deng Xiaoping and other leading opponents of the Mao line constantly supported the actions he took to nullify the decisions of the Congress for which they had fought and on which they had defeated him. It looked like collusion but turned out not to be.

Marine Andrew Condron was the only British prisoner in Korea who chose to stay after the armistice agreement under which the Americans insisted on 'voluntary repatriation'. It was one of their delaying devices and held up the cease-fire for a long time.

The Chinese agreed that Condron could settle in Beijing, which he did, as a language teacher which is one reason why a number of Chinese speak English with a strong Scottish accent. Andy was a family friend and used to call in and make himself what I believe is called a chip butty, fried potatoes with vinegar and salt between two slices of bread and butter. Solid fare.

He was the unwitting cause of my next trouble which actually arose out of differences of tradition. Chinese have a traditional scorn for prisoners of war. There is also no, or very little, sympathy for the underdog, rather the superstition that trouble may be catching and helping a person out of a difficulty may transfer it to one's own shoulders. Promises are often regarded as a means to an end and not especially binding. All these ways of thought combined to create the Condron impasse.

One day he arrived at our house breathing tautly with the news that he had been officially told that he must leave Beijing, where all his friends were, and live in Wuhan, a dreadful town, known as one of China's ovens. 'They promised me that I could stay in Beijing, I'm not going,' he said. It was true. I heard the promise made in Korea.

'Some bureaucrat,' I assured him. 'I'll go and talk to the Foreign Ministry.'

It was indeed some bureaucrat, or several, but it was also policy and not mere carelessness. My arguments encountered the inspired passivity which makes clear only that no hope should be entertained of changing the decision. Having ex-prisoners in Beijing was *bufangbian* ('inconvenient'). Reminded of their promise that Andrew Condron could stay in the capital only brought the statement that his return to Beijing could be considered in the proper quarters and in the meantime he should carry out the decision and go to Wuhan.

It would have been impolite on my part to suggest that this was a typical get-out, but we both understood this to be the case. He and those behind him in the Foreign Ministry evidently thought that I was making a gesture and that it would be absurd of me to go further on behalf of someone to whom I owed no obligation and who was no more than a former prisoner. Loyalties which are not political or filial but personal are not rated highly by the Chinese. They saw the whole thing through their own eyes.

But for me, Condron was a friend to whom I owed a duty as such and because he was a fellow Briton who had like me got a rough deal out of the Korean War. There was only one thing to do, which I felt sure would not have been taken into the calculations of those who had issued the ukase – I invited Condron to be my guest for as long as necessary and that afternoon he arrived at 17 Yong Xiang Li in a pedicab bearing his few possessions.

Nothing happened. His teaching job had been phased out and I could not imagine how the affair would end. I had taken a serious risk because my decision to provide him sanctuary was a flagrant interference in matters that were not my business. I was attacked by quite a few Sinified 'foreign friends' for displaying bourgeois romanticism and taking advantage of my special position as a representative of the British Communist Party. True, I agreed, but were not the Chinese taking advantage of state power to break a serious promise? If promises could be broken they became mere deception which was impermissible in normal social dealings. We were both wrong but they had started the trouble.

Weeks passed and no official word was spoken. It seemed as though the uneasy contretemps could continue for ever. If it were to be ended, something had to give. So far nothing irrevocable had been done but in my case, I could not take the only step possible – kick out Andy. On the other hand, for the Chinese to withdraw the order that Andy must go to Wuhan would be a serious loss of 'face'. If any solution were to be found it must lie in the middle. Was there a middle?

In the past Andy had made some extra money 'polishing' the English of film captions and similar rough translations and since he moved in with us had regularly gone around offering himself for such work. He was allowed to wander fruitlessly until someone somewhere considered that he had been punished enough and then he got a little work by dribs and drabs.

But that could only have happened with official sanction and so it was clear that the Chinese had decided to let him stay in Beijing. Not a word was said. Then he found or was cleverly directed to a pretty little two-room place just off Chang An Boulevard and nobody stopped him from moving in. The incident was over and no 'face' had been lost. It was a perfect example of the skill Chinese can show in smoothing out difficult personal problems. I personally never heard a word about the incident since my talk at the Foreign Ministry and nor did Andy. We had both been silently reprimanded, the Ministry had given way. The rest was silence.

As 1957 drew towards its muddled, turbulent end with the critics in flight before the Anti-Rightist movement, Mao had established that any strategy of advance which enlisted the services of intellectuals was built on sand. And the chasm which had been opened between the Communist Party and the intelligentsia included those who had come from overseas at the urging of the party to contribute to China's renaissance. Decisions taken by the congress a year before were being shredded, reversed indeed, without a sound of public complaint from Liu Shaoqi and Deng Xiaoping or any other leader.

The rectification and Anti-Rightist movement slid quite naturally it seemed, in a skilfully inspired way, into asserting that Redness – which the masses had – would establish 'communism' quicker and better than Expertise – which the intellectuals were supposed to have. The great Red Before Expert storm did what we were to see so often from that time.

Its pattern was to pose essentially complementary factors as mutually exclusive. This was an offshoot of 'On Contradictions', Mao's barnyard concept of dialectics.

After the Hundred Flowers pitfall the *ganbu* were treading carefully. They were urged to 'dedicate your heart to the party' as the next step. They looked for ways to get through that next stage without too much trouble, knowing that some were certain to be tangled in the mesh. I made notes of some of the arguments I overheard from people who did not realise how much Chinese this foreigner knew.

'It's no use to be a crane among chickens or a chicken among cranes. Try not to be conspicuous.'

'Find a middle way. If it's impassable, turn a bit left.'

'It's easy to be Red, hard to be Expert. Expert knowledge needs diligence but politics is only lip-service.'

'Technical knowledge is the essence. Politics is the façade.'

'No. It's easier to be Expert; hard to be Red. Political consciousness can easily be learnt but it's hard to practise. Being Expert is harder to learn but easier to practise.'

'To be Expert takes three years but to be Red much longer, if ever. To be Red *and* Expert or vice versa is impossible.'

'Best to be pink. You must have some politics, more or less Red, say pink. Evade being a Rightist, that's Red enough.

'You can be tested for your technical knowledge but, in the end, who knows what Red is?'

In Xinhua journalistic proficiency became a term of belittlement. What 'face' I possessed by being in Chinese eyes a *zhi-shi-fen-zi* ('intellectual'), now disappeared. Ah Lan's insistence on timeliness, brevity, accuracy, clarity, story and sentence structure and the rest were after all no more than bourgeois technique. It was safer to write down what happened chronologically. If you tried to put the 'main point' prominently you might easily select the wrong point. For the sake of brevity you might leave out something that might be regarded as important. Better leave nothing out.

My lectures at Beijing University (*Beida*) were not cancelled out but they did not happen. Meetings took the place of my training classes in Xinhua. When I revisited Xinhua in 1981, I learned that the printed notes of my lectures had been buried for safety by a member of the staff and dug up after the

Cultural Revolution. They had again become basic training material. I also learned that a cardinal crime committed by the Xinhua *ganbu* had been their association, willy-nilly, with the arch-enemy Winnington.

Next Lu Dingyi, an alternate member of the Political Bureau and Chief of the Party Propaganda Department, came to Xinhua and made a long speech about journalism as a weapon in the class struggle in which he devoted his main attack against timeliness in news and emphasis on journalistic technique. In three hours he reduced the whole thing to pudding and contradicted almost everything I had taught about news-work without mentioning my existence.

In one thing the Rightists had been right. It was quickly seen that Expertness can be judged whereas Redness can be deception. That, however, was evidently not the point. The movements of 1957 were intended to destabilise the intelligentsia and degrade technique. To serve notice: there will be no resurfacing of the literati in this dynasty. Also, it seemed, to demonstrate that regardless of the Eighth Congress, movements were what they would get and not a code of law. And the next movement seemed gratuitously absurd in order to rub it in, as though the people were being made to jump through paper hoops to punish them for their temerity in criticising the party, with or without by-your-leave.

China, miles ahead in population, aeons behind in productive capacity, was to concentrate its enormous manpower on the task of wiping out the Four Evils – rats, flies, mosquitoes and sparrows.

Ideologically pure, children were empowered to stop people anywhere and inspect their fly-swats, no doubt giving them the taste for authority which years later drew them into the disastrous *Hungweibing* ('Red Guards'). Incalculable man-days were wasted collecting, counting and book-keeping dead flies. Beijing ran out of flies. Desperate to fulfil quotas, people, including my wife, solved their personal problems by breeding flies in boxes in order to have something to wipe out.

Long preparation went into the ridiculous three-day Beijing battle to kill the small birds. In my dwindling role of adviser to Xinhua I suggested that it would make China a laughing stock. Xinhua should at most give it a paragraph or two. I argued that it would anger bird-lovers and almost certainly have negative ecological effects. We had been told that sparrows eat a lot of grain which people should be getting. In Beijing this was observably not true. Any sparrow who could find a grain of millet unattended deserved a medal.

Banter of this kind did not go down well since it was known that Mao was personally the initiator of the Four Evils campaign. I suggested that perhaps he had not considered the environmental question, though this itself was near blasphemy in the current atmosphere. My remark reached Xinhua's director who, it appeared, mentioned it to Mao himself, Mao's response was staggering.

If wiping out sparrows had a negative effect, the Chairman said sardonically, China would ask her Soviet friends to supply replacements. Not even Confucius, he added, had conceived the idea of wiping out the Four Evils. So far as I knew, Confucius had never thought of importing barbarian sparrows.

For three days and nights, all over Beijing, people remained up trees, in open spaces, on roofs, banging gongs, clashing cymbals, dustbin lids, pots and waving flags, forcing the exhausted birds to fly till they fell into the dust and could be killed.

My house was surrounded by a high wall and those feathered enemies which fell inside it were given sanctuary, food and water in an outhouse. We ignored the clamour of the street committee *ganbu* to have them handed over for killing and adding to the Yong Xiang Li score. When the din of battle died down our counter-revolutionary birds flew off. Another black mark, of course.

Soon we began to notice fine webs attached to slender squashy caterpillars in our hair, on our faces, down our necks. In a few days they covered the trees and the leaves disappeared. The caterpillars got into the food and were almost impossible to get out. My suggestion that possibly the Chairman's concealed aim was to increase the supply of edible protein raised no laugh. But it had to be admitted eventually that the wiping out of the birds was a terrible error whose effects are still felt. Bed bugs were promoted to take the place of sparrows as an evil.

16
The Great Leap Forward

Not long after Beijing's dying birds had flopped into the dust, a phone call from Xinhua asked me to go in to give the final English polish to a long and 'very important' speech by Liu Shaoqi. I cycled, as I always preferred, through the narrow adobe *hutungs*, along Wine Vinegar Lane, down toward Execution Gate to Parliament Street, brushing webs and caterpillars from my face. It was a glorious evening in early spring, 5 May 1958.

Liu's speech was not merely important, it was his historic report on the work of the Central Committee. The Second Five Year Plan had been approved at the Eighth Congress two years earlier and Liu's report seemed at first to be the ordinary kind of CPC self-approbation on that subject. But somewhere about the middle the tone changed completely; language of a different kind took over.

Liu said, 'Comrade Mao Zedong has put forward the slogans "overtake and outstrip Britain in fifteen years", "build Socialism by exerting our utmost efforts and pressing ahead consistently to achieve bigger, faster, better and more economical results".'

As Liu's report went on it seemed that lyric had displaced economics and resounding phrases had taken over from reality. 'Hard work for three years, happiness for a thousand,' Liu said, 'A mighty torrent of Communist ideas has swept away individualism, departmentalism, localism and nationalism,' now we were at 'the actual beginning of Communism'. All this from the man who had denounced 'leftist' ideas of achieving socialism 'overnight'.

The Great Leap Forward had begun.

The Great Leap Forward

The First Five Year Plan, ending in 1957, had increased industrial production by 141 per cent and agricultural output by 25 per cent.

The Second Five Year Plan had been worked out carefully in co-operation with Soviet specialists by my old Harbin friend Chen Yun, almost the only man at the top who knew something about economics. It was a demanding programme but regarded as possible: to double industrial output and increase agricultural output by 35 per cent in five years. Many had attacked it as too ambitious.

Suddenly, without explanation or any planning, those aims were to be reached in a single year. In the period of this Five Year Plan but without any planning, industrial output was to be multiplied by six-and-a-half times and agricultural output by two-and-a-half times.

Taken as a whole, the CPC leadership knew no other way to proceed than along the lines which the Soviet Union had used. Soviet credits and aid in the form of hundreds of factories and thousands of technicians had helped to bring results which were admitted as tremendous by any standards. Those successes were not the results of Mao's work and the praise he gave them was less than warm.

Duo, kuai, hao, shenq (literally: 'more, quick, good, frugal') would take the place of management. Mao had said there were two possible methods. 'One will result in doing the work faster and better; the other slowly and not so well. Which method shall we adopt?' The usual twaddle, I thought. How about faster and worse or slower and better or some other variation?

There was a vital point in Liu's report which I knew to be a lie, which he knew to be a lie and so did everyone in a leading position. He referred to the 'upsurge' in the countryside in autumn 1955 and spring 1956, based on Mao's ideas, as proof that bigger and faster meant better.

I recalled one of my last confidential briefings in Xinhua before I became a bourgeois lagging-behind element.

The First Five Year Plan had been endangered in 1955 when agriculture had failed to meet the needs of industrial development. Mao proposed the rapid conversion of small co-operatives into large collectives and ran into opposition in the Party leadership. It was then that he lashed out – in what later became a much-quoted phrase – at 'some of our comrades who are tottering along like a woman with bound feet, always complaining that others are going too fast'.

Among those totterers had been Liu Shaoqi and most of the other top CPC leaders who argued that large farms could not be operated without machines, fertilisers and power as well as skilled people. Liu had scorned 'utopian' agricultural schemes and stressed that agriculture could only be collectivised 'step by step ... within a relatively long period'. The totterers won the day but somehow Mao circumvented this decision and almost all peasant households were incorporated into large Agricultural Producers' Co-operatives. The move was a fiasco but its worst aspects never became public.

I attended a strictly confidential briefing in spring 1956 about the near disaster which had resulted from Mao's haste. The peasants had suspected that this collectivisation was a trick to turn them back again into tenants, this time of the state. They hid their farming implements, neglected the fields, killed their animals to sell and eat and many fled to the cities.

Food hoarding became widespread and attempts to attract food to 'free markets' brought about speculation. The person who gave this briefing (he is still alive and I leave his name out) put the blame for this failure on local *ganbu*, which was nonsense.

Now Liu Shaoqi was claiming this fiasco as a success, proving the correctness of Mao's new policy.

It may always remain a mystery why, so soon after having defeated Mao on 'overnight socialism', collectivisation, movements, legal code and the deification of persons, such powerful figures as Liu, Deng and others should let him pluck all those decisions back and reverse them.

Mao with extraordinary daring, half-way to madness, by setting hundreds of millions into planless activity, paralysed the advocates of step-by-step planned advance. He leapt, blindfold, past those who were 'tottering' with their eyes open.

No satisfactory explanation has yet been found why some 500 million peasants, officially 121,936,350 families, flocked into the short-lived people's communes in a space of 45 days after so recently rejecting the Agricultural Producers' Co-operatives.

Coercion alone could not have achieved this.

Deliberately created hysteria was an essential component. They had been through bewildering changes reaching deep into the fabric of life – the land reform with its violent class battles, mutual-aid teams swiftly transformed into co-operatives which many saw as taking back the land they had won, the Agricultural Producers' Co-operatives which enhanced that disappointment.

And now the gigantic confidence trick of the Great Leap which seemed to offer the peasants' ideal of a welfare state: the 'eight frees' put out as 'communism' – security of food, clothing, housing, transport, birth, old age, sickness and burial – to each according to his need regardless of his work, and such vulgarisations of Marxism. Who would want to risk missing the new heaven? Cymbals, drums, gongs, trumpets and songs swept them along.

On 12 August 1958, Xinhua put out the following reporter's description of the morning scene as peasant members of the Zhaoyang Commune in Henan Province began their day:

> In about a quarter of an hour, the peasants line up. At the command of company and squad leaders, the teams move to the field, holding flags. Here one no longer sees peasants in groups of two or three, smoking or going leisurely to the fields. What one hears is the sound of measured steps and marching songs. The desultory living habits that have been with peasants for hundreds of years are gone forever.

After inspecting such scenes – enhanced by the Chairman's presence – Mao was convinced that his dream was being realised. 'I have witnessed the enormous energy of the masses,' he triumphed. 'On this foundation it is possible to accomplish any task whatsoever.'

What he had actually seen were landscapes filled with simple, cheated people whose time, energy, resources and *élan* he was squandering on worse than useless tasks, most of which had to be reversed and many of which were doing irrevocable damage; people caught into this mad vortex by infantile agitation: 'Communism is Heaven and the People's Commune is the ladder.'

In a commune near Tianjin, well-rehearsed peasants happily

told me that quite apart from wages and personal purchases such as radios, bicycles, alarm clocks and thermos flasks, within three years standard free supply would include: meals with a daily average per person of half a pound of meat, two eggs, four ounces of milk, a pound of vegetables, a pound of fruit, noodles, beancurd and grain. They would get annually two cotton suits, two boiler suits, six pairs of socks and six pairs of shoes – three cloth, one padded, one rubber and one leather. At least! Who would risk missing this?

Could it be done? Of course. Under the leadership of Mao Zedong and the Communist Party and with mass initiative. As an example of the last I was shown one *mou* (one-sixth of an acre) of paddy planted to rice so thickly that 'you could sleep on its surface'. That, they said, showed what was possible.

Ganbu from other communes were making notes in their little books. Deep-ploughing, super-fertilising, seed selection by hand, ultraviolet light, forced ventilation, had produced this phenomenon. It was equivalent to one hundred tons per acre calculated on the basis of sample ears. Follies like this bred new follies.

Showplaces where visitors to Beijing were taken, such as the Huang Tu ('Yellow Clay') People's Commune on the city's outskirts had some people who did little else but talk to foreigners and show them round its facilities. It had plenty of fat pork, dumplings, unlimited rice, spotless clinics, well-equipped schools and nurseries, an old folks' home and canteens.

I heard, long before any details became available, that in August 1958 at Beidaihe Mao Zedong had denounced wages as 'bourgeois' and demanded a return to the military 'communism' of the civil war period. He had equated free supply with communism which meant, as he said, 'all eating from the same pot'. Challenged by Liu Shaoqi, who said that free supply was a guerrilla habit and would negate initiative, Mao had attacked Liu as a 'Rightist'.

Much later this quarrel was confirmed but already it was obvious that the struggle at the top had not been resolved. In the meantime, and for unexplained reasons, the CPC had turned away from the awesome, real tasks of planned, step-by-step industrialisation and socialisation which it had set

The Great Leap Forward

itself and it seemed that Liu and others of his view – probably a majority of the leadership – had retreated before Mao to preserve an appearance of unity out of fear.

In place of the agreed Second Five Year Plan, China was left with mass spontaneity.

It was impossible to avoid arguments, often caustic, with born-again 'foreign friends' – converts to the prevalent faith in instant communism, claiming to be true friends of China and only too happy to eat from the same pot.

In those days of the Great Leap people either jubilated or else. Second thoughts, not to mention actual dubiety or opposition, signified various degrees of right deviation. Not surprisingly Liu Ningyi, a member of the Central Committee, asked me to tea. This was the man whom I first met ten years previously in Harry Pollitt's office. He was the most travelled of all China's leading people. Travel had not broadened his mind.

He assured me that soon, when everyone had a high political level, China would 'go on the supply system, as in Harbin [during the revolution]. Work according to ability, take according to need.'

In Harbin it had actually depended on rank. He and I had done quite well. Most *ganbu* were on third-kitchen rations.

'How soon?' I asked.

'Rather soon in China. The peasants are politically advanced. They know the benefits of collective life. The communes are a great leap to communist society. It will take time to harden the intellectuals by labour and break down the little haven of the family. Our family is the world. Communists should pay less attention to the family.'

Time passed.

'I have heard,' he resumed, 'that you have other opinions.'

Liu Ningyi's few smug assertions seemed to confirm what I had assumed about Beidaihe and embraced so many absurdities that I was – a rare thing for me – lost for words.

His right heel was bobbing up and down in a nervous manner and time continued to pass.

At last I said, 'On the subject of the transition to socialism and communism I agree with Marx, Engels, Lenin and Stalin.'

'And Chairman Mao?'

I ignored this and went on, 'Communism is not egalitarianism; it is not a means of sharing poverty. I still think that the decisions taken at the Eighth Congress remain correct.'

Well that gave him something to grasp and he launched into a long, memorised, *People's Daily* editorial about quicker and better or slower and worse and *duo, kuai, hao, sheng* until he came to myself with a long parable about however good a locomotive may be, it is useless if it goes off the rails. It emerged that I was the good locomotive.

Communists are accustomed to having absurd policies pinned on them and being attacked for ideas they do not have – abolition of material incentives, private property and the family, regimented work and levelling down living standards. These fabrications are the stock-in-trade of red-necked anti-Communists and street-corner hecklers and constitute a prime barrier to the spread of scientific socialism among working people.

Now here in front of me, was Liu Ningyi, member of the CPC's Central Committee, leader of China's trade unions, matter-of-factly, self-confidently and ignorantly enunciating those vulgarisations of Marxism, copy-book examples of the infantile leftism denounced by Lenin and all serious Communists, as *policy*.

Marx wrote in *The Eighteenth Brumaire*, 'Men make their own history, but they do not make it just as they please; they do not make it under circumstances chosen by themselves.' There were among China's leaders, people who knew that there was no escape from economic principles via the 'Thought of Mao', people like Liu Shaoqi and Chen Yun, but they too had bowed to the Beidaihe concept that Marxism had become a right deviation from the Chairman's Great Leap.

Three names are especially associated with the early popularisation of the Chinese Communists: Edgar Snow, Agnes Smedley and Anna Louise Strong. Anna lived in Beijing during and after my time there and gave me the impression of an embittered and arrogant woman. Intellectually she was a lightweight compared with Snow and quite lacked the burning sincerity and selflessness of Agnes, whom I met not long before her death.

Snow had, as it were, taken up Mao in *Red Star Over China*;

Agnes Smedley's *Great Road* had done the same for Chu De. I thought that Anna was jealous of both: Snow for the enormous publicity he had made and Agnes because she had become a trusted friend of the modest General Chu De, Commander-in-Chief of the Chinese People's Liberation Army, one of the most outstanding military leaders of the century and, among people who knew, more respected than Mao. But Agnes was dead and Anna was not.

Anna Louise Strong held court – it is scarcely an exaggeration – in a magnificent flat not far from the Beijing Hotel. From the time I first met her until her death she reflected every twist of official policy and was given flattering opportunities to do so. Her international reputation was built up by Mao and Zhou Enlai and she paid with hypocrisy for the dubious honour of becoming their trusted mouthpiece.

Rough words maybe, but Anna was not a newcomer to the Chinese scene like most foreign sympathisers who turned up to help and showed equal agility in following the vacillations of the CPC after 1956. Those newcomers were in the main middle-class and self-conditioned to fall instantly in love with '*ganbu* China', without realising that all those people dragging overloaded carts and making things on the street were the real, '*lao bai xing* China' and usually very hungry.

Such foreigners might be excused for not knowing what Anna knew and chose to ignore.

Mao's Great Leap was a fine chance for her to move in front and every facility was given for her to write a quick book from which two quotations are enough:

> Changshih (Commune) today offers its members not only wages, but three good meals daily for everyone, children and aged included, for which they have not only more rice than they can eat, but also pork, fish, chicken, vegetables, fruits, mushrooms, peanut oil, tea and honey, all produced by themselves. 'Salt is the only thing we have to buy,' they boast.*

In fact, if every one of China's then six hundred million

---

* Anna Louise Strong, *The Rise of the People's Communes*, New World Press, Peking, 1959, p.23. Before Anna's book appeared it was known, but not announced, that the communes and steel ovens had failed, but they let the printing go ahead because the failure was still an official secret.

people had eaten one pound of pork more *per year*, it would have wiped out the export of that article. She, an old China hand, must have known that.

People all over the world associate the Great Leap with the extensively publicised 'backyard steel furnaces' and Anna Louise Strong lent her prestige to publicising this dream of Mao. She was taken on a trip 'with a small group of Americans' by car from Shanghai to a 'steel base' on Paimao Commune. One can imagine the preparations to receive these foreign friends. Anna wrote:

> Here on a large area of wasteland containing ore, some 11,000 people had come between 15 September and 15 October, camped and dug in, erected furnaces and begun making steel. They had built 1,100 furnaces, 800 of them small ones while 200 were relatively large, some five feet in diameter ...
>
> When the visitors from Shanghai appeared in autos, a band quickly formed to greet them with music. A good time was being had by all.
>
> In five weeks they had not only built the furnaces but had begun turning out forty tons of steel per day which would reach 200 tons easily within ten more days ...
>
> This was how China, in a single year, doubled steel production from 5.35 million tons to more than eleven million. At the height of this drive it was said that sixty million people made steel. Foreign experts stared in amazement, and said that if the costs of labour were counted, this steel cost a good deal more than gold.*

It had cost perhaps more than moon-dust and was unusable. Some of it could be resmelted at enormous cost. The rest was abandoned *in situ* and became interesting modern sculptures littering the landscape.

A real steel expert named Yeh Chou Pei – we called him Yap – was one of the regular visitors to our house. He was as American as a Chinese could be and also as patriotic as a Chinese could be. He was really high level in steel technique and left a big job in the United States – as so many other experts did – to put his abilities at the service of the New China. He and the others were now being damned on all sides like the Jackdaw of Rheims and shunned by Zhou Enlai who

† Ibid., pp.65ff.

had been largely responsible for inviting them to come to China's industrial aid.

Yap was one of those all-round scientists, a tremendously intelligent, modest and lovable man. When he first arrived he had been drawn into the birth-control business as an adviser and was appalled to find that even with the then available figures and trends, China's population could be up to a billion in a couple of decades, and should be kept to half of that or less; he prepared proposals to achieve that result. At that point Mao Zedong concluded that people were China's greatest asset and countermanded the birth-control drive.

Among his other jobs, such as training steel technicians, Yap was working on some new development in continuous steel production, too technical for me to grasp at all. He sent his ideas to the proper people in China and also the Soviet Union. He was overjoyed when the Russians accepted his method. It was ignored in China.

Soon after, I came home and found Yap weeping. He had been publicly denounced by his pupils, the sort of thing that later became a commonplace. In China, for pupils to insult a teacher is, from the point of view of 'face', the end. They had called him a bourgeois, conservative, reactionary element. 'Your methods have no meaning here,' they told him. 'As long as a person is Red, he can make high-speed tool-steel with a candle and *Mao Zedong di Si Xiang* (The thought of Mao Zedong).

Yap was finished. Later I heard that he had been denounced variously as a spy for the Soviet Union, America and Japan. Busy man. It also happened to me, I was told, but I was not 'in the jurisdiction'. He died, of sorrow they reckoned. His American wife went to gaol and later was rewarded with a personal apology from Zhou Enlai.

At the level which mattered, where ignorance ruled, nobody was willing to listen to voices urging caution in the use of machines. There was an underlay of superstition in believing that the Thought of Mao Zedong brought special properties to real things, as the Tibetan 'army' held up their amulets while they were being mown down by Younghusband's Maxim guns. People were not only unwilling to listen to advice that a given lathe and tool would not cut faster, they were ready to treat such advice as anti-Mao.

This must have applied also to the Soviet experts, serious technicians, sent to help build factories and train technicians. I didn't know because they kept to themselves but it must have happened and it must have been hard for trained people to accept the wishful beliefs of people who scarcely knew what a spanner was.

For the general picture the best example that came my way was Albert Belhomme, an American soldier whom I knew in North Korea when he was a prisoner and decided to settle in China as Condron did. He married a Chinese woman and settled down as an electrician in a local paper factory, built by the Japanese during their occupation in the thirties.

I was able through these contacts to talk to a Westerner who had the almost unique experience of going through the Great Leap Forward as a worker. He told the same story that one could tell in Xinhua about the persecution of the intellectuals and of several who killed themselves under the strain.

'After that, only production counted. They went nuts. We worked night and day to build seven extra generators. I hardly slept for a week. Then we got a Polish engine to drive the generators. It did not have enough power but they went ahead. Mao had said we can do anything. In no time the engine's bearings went. After we went through three engines we had to go back to municipal power and the city could not produce enough.

'We had to push the paper-making machines far beyond their capacity of 75 metres of paper a minute. They got it up to 200 metres, got all kinds of mechanical and belt trouble and ruined the machines.

'That was convenient because we were free to go and make steel. Everything that would move was used to transport bricks, coal and ore and I was taken off my work to tend the ovens.'

'I believe,' Belhomme went on, 'that all those peasants ought to have been maintaining ditches and so on during that time and the bad crops later came because of neglected field work not bad weather. Anyway, the peasants said so – but quietly of course.'

Xinhua's *ganbu* saw the campaign to produce steel as great fun. Soon Chingling – Sun Yatsen's widow – lent the thing prestige by having a well-publicised steel oven in her garden into which,

The Great Leap Forward

no doubt, she sometimes dropped a bit of coal with chopsticks.

Two furnaces in the Xinhua compound were spotlit all night and there were two very large and powerful electric blowers forcing cold air expensively into clumsy-looking blocks of brickwork, while translators, editors, typists, reporters, drivers and cleaners threw coke, scrap-iron and various things into a hole at the top.

Part of the dreams was that urban communes would be developed and one of their advantages would be to set the women free from cooking tasks by establishing mess-halls. These did not exist then, and never did, but when a shortage of scrap developed, enthusiasts went from house to house confiscating anything made of iron or steel, including cooking pots and if people resisted, smashed them on the spot as being, at any rate theoretically, redundant.

Xinhua's *ganbu* found it much more interesting to stand around drinking tea and smoking all night than sitting at a desk. A few times I watched a 'pour'. This had nothing to do with the furious battling of half-roasting steelworkers in protective clothing, tapping and containing the furies of white-hot molten metal. Out of all the expenditure of electric power, coal, scrap-metal and idle chatter crept or was dragged a sluggish mess looking like the asphalt used on roads – not even Red and much less than Expert.

Xinhua produced no steel but it managed to produce a scandal. Hanging in the compound was a banner quoting from some poem, I think, 'For the party secretary sleeps by the blast furnace and makes it glow ...' In this case, the (married) party secretary of the *Dui Nei Bu* ('Home Service') made use of one of the empty offices to get a single girl in the family way and was duly charged with rape. For traditional reasons, in China, little distinction is made between rape and extra-marital sex, especially if the man is married.

Xinhua's lack of results on the industrial front was compensated by an invention which must have been conceived by the laziest man in the office. As a contribution to hygiene he devised the Great Leap Forward Extended Water-Closet Flush Chain. By lengthening the usual chain to a lever on the floor, the user could flush the toilet by a mere movement of the foot. This was actually taken seriously and installed all over Xinhua and in some other offices to improve hygiene, though owing to inadequate plumbing, used toilet paper continued (and still does) to be put in baskets at the side. My suggestion that it was wasteful of the extra chain and the specially-made lever was ignored. Xinhua needed something to counteract the rape case.

My Xinhua colleagues were politely cool. Their bush telegraph told them that things were going badly and they knew I knew. Their safest course was to lie low and send out whatever came into the office without discrimination. I never found out, but I think that discrimination was what led Chen Long, the Ancient Dragon, to disappear for a spell and come back much later silent and chastened, demoted from department head to typist and avoiding one's eye.

His place was taken by a man of stupefying solemnity named Xiao Ximin who wordlessly passed items across the desk for my perusal. A typical Xinhua item at the time read:

> Huayung County in Hunan Province has found a way of making its pigs grow fat quickly, not in weeks or months, but days. By removing the thyroid gland, clipping the ears and cutting the tail a pig can be made to grow an average of six jin (three kilograms) a day. The quality of the pork is not diminished in any way.

I wrote 'Kill' and passed it back. It was sent out.

Much worse things happened. One night a report came in about an ingenious Sichuan peasant who had succeeded in cross-breeding pigs with cows. Here we had an animal that gave more meat and at the same time milk. I admit that I laughed.

Xiao Ximin had a habit of holding news items as though they were likely to burst into flame and staring at them, putting them down and picking them up, almost speaking and deciding not after all. I had written 'Impossible' on the item.

At last he said diffidently, as though in absolute proof of the correctness of the item, 'It was sent by the Xinhua branch in Chengdu.'

'If this is true,' I countered, 'it is of the greatest importance. We must send a reporter, find out all the facts, does it have horns, is it a ruminant? How is it done?'

He continued to stare at the piece of paper. As I left for the night, it still lay on his desk. When I had gone, he put it on the morse-cast.

Next came a report of a peasant genius, maybe a third Wright brother, who had invented a bicycle with a propeller on the front. It was said that the harder the wind blew against the cyclist, it turned the propeller faster and the bicycle went more quickly forward.

We had the same argument with the same result.

On that day, ten years after joining Xinhua, I decided that, as with the RAF two decades earlier, my services were no longer required.

'Two-Gun' Morris Cohen, former bodyguard of Sun Yatsen who was for more than thirty years intelligence adviser to successive Chinese governments, was a regular visitor to our house. We named our tough pet cockerel Two Gun after him.

Two Gun the rooster and his playmate, a young tortoise-shell alley-cat named Moll Flanders, were the only pets I ever had. Moll, who died a virgin despite her name, was a product of the Beijing jungle. Her two sisters were snatched from their basket in the kitchen on consecutive nights by a powerful savage tabby. My wife waited for him on the next night and killed him with a poker after a wild crockery-smashing batle, watched in awe from outside the windows by the *baomu*, children and some neighbours.

Moll, whose mother disappeared, and I were friends. When I came home from night shift, she would be waiting in the watergulley at the bottom of the wall, where she had been born. Tail high she led the way in and at once rolled her glass marble across the tiled floor to start her nightly game.

She was clever. A favourite trick was to drop the marble into a shoe a few times – letting me find it – then appear to do it again but actually keeping it in her mouth and seeming to laugh while I looked for it. If I sat down, defeated, or sometimes before, she let the marble drop with a click and flick it across the floor, racing me to it. Maybe other cats do this sort of things and I am merely being partial. But most cats do not seem to me to have much sense of humour.

She caught some cat-illness and lay shivering under the stove while I raced all over Beijing trying to find some means to save her life. When I came home she was on her way staggering to the coal-bin, where she died, privately, as cats do. Two Gun survived her for a while but marbles meant nothing to him.

Morris got his nickname, he told me, from an incident when he accompanied Dr Sun to an appointment where it was stipulated that weapons must be left at the door. He left his revolver but went in with a cleverly shoulder-holstered automatic. There are other versions. Anyway, he always carried a tiny gold model of a long-barrelled Colt on his watch guard. We believed that in his retirement his frequent visits to China were to sell aircraft, a reward to him for loyal service to China since the beginning of the century.

On his way to us for a cup of 'real tea' he rang the bell and was suddenly confronted by Di Di – our four-year-old – equipped with a home-made submachine-gun and shouting: '*fandui yingguo diguo juyi*' ('oppose British imperialism') which he did not know anything about but it had been explained to him that the British were *huai dan* ('bad eggs') and he was posted at our door keeping the bad eggs out, not realising that there was one inside – myself. 'You seem to be in trouble, Alan,' Morris joked.

Actually I was. We were. Both boys were getting muddled by being pumped full of high-pressure politics. Children were being encouraged to denounce their parents for ideological sins or were being hounded at nursery and school for defending their parents. *Bao jia*, the ancient system of mutual responsibility or guilt by association may have changed its form, but the tradition was there and had deep roots.

In the radio station where my wife worked, group ideological pressure shifted from individual to individual according to some silent planning that went on intangibly behind the scenes. Remoulded *ganbu* were only too happy to subject others to the misery they had experienced. It was like tamed elephants being used to subject others.

Being married to a foreign friend, although no longer of the best kind, protected her from the worst features of remoulding or restamping. She was a political crane among chickens and it must have been extremely frustrating for the manipulators of

The Great Leap Forward

the movement at the radio station to cope with a far-gone bourgeois rightist who could not be pressured into confessing, reforming or begging forgiveness and still not be subjected to the ultimate retributions. At that time, it was still unthinkable to go to the limits of struggle against the wife of a foreign friend. If only I had been an ordinary correspondent I could have been ejected, but I was also a *ganbu* wearing the blue cotton.

There were plenty of petty devices to make her run the gauntlet in excusable ways. Endless boring articles had to be read on to tape 'for practice' under constant barracking. Her announcing was said to have deteriorated because of ideological weakness and she lacked revolutionary enthusiasm. She was not Red and did not stress the main points.

Her fellow *ganbu* found it very improper that she could accompany me to diplomatic functions, wearing 'reactionary' Chinese dress, go dancing, swimming and skating at the International Club, talk to foreigners without being made to write a report. That a *ban-ban*, 'a false foreign-devil', should get all these titbits and even shake hands with the top people including Mao was indeed unjust.

My original purpose in coming to China had been left behind. Work at Xinhua had become useless and degrading as it had for so many technicians and specialists whose advice was no longer needed.

We decided to resign from our jobs in Chinese organisations. I applied for Esther's release to become my assistant as a correspondent. I imagine that the Chinese were glad to get us out of the anomalous position of being both *ganbu* and quarrelsome.

Our situation was still precarious. I was passportless, she now only had a Chinese passport and we did not want to apply for British citizenship for her in Beijing. If the British Embassy refused there might be more trouble. We left it, kept the children home to stay and Esther had a good year coming on trips round China with me and to Korea and Vietnam where she had a talk with Ho Chi Minh – her ultimate ambition.

17
Nuclear Bombs and Paper Tigers

In the Yellow Sea, there is a single bay where everyone used to go who was fortunate enough to go to a beach during the dreadful monsoon time in Beijing. Beidaihe looked as a resort must have looked fifty or even one hundred years before. There, the Political Bureau members could sometimes be seen floating, unsinkable, in air-rings, wearing straw hats almost a yard in diameter. They were there that summer, 1958; so were my wife and the two children, so were many of our friends. I was not. Xinhua, in unspoken punishment for my various sins, said that owing to this and that I could not have time off to write my book on the ethnic minorities I had visited (*The Slaves of the Cool Mountains*) and I had to write it during my holidays.

Wearing only a towel, sitting on another towel, with clothes round my arms to prevent sweat dropping from my elbows as I typed, showering every hour, I finished the book.

In Beidaihe one of the most momentous events was taking place, but had I been there I would have had just as much information as I got in Beijing – none. Not till long after did we find out that at Beidaihe, only a few months after it was launched, the Communist Party of China, moving very cautiously, began to dismantle the Great Leap.

Actually, by staying in Beijing I learned a great deal more because Chinese friends from the provinces dropped in and told me what was going on. Nobody had any good to say about the Great Leap. There was despair over failing crops, substandard products, invented statistics, corruption, inexpert water conservancy. While some people near starvation fought over grass and leaves, fat extortioners waxed again and officials grew rich. All that the people had as the practical gains of their revolution was being rapidly wiped out. There were local uprisings; people fled from the communes and turned vagrant or bandit.

Soviet technicians, according to what news could be got, were bewildered by the sudden anarchy, the flouting of technical usage, the havoc caused by puerile attempts to speed up. New plants stood idle, ruined by flagrant abuse.

Emi Xiao, an eminent Chinese poet who knew Mao intimately and was at school with him, told me that one of Mao Zedong's favourite sayings from the old Chinese was, 'When the first cart breaks down, the second stands in thought.' But the Chairman ignored this valuable piece of advice. As the failure of the Great Leap became daily more evident, praise for it grew and Mao became godlike. After the Stalin disclosures, Mao did not stand in thought; he took over the cult and hung bells on it. He was without error; the light he shed was the source of the new material force driving China forward; he was more than a Chinese Marx, he was an advance on Marx, being more modern; he was in fact the Great Helmsman charting a short cut to Communism. On the other hand, the Political Bureau had privately, but with Mao's knowledge, taken the first steps to return to planned industry.

The vast force that had been engendered rolled on. Trees had been felled on Mao's advice, to plant grain; grass and lawns had been eliminated as bourgeois. Beijing became more than ever a dust-bowl, choking on grit-filled air, bald of leaves and birdless. There was almost nowhere for the new assets – the burgeoning baby population – to play. The street committee called to tell us to dig up the lawn we had nurtured into dusty life.

Instead of songbirds and vegetation we had a fine crop of art shops with rows of plaster busts of Mao Zedong, mole and all, and priggish statuettes of pioneers with red scarves and peace doves on their fingers. Medicine stores no longer displayed contraceptives or diagrams explaining birth control. Loudspeakers endlessly boomed out *Dong Fang Hong* ('The East Glows Red'). In a loose translation, the first verse of the song goes: 'From the red east rises the sun. There appears in China Mao Zedong. He works for the people's welfare. He is the people's great saviour.'

My brain fought my sentiments that autumn. I had become emotionally snared, in love with the China of the endearing modest millions; convinced too of the perspectives opened out for mankind by the unity and contiguity of one third of the world's peoples united and moving to peace and socialism.

Could all that be jettisoned in favour of a set of preposterous fantasies? Was it possible that China's steeled and intelligent leaders had gone crazy overnight?

In that hot summer of 1958, through the turmoil of the communes and the Great Leap, the rain and the dust and the confusion, the pattern of a policy began to take shape.

While I was in Korea I had become friendly with a number of Indian diplomats on the Armistice Commission and through them met others in Beijing who were in the need-to-know class and relied on my discretion. From them I heard first of Mao Zedong's discussions with the Indian leader Nehru about nuclear war.

At that time Mao envisaged a world nuclear war in which as many as half of the world's population of 2,700 million might be killed. Mao said that half would still remain and imperialism would be destroyed, socialism established and there would soon be as many people as ever.

This sounded as though it might be Mao trying to shock Nehru, or even get his reactions, but the same 'theory' next cropped up when a Chinese friend from my early days in Manchuria turned up at my house almost in a state of shock from having heard a report given by Mao Zedong to a Chinese party conference. In it Mao said, more or less verbatim:

'Wars should not be feared. We comrades here have seen death and it is not frightening. If out of our 600 million half die, there will still be 300 million.

'As I see it, the atomic bomb is no more terrible than a big sword. In the Second World War the Soviet Union lost twenty million people and other countries in Europe ten million, a total of thirty million. After the Tang and Ming emperors wars were fought with swords and forty million people were killed in these wars.

'If half of mankind dies in a war it will be of no consequence. It would not be terrible if one-third of the population remains. Within a certain number of years the population will again increase. I spoke of this to Nehru. He disagreed. If a nuclear war does break out, it will not be so bad because capitalism will perish and eternal peace will reign in the world.'

In fact, Mao did not believe in eternal peace but in continuous violence.

As I understood from another source, Mao Zedong had tried to sell this grotesque thermonuclear argument to the International Meeting of Communist and Workers' Parties in Moscow in 1957 where his statement was not taken seriously. But views of this sort were by no means an aberation, he went on developing and 'perfecting' them into a system which he imposed on the Chinese party's philosophy.

Mao dressed this charnel-house concept of human social progress in a sort of theoretical sounding terminology. He was far from deeply read in economic and social science and one of his recurring philosophical simplifications was the 'contradiction' that everything, including world nuclear war, had a good side and a bad side, and this he liked to illustrate with an ancient Chinese fable about an old man who lost his horse. His neighbours commiserated with him.

'This may be a good thing,' he said.

The horse came back with another horse and the neighours called to congratulate the old man.

'This may prove unlucky,' he responded.

His son trying out the new horse, fell off and broke his leg. Once more the neighbours expressed their sympathy.

'This may turn out for the best,' the old man said.

Then the Huns invaded the country and most able-bodied men were pressed into the army and killed in battle. Thanks to his broken leg the old man's son survived.

I wondered how all those press-ganged soldiers who did not have broken legs got on, not to mention all the Huns. As an argument in favour of nuclear war as a means of achieving socialism I found it unconvincing, and Mao had not even mentioned the effects of world-wide radioactive fall-out.

Possibly he did not know about such things any more than he realised that killing all the birds in Beijing would have disastrous results on the environment.

Toward the end of July there was a curious paragraph in the *People's Daily* which I clipped for filing. It said:

> Today in the Middle East another link [Iraq] in the imperialist chain has been broken. Tomorrow yet another will be broken in Asia, Africa or Latin America. Now that the east wind continuously prevails over the west wind, colonialism and imperialism will find no avenue of escape from ultimate doom.

Where was 'east' in relation to where? What had happened to the socialist countries and to the working class of the capitalist countries in the struggle against colonialism and imperialism and the establishment of world socialism? When I put this question, pointing out that Lenin had advocated the formation of an anti-imperialist front embracing all democratic movements including anti-imperialist capitalists, I was told that the working class of the industrialised countries had been corrupted. They had been bribed by the high standard of living that was derived by their capitalist masters from the super-exploitation of the colonial territories and peoples. But this entirely revised version of Communist policies was *nei* (internal) and was not published but spread by word of mouth.

Nikita Khrushchev flew into the sweating capital for talks with Mao Zedong but their joint communique tiptoed round the questions of nuclear weapons and the communes. The Soviet leader had scarcely left the Chinese capital when *Hongqi* ('Red Flag'), the official theoretical journal of the CPC, asserted that nuclear war was nothing very special and would speed up the advance to world socialism. In its next issue it acclaimed the people's communes as a historic product of Mao's thought.

The *Hongqi* article of 16 August 1958, judging from style, authority and argument, appeared to have been written by Mao as a parting shot at the tail-fins of Khrushchev's plane.

> The atomic bomb is a paper tiger, 'It looks as if it is a fearful thing: it is not so as a matter of fact ... The emergence of the atomic bomb marks the beginning of the end of US imperialism.'
>
> To the people who fought bare-handed in the past, swords,

spears, bows and arrows were the ancient equivalents of 'atomic bombs'.

To the Chinese people's armed forces in the revolution who had 'only rifles and millet', the complete arsenal of weapons and equipment possessed by the imperialists and their lackeys could also be regarded as the 'atomic weapons' of that time ... There is only one way to deal with (atomic war maniacs) – to expose and fight them ... Those who want to run amok must be warned that once they start an atomic war, the result will be the destruction of imperialism which has brought untold suffering to mankind. Socialism far from being destroyed, will be realised all the more quickly throughout the world.

How did such fantasies as the wind-driven bicycle and the bovine pig get into the Xinhua office and land on the desk of Xiao Ximin who had an education and knew they were lies and could only be lies, but still sent them out to the world?

Somebody must have had the idea. From a concept to the method of ascertaining its properties by logical deduction is an attractive method. It is *a priorism*. But it has nothing to do with Marxism, and it is certainly not based on experience as the starting point of knowledge. Nobody ever saw that bicycle riding off into the wind or that bovine pig being born.

And now Mao Zedong had outlined his new world concept, the product we were told of sleepless nights, with all the logical simplicity of the Sichuan peasant's bicycle. The Great Leap and the new world that Mao was conceiving was hard to accept as intentional because it seemed too mad, but there was within it a mad logic and there was a pattern as well if you started from the position of a world ruled from the Central Kingdom by the Son of Heaven.

Nuclear war should not be feared since it would wipe out 'imperialism' – all the industrialised countries in fact, though it would be tactless to mention the Soviet Union in this connection. That aside, Asia, Africa and Latin America would suffer relatively less and undoubtedly China could reckon to be the most powerful force in that brave new world of radioactive ash.

In this scheme, the communes, included in the state administration, as Xinhua recorded in that monsoon August of 1958, would merge industry, agriculture, commerce, education and the military forces, able to function as units amid the devastation. Those would, in Mao Zedong's scheme, comprise a large portion of the survivors. They would advance under Mao's leadership to a life of 'communist' barracks, equalised poverty spread thin, militarised work, canteen food and free burial. It happened without the bomb in Kampuchea.

Even the halting of birth-control fitted in. A lot of extra Hans would be needed to maintain a world surplus if, say, a third got wiped out.

Nothing remained to do but start a nuclear war, for which China had not the means and when Khrushchev had come the Soviet delegation had evidently not approved this scenario. All this was very much *nei*, but little as I could get between the lines, it was enough to provoke the *ganbu* into unwittingly confirming that their *nei* briefings were moving in the same direction as my deductions.

I said that nuclear war was obviously a non-starter for quite a few countries including my own, which would be wiped out. In my opinion the only way for humanity was to prevent nuclear war. The copy-book answer was that world progress may demand the sacrifice of partial interest to the overall goods – of national interests to internationalism. It was implied that my standpoint was if not cowardly at least lacking in international solidarity. And if I liked I could remain in China, as though China would be safer, which apparently they thought it was.

Among western Communists, Sinophiles and free-loaders in Beijing, many swallowed the new line of Mao thought complete – Great Leap, communes, atomic paper tigers, the prevailing east wind, the new zonal theory and the belief that ideological change must precede quantitative advance.

For these, and they were a majority, the Great Helmsman was the Marx of the world's backward peoples – more, he was the Marx of a new era, of the peasants counterposed to the industrial workers who had missed the ferry and would suffer nuclear punishment for that.

This kind of Maoist failed to observe that Mao was not in any sense a major theorist, social philosopher or economist. His concerns were with pressing issues, political in-fighting, and were always liable to basic change. He was eclectic. He selected and compounded Marxism, fringe-Marxism, anarchism, Trotskyism, ancient and more recent Chinese theories and beliefs such as the Taiping Great Heavenly Kingdom, and made basic changes as the whim struck him – birth-control for example, and the Hundred Flowers, turned overnight into a single weed.

Uncritical adorers, believing themselves to have ringside seats in the new historic era of Maoism, cheerfully threw out Marx, Engels, Lenin and Stalin in favour of a confused, vacillating and essentially poorly educated ideologue who was more a capable and ruthless soldier-politician than the great new world teacher of mankind.

Another category of foreign friends became stuck at the point of euphoria about the access of strength to the socialist camp brought about by the success of the Chinese revolution and could not bring themselves to believe that there could be a split within the leadership of the CPC or between the CPC and the Soviet Communists.

A much debated view in those levels was that it was all a deep game of bluff to mislead the Americans who would then be less on their guard than if faced with a united Communist camp. It was a little naïve since it presupposed that the Americans would not see through so transparent a trick.

In the two years since the Eighth Congress nothing had happened to change my mind about the correctness of the decisions taken then. Only harm had been done by departing from them. All the lyrical propaganda about the Great Leap went on but I knew that it was actually a catastrophe.

Suddenly the signal to retreat from the Great Leap and the people's communes was given by the Central Committee of the CPC after a long meeting from 28 November to 10 December 1958, in Wuchang (part of the triple city of Wuhan). Its resolution praised the communes as 'a new social organisation, fresh as the morning sun, on the boundless horizon of East Asia'.

But a careful study of the text showed that what was actually being announced was a return to pre-commune organisation without actually saying so in as many words. After the Great Leap fanfare the naked truth would have been too bitter especially as Nikita Khrushchev had scoffed at the Great Leap and the communes from the first.

No serious analysis was therefore made. The Central Committee rallied to protect those responsible, especially Mao, who grudgingly conceded his position as head of state to Liu Shaoqi in order to retain the more vital one of Party chairman, with its unlimited possibilities for manoeuvre.

In retrospect, this was the turning moment of China's post-1949 history. What Lenin had described as 'the most dangerous mistake that revolutionaries can make' had been made on a gigantic scale – mistaking desire for objective reality. Impatience to achieve 'communism' the day after tomorrow had been turned into a theory, with what Engels had once characterised as 'childish innocence'.

And the scale of this folly, pressed through in reversal of the CPC Congress decisions, had already caused devastating losses in a country and situation which could not afford them. The need for an analysis was imperative.

Instead, the Central Committee conspired to hide the error, pretend that it was a success requiring light trimming, and failed to take power away from the leader whose brain had visibly been turned by adulation, age and megalomania – the desire to step into the shoes of Marx.

There was no evident excuse; they had before them the fresh example of Stalin – the overturned cart. Later most of those Central Committee members had time to regret, in Mao's gaols, their failure to curb him when they could.

We who were not at Wuchang but only able to study the entrails in Beijing were happy at what appeared to be a U-turn to sanity. I decided to defer asking Pollitt to find me a new assignment and went ahead with plans for an anthropological field trip among a small ethnic group in Manchuria which subsisted on hunting tigers. How apt!

Then I had to cancel all arrangements. The Dalai Lama, God King, Reincarnation of Chenresi, the All-Embracing Lama, Precious Protector, Holder of the Thunderbolt, had fled from Lhasa to India with his entourage.

I at once asked for facilities to go to the Tibetan plateau again.

18
Back to Tibet

When in 1955 I first crossed the Tibetan plateau – the so-called Roof of the World – the road was unfinished but passable. Sometimes the lorry in front of my jeep, inching along a ledge, did not have all its six tyres on the road. Most of the time my stomach was somewhere else. I knew that my uncontrollable fear of heights would disappear if I could drive myself, but that was against the rules and I had to bite the bullet.

Rough as it still was in places, the road was already an engineering phenomenon – shortening the 2,000 mile journey from Ya-an in Sichuan to the Indian border from two years by yak-caravan to a fortnight by jeep. It had been built by men of the Chinese People's Liberation Army in four years, working along its whole length at the same time. 'We want,' as one said to me, 'to prevent another Korea.'

We drove along narrow ledges, over moraines, on hills of sliding sand, over hidden waters, swamps and glaciers, over the Mekong and Salween Rivers to Lhasa and Shigatse. I had the curious experience of being the first visitor by road to Gyantse, where half a century before British troops under Colonel Younghusband had pitted their maxim guns against the matchlocks of the Tibetan 'army' and wiped it out in minutes.

About the time that William conquered England and imposed a unified feudal system on its inhabitants, Tibet must have been in a comparable situation. And there it stuck. For almost a thousand years as near as can be judged, life in Tibet, for rulers, serfs, slaves and herdsfolk, had followed an invariable pattern.

I was fortunate to have seen a period of mummified history,

almost unchanged while elsewhere men were inventing aircraft that could fly over this vast plateau where on the ground everything was transported on the backs of men and animals, for the use of the wheel was forbidden as conducive to change.

Living and travelling in Tibet made it no easier, in some ways harder, to credit the existence of anachronism on so vast a scale, and yet it was precisely the scale that made the anachronism not merely possible but inevitable.

Tibet was practically impenetrable. It is half a million square miles with a mean altitude of 16,000 feet. Huge peaks of perpetual snow and ice dot its endless mountains. Among this desolate waste lived an estimated 1.2 million people. The new southern road had an average altitude of 13,000 feet, crossing sixteen major mountain ranges and twelve big rivers. Its highest point was about 17,500 feet – at that time the highest road section in the world.

Westerners had never been welcome. Strangers who risked the natural barriers had to seek out villages to find food. There they encountered the vigilance of officials who were ordered on pain of terrible punishment to keep out all *Feringhi* (Europeans) – as being warlike and annexationist. Foreigners found even the air inhospitable, so thin on high ground that the locals called it 'the poison of the passes'. Colonel Younghusband, who had no difficulty in defeating the Tibetan serf army, was himself defeated by the weather after a token victory.

Tibet had remained in isolation since the tenth century when the lamaseries – practising a blend of *Bon* animism with a crude adaptation of Buddhism – had become the only places in those isolated valleys where there were concentrations of armed men; the retainers of the nobility being spread thinly over their overlords' estates. The lamas challenged the monarchy.

Legend has it that the last lay king, Lang Darma, headed an attempt to smash the church but that a monk, dressed in black and riding a white horse blackened with soot, got close to the king and killed him. He escaped by taking off his black robe and riding the horse through a river to wash off the soot.

Terrain and cohesion made the monasteries all-powerful and the nobles sent sons into them. So the clerical-lay regime emerged. The serfs too had to provide manpower for the lamaseries, each family being forced to give a son or pay for a substitute.

In this unique social system the ruling aristocracy – clerical and lay – were at the same time officials and merchants. Lay commoners who made their way as merchants were not class rivals but were elevated to the noble-official class. So no 'third estate' could develop to challenge the ruling gentry and their figureheads – the Dalai and Panchen Lamas.

Such a power vacuum as Tibet was a standing temptation to the surrounding nations. Since 1720, a Chinese *Amban* had sat in Lhasa but the Chinese had taken no action to prevent the British incursion in 1904. Chinese suzerainty had suited the Western powers until the Communists took over, and then they began to demonstrate interest. Beijing could not leave things as they had been for the last 1,000 years.

Tibet had to change and it seemed to me that socialist China had the means and the desire to consolidate its position by making those changes come about peacefully and painlessly. It was not easy to work out how to achieve co-operation with the ruling nobility in putting an end to their own privileges. As one puzzled noble, educated at an English public school, asked me, 'How can one live without serfs?'

I had long talks with the two Grand Lamas and their advisers who confirmed the view that Tibet should remain part of China and that there had to be reforms going along with self-government to bring it into the twentieth century.

Mutual trust was growing; the air of optimism and progress was comparable with the *élan* in the rest of China, especially among the young nobility.

I attended a meeting of all the lay and lama leaders to prepare the way for Tibetan self-government. The Dalai Lama became Chairman of the Preparatory Committee for the Autonomous Region of Tibet, with the Panchen Lama as the First Vice-Chairman and a Han, Chang Guohua, as Second Vice-Chairman.

Chang Guohua enunciated what he defined as 'the established policy of the Chinese Central People's Government on the question of reforms in Tibet'.

He said:

The Tibetan region differs greatly, socially and economically, from the areas of the Han people and other minority nationalities. The measures to be taken in future to carry out reforms in the Tibet region must also be different from those adopted in other areas.

According to the instructions of the Central People's Government, future reforms in the Tibetan region must be carried out from the upper to the lower levels and by peaceful consultation, in accordance with the will and desire of the majority of the Tibetan people.

During and after reforms, the government must take whatever steps are necessary to ensure that the political status and living conditions of the upper-class Tibetan people (including upper-class ecclesiastics) will not be reduced but will possibly be raised.

That is to say changes can only be for the better and not for the worse.

This method is to the advantage of the aristocracy and of the monasteries and also of the people.

After future reforms in Tibet, the religious beliefs of the people can remain completely unchanged.

Speaking at the same meeting, Vice-Premier Chen Yi said that reforms in Tibet 'can only be carried out when the Tibetan leaders and people unanimously demand them. They can never be carried out by any other nationality'.

If stability was to be maintained, reform in Tibet could only come from above, winning at each step the co-operation of its historic rulers. Any attempt to rally the unimaginably abject serfs, slaves and other commoners to revolt against their lama and lay rulers was almost guaranteed to play into the hands of powers hostile to the new Chinese republic. At that time Beijing's policies were carefully worked out and realistic.

As I wrote in my book *Tibet*, it was perfectly feasible to raise everyone's standard of living. Tibet's wealthy were far from well-to-do by Western criteria and like everyone else they suffered from a lack of social amenities. The younger generation of nobles were turning to modern things. They were more interested in radios, aircraft, motorcycles and gramophones than horses and prayer-mills. Beijing could afford to pay a Lhasa school-teacher more than the income-equivalent of a large estate with its output of rancid yak butter, poor barley and wool.

China had nothing to gain from alienating the Tibetan rulers and everything to gain from winning their good will. I was convinced and still am that the policy expressed at the Eighth Congress of the CPC toward the ethnic minorities was genuine although it later became obvious that Mao and presumably others silently dissented from Liu Shaoqi's plain words: 'In carrying out reform, peaceful means must be persisted in, and no violent struggle should be resorted to.'

Liu and others speakers denounced *Da Han Ju Yi* (Great Han arrogance) – the assumption by the Han Chinese of their superiority over all other peoples – a besetting sin in their treatment of the minorities. Liu warned, 'Although the minority peoples comprise only 6 per cent of China's total population, they occupy about 60 per cent of the country's total area.'

Zhou Enlai had made the point another way in a talk with me in May 1950. 'The Han people wronged the fraternal nationalities and drove them to the mountain tops and border regions. We have to make good the wrongs of our ancestors. There must be no hasty reforms.' There was more than humanitarianism and righting wrongs in the policies enunciated by less extreme spokesmen at that time.

The 60 per cent of China's territory where the minorities lived was largely on its borders but, apart from its strategic significance, was reckoned to contain most of the countries richest resources, especially minerals.

One of China's serious problems, which Liu's policy would have solved but which the Great Leap and the Cultural Revolution compounded, is that its border regions are inhabited by non-Hans who are traditionally and with reason hostile to the Hans.

China has now confessed to the arrogance and negative effects of her policies towards the ethnic minorites. These will not be easily overcome.

This great-nation disdain is a folly into which the Russians have not fallen. Remarking on the differences, David Bonavia, who served as *The Times* correspondent in China and the Soviet Union, wrote:

*

The Russians have on the whole shown a greater respect for the cultural traditions of the racial minorities, and studies in Uzbek, Tadjik, Georgian and Armenian subjects, for instance, are pursued vigorously in the various Union Republics. Moscow's attitude toward its minorities is to let them have whatever cultural freedoms they want provided they are not disruptive to the stability of the state. China has still to learn this lesson and put it into practice if it is to keep or restore the goodwill of its ethnic minorities.*

Almost half a year passed after the flight of the Dalai Lama and his supporters to India. All enquiries at the Beijing foreign ministry went unheard. I had just begun a holiday in Beidaihe in 1959 when there was sudden call to Beijing and a hasty flight to Lhasa.

It was no surprise to myself and a few other correspondents that we were in time to see the first land-reform – well-choreographed – and to interview word-perfect poor lamas, ex-serfs and ex-slaves, to be shown Lhasa's first public latrines which were situated near an absurd bandstand-style gazebo from which a Han traffic policeman directed non-existent traffic. Both had been built at the entrance of the Jokang Temple – the Holy of Holies of Tibetan Lamaism – the true Lhasa or Place of God.

The stage-management was as obvious as it usually is. In such cases the *ganbu* regard it as rather easy to hoodwink an assortment of foreigners most of whom could speak neither Han-Chinese nor Tibetan. And suppose one was not taken in, nothing could be done about it, being a guest.

I had spent quite a long time in Tibet some years before, and a look round Lhasa on arrival demonstrated with what blinkered crudeness the central authorities had outraged Tibetan custom since 1955. A few indirect enquiries established that all the gratuitous vandalism had happened in the last year as a result of the Great Leap.

An ugly whitewashed hostel had been built facing the glorious facade of the Potala, as discordant as a chrome supermarket on the steps of Notre Dame, pitilessly ruining

---

* David Bonavia, *The Chinese*, Allen Lane, London, 1980, p. 266.

what had been the only example of unalloyed architectural perfection I had ever seen.

On the former luxuriance of the Plain of Milk, between the Iron Hill and the Jewel Park, massed rows of tin-roofed huts had been constructed.

The toilets and the road paving were visible signs of the haughty Han assumption of their superiority over the ethnic minorities, who like the English until recently were accustomed to do their business where they happened to be – a custom as much frowned on by the Hans as Tibetan sexual mores.

There were many more such signs and they represented a very drastic change of policy compared with the extreme prudence displayed a few years earlier. My belief – that had dawned during the long wait for facilities to go to Lhasa – was confirmed. The Beijing authorities, suddenly taking over Mao's 'General Line' of more, quicker, better, frugally had deliberately provoked the Tibetan rulers to revolt and driven them, with the Dalai Lama, over the Indian border.

Central government troops were deployed on every route between Lhasa and the Indian border and the whole entourage could have been prevented from leaving Tibet. I believed, and still do, though I have no means of proving it, that this was the Tibetan aspect of the Great Leap.

In an interview I had in Lhasa with General Zhang Jingwu, the senior CPC official in Tibet, he did not hide his exultation. 'After the rebellion,' he said, 'we can mobilise the masses and do as we like. The faster the better. The more chaotic the better. After the open clash the political responsibility is not ours but theirs.' He described these events in *Hongqi* as a 'Chinese victory'. Actually it was a defeat for the CPC policy of peaceful change among the ethnic minorities.

But if we give people like Zhang Jingwu the benefit of a big doubt and accept their charge that the Tibetan nobility rebelled treacherously, without cause, in breach of agreement (and suicidally) we are still left with the conclusion that this was a unique opportunity to make, for the first time, a deep study of the 'land of mystery' while there was still time, before changes wiped out the possibility for ever.

Those foreigners who had risked their lives on Tibet's frozen stony mountain trails in the past had never been anthropologists, but at best explorers and mostly spies or adventurers who, when they were lucky enough to make contact with the Tibetans, met only the noble class. They saw in the ordinary Tibetans abject, filthy, tattered creatures, bowing their heads away from their betters in lifelong humility. They were not interested in how the yak butter, barley, wool and leather which the serfs and herdsmen produced became metamorphosed into gold and silk brocade for an idle group of aristocrats and noble monks. None tried to examine Tibet's social system, economic structure, class relationships or marriage customs. Very few mentioned that it was customary for a host to provide his guest with a woman for the night or to entertain him by having a serf flogged or tortured after supper.

Tibet's small population embraced life modes of great complexity – feudalism, nomadism, slavery and small traces of wage labour. A study of their interpretation would have been of great value. It was possible the largest area of the world where polyandry was the commonest mode of marriage. There was now an opportunity to study this marriage form and it would never recur.

It was missed, or rather evaded. During my previous journey, the Han *ganbu* had begged me not to attempt to investigate sexual customs for fear of offending the nobles. Actually the Han officials were even more shamefaced about what they regarded as sexual debauchery than they were about the Tibetans going to the toilet in any other places on this vast plateau than houses specially built for that purpose, which Tibetans regarded as madness.

There was no offence. Tibetans regarded polyandry, polygamy, monogamy, and their other sexual customs as normal.

Prince Peter of Greece and Denmark, who made a very deep and valuable study of Tibetan polyandry cites a talk with a Tibetan in support of this:

> Lobgesang Tok-Tok complained bitterly of the 'immorality' of the young people in Leh. He said that polyandry was no longer desired by the younger generation, and that this was all due to

outside influence from Indian and Turki traders from Sinkiang, and from European missionaries and travellers who were perpetually speaking against the time-honoured customs of polyandrous matrimony such as Ladakis and Tibetans had always practised, and were introducing the bad habit of monogamous marriage ...

He had noticed, he said, that those Ladakis who were converts to Mohammedanism ... ceased overnight to be polyandrous and divided up the property immediately they got married. The result was that there was not enough to go round for all of them ... They had to look for work.

(He said) he could now grasp why Europeans had colonies throughout the world, why they came to India and even to Ladak. It was obviously because, with the family system they had, they did not have enough to live on at home and the fact that they did not practise polyandry led them to go overseas to seek a livelihood ...*

Now that the nobles were no longer concerned, the Han *ganbu* still dodged my requests to make anthropological studies among the serfs and herdsmen with the embarrassed persistence of Victorian missionaries. They treated my interested in such matters as prurient and evaded my questions with blushes. I could not find a single *ganbu* prepared to take a scientific position. It was a 'face' question. The 'incestuous' non-Hans were, after all, citizens of the Chinese People's Republic and would soon become as civilised as the Hans.

All the same, in that year, by display of temper I got some facilities by means of which, together with my knowledge of Chinese (though unfortunately not Tibetan), I was able to make a study of the economic relationships in the agricultural valleys and among the nomadic herdsmen on the high grasslands. Restricted though I was I managed to gather unique material which has so far not been published.

Prince Peter pointed out that preoccupation with property was what underlay all Tibetan marital oddities (fathers and sons marrying the same woman – women marrying their husband's sons). He adds:

---

* Prince Peter of Greece and Denmark, *A Study of Polyandry*, Mouton, The Hague, 1963.

From his recent journey by car in Tibet, Winnington has brought back the impression that whatever the origin of polyandry among the nomads, it now has a compelling economic motive. If the herds and grazing rights were sub-divided there would not be enough for several sons each to support a wife, and the solution is therefore for the eldest to marry and for his brothers to share his wife as long as they remain living together.

If Beijing had persisted on the line of Liu Shaoqi and Deng Xiaoping, a systematic study of Tibetan society – the first ever and the last chance before the agreed reforms – could have been made in the course of working and co-operating with Tibetans of all social classes. Only a few more than 1.2 million people were involved so the policy of slow and agreed progress with financial help to all social strata was exactly right and could have salvaged this unique fund of anthropological knowledge. Already, the presence of the Hans had stopped the worst excesses of the nobles. There was absolutely no need to hurry and this has now been ruefully admitted.

The two trends in the CPC – Great Leap versus Planning – were reflected with dire results in the policies adopted toward the ethnic minorities.

Predictably, those who favoured consolidation, industrialisation, step-by-step progress and all the other decisions of the CPC Congress which Mao had privately characterised as stinking 'Soviet farts', also favoured winning the support of the non-Han minorities. 'Primarily,' Liu Shaoqi stressed, 'this requires overcoming Great Hanism.'

Those who favoured the Mao line, *duo, kuai, hao, shenq* logically stood for 'Hanifying' the non-Hans and merging them willy-nilly into a single 'Chinese' culture. They saw no virtue in the survival of local languages and cultures.

Tibet's tiny caste of rulers were themselves divided after the Communist victory. For centuries they had lived in a state of uneasy peace with Beijing while its power was distant and not used. Beijing's envoys to Lhasa, the *ambans*, traditionally had occupied that post as exile, a punishment. Reluctant and bitterly-argued acceptance of gradual reforms from above, with the costs borne by Beijing, placed the nobles, other than financially, on the level of their former serfs and slaves.

Any signs of a breach of faith on the Han side would better account for the rebellion and the removal of the Dalai Lama than the lame tales of the Hans and the exultations of Zhang Jingwu.

And such signs were plentiful. As I saw, not even remote Tibet was spared the determined follies of the short-lived Great Leap. What the enlightened Liu Shaoqi had denounced as Great Hanism – the chauvinism, obscurantism and ignorance of the Han *ganbu*, the scholar-intellectuals – was given free rein.

Tibet was a place where even the simplest things were works of art. I bought for coppers several household pots and implements which are marvels of simple beauty. If the beauties of Tibet were at the cost of a slave system that is still no reason for destroying them any more than, in Greece, destroying the Parthenon or smashing the sculptures of Praxiteles.

I saw a little, but few visitors have been allowed since the Red Guards vandalised it. Such visits have been brief, circumscribed and with the belated aim of reversing some of the propaganda damage done to China by the infant cultural revolutionaries in Tibet at the behest of Mao's termagant wife, Jiang Qing.

Among this tiny band of pro-Mao propagandists was, in fact, Jiang Qing's old friend Han Suyin whose trip resulted in a book astonishingly labelled *Lhasa, The Open City*. As an unconscious exposure of her own Great Hanism it was chilling but worth reading for that alone.

It was a patchwork of guided interviews with quotations and descriptions from writers who had earlier been where she had not been able to go. She quotes me as writing: 'Tibetan women regard polyandrous marriage as an institution conferring great prestige on women.'

Han Suyin's typically irascible response was:

> I don't believe him. He got this information from a man, to begin with [this is not true, AW]; and secondly, I just don't see how any prestige or self-respect can redound to the credit of a woman compelled to marry up to five men, not of her

choosing, because they are brothers. She becomes the 'labouring beast' for all of them.

If Han Suyin had visited the high grasslands, she would have found, as I did, that the herdsmen had to provide the nobles, lamas and trading usurers with animal produce, forced transport (*ula*), one male child to serve the lamasery and various unpaid services that came under corvée duties. They were never out of debt.

I had written:

> If the herds and grazing rights were subdivided, there would not be enough for several sons each to support a wife. A wife is therefore found for the eldest son, and his younger brothers share the wife so long as they remain living together ... Generally one son, the youngest, is a monk, one out with the herd, one hunting; someone had to go to fairs and so on. There would be few occasions on which they were at home together for long periods.

Polyandry seemed to be the only possible solution, and what was possible had the usual tendency to be regarded as normal and respectable. A woman married to several brothers did have prestige and an easier life, looking after the tent and bringing up children while her husbands performed the harder tasks of a nomadic life. She was envied by other women who had to become servants, concubines, prostitutes or beggars.

What emerges from Han Suyin's book – one of the few since the years of the infant 'revolution' – is that the Hans had liquidated Tibet's ancient modes without attempting to make a study of them and that the tales that officials tell visiting writers will in the end become official history (Great Han variety).

Tibet was saturated in Lamaism for centuries. I never saw such a concentration of religion. Han Suyin saw only one prayer-wheel and asserts that religion has almost vanished. Perhaps it is my turn to say 'I don't believe it.' After centuries of submission, the Tibetan serf knows how to keep a low profile.

She visited the Jokang, the holy of holies, the true Lhasa or Place or God.

There I drank my first buttered tea, served by the keeper of the Jokka (*sic*) Kang, who had been a lama but is now some sort of a curator. For it is obvious that the Jokka Kang is no longer a place of worship; no crowd is here, and except for some incense burning in front of some of the statues, I only noticed one old woman who seemed to be doing some praying.

It is enough. The Tibetans are being done good to.

She reports that parts of Lhasa are being bulldozed to be make space for 'modern conveniences'. In all the vastness of Tibet, Lhasa covered less than a square mile – a unique medieval city graced by the breathtaking nobility of the Potala palace, which she finds 'evil'. Lhasa itself was a museum. Bulldozers!

There is always the danger for writers of travel books to be led by their guides into the most horrible sins against reality. In China especially the deception of foreigners is almost universal and derives from a mixture of Great Han chauvinism and shame.

In Kunming, before I set out in 1957 to investigate life among the head-hunting Wa in the mountain jungles of south-west China, I asked to meet some Wa people who were being educated in the Kunming Institute of National Minorities.

Two young men were brought to see me, dressed in brightly coloured and very expensive silks, sashes and embroidery, and carrying swords in solid silver scabbards. I was assured that this was their 'national costume'.

'Head-hunting?' I asked. They laughed. In the old days that kind of thing happened but since liberation, under the guidance of the CPC and Chairman Mao, this nasty custom had ended.

But when I got into the Wa jungles, where the Wa were still in a mainly primitive state I found that this nasty custom was very much still in vogue. I interviewed and photographed a young man named Aileh who, two weeks before, had cut off the head of a man called Aidong from neighbouring Gotgor village. Aidong's head was now swaying in a basket on a tall bamboo above the sorcerer's drum-house in Aileh's own village of Masang, in order to ensure good crops.

There was also no national costume. They wore whatever they could get and Aileh had on an ancient, cheap Fair Isle jersey. The young men I had met in Kunming earlier were playing their part in deceiving a foreigner. Whatever they felt before, they had been made to share the shame of being more backward than the Hans and turned into hypocrites displaying a concocted national costume.

Dressing up for foreign visitors is normal on those invisible tracks along which tourists and others are guided and where the Chinese public are well-trained in what is expected of them. The stupid take it in, the intelligent feel that their intelligence is being insulted. What the Chinese feel about entering as they do into a conspiracy is impossible to judge.

If anyone sees a Wa now it will be a tame one who will repeat the now official history that head-hunting ended in 1955 although I knew a case in 1958 and, if it is not still going on in those border jungles I will follow Mr Grimwig's example and eat my own head.

19

Comrade Ah Lan Becomes a Non-Person

Mao had outfoxed the other Communist Party leaders in the showdown over the Great Leap. He had resigned under pressure and appeared, even with wry good humour, to accept the statement that 'our sincerely beloved leader will in future concentrate on Marxist-Leninist theoretical work.'

The beloved leader did no such thing. He commented later that 'They treated me with the respect they would have shown their dead father at his own funeral.'

On the contrary, the beloved leader concentrated on fragmenting the party leadership which in his opinion had humiliated him first by carrying through a 'Soviet-style' Second Five Year Plan and then demoted him for the failure of the Great Leap.

I returned from Tibet, frozen in an unheated military aircraft, my head ringing with the new statistics that proclaimed the reduced results of production, though with hopes that a new start could be made.

But in fact, with teeth and nails, Mao had again managed to regain control.

While I had been in Tibet, what had been essentially a continuation of the showdown with Mao had taken place at Lushan, where Mao had been challenged by the Defence Minister Marshal Peng Dehuai and almost defeated. I was fortunate in having such good contacts that I was able to piece together the dramatic happenings that came within an ace of bringing about Mao's downfall.

Peng Dehuai, the crusty forthright soldier whose generalship had blocked the way for the Americans and their allies in Korea, disagreed with Mao all across the board.

Korea had taught him and most other soldiers there that China must advance from Mao's concept, successful as it had been, of peasant armies with captured small-arms drowning their attackers in a sea of popular resistance when needed, and doing duty as farmers for the rest of the time.

Peng and his Chief of Staff, General Huang Kecheng, my old Manchurian travelling companion, were among the many who favoured a modern army, sophisticated weapons, close technical and military alliance with the Soviet Union, planned production, industrialised farming – all the policies agreed at the 1956 Congress and thrown overboard by Mao in the Great Leap.

Peng Dehuai took Marxist studies seriously. He read laboriously but always had his pockets stuffed with notes and Marxist works; he had a poor opinion of Mao as a Marxist, none at all for Mao's economic understanding and he knew that Mao was anti-Soviet. He detested the cult of Mao whom he thought had ambitions to establish himself as leader of the world Communist movement following the death of Stalin.

Peng Dehuai was not willing to allow Mao's errors and especially the Great Leap to be swept out of view. Reminding his colleagues of the dangers of failing to learn from mistakes he recalled the words of Mao himself in 1937: 'Liberalism negates ideological struggle and advocates unprincipled peace.'

At Lushan, the Marshal made a prepared assault on the whole concept of the Great Leap. He charged that *ganbu* everywhere had been encouraged to falsify production figures; that essential resources had been squandered in the backyard furnace campaign and that the combination of the communes and unplanned water conservancy had brought disaster to agriculture.

Pouring scorn on the Great Leap Forward concept as a reversal of Marxist methods he classified it as 'petty-bourgeois fanaticism' and 'left radicalism', charging that 'In the view of some comrades, putting politics in command was a substitute for everything ... But putting politics in command is no substitute for economic principles, much less for concrete economic measures.'

The Marshal's legendary cunning against the enemy seemed

to fail him in facing his own colleagues. Possibly he believed that it was enough to have right on his side. His attack was simply an effort to return the party to the policies of the Eighth Congress, which they had all endorsed and from which they had no constitutional right to depart.

But that had been three years earlier and so it was in effect a denunciation of almost all the leadership, who had failed to curb Mao when he made his first departure from Congress decisions and afterwards retreated further. For them too it was a 'face' question.

How many of the CPC leaders agreed with Marshal Peng but faltered when it came to a showdown which must expose their own vacillations? Maybe some of them, perhaps even those relatively well-versed in economics, had wondered whether or not, against all odds, Mao had stumbled over some economic miracle which Karl Marx and every other economist before Mao had overlooked. Some miracle that belonged to a non-industrialised era and could rely for its purpose on the 'tremendous energy of the masses', and on nothing else.

Old Peng's feet were closer to the ground, for in a way, General Chu De's military – and realistic – experience had ended before the Americans had to be directly faced. Peng knew more about logistics and economics. And of the few who backed Peng Dehuai, only Chu De could see what it was about.

As it was, Peng, more at home deceiving the enemy, was outpoliticked by Mao and his natural backers fell apart. He had tried to storm the citadel only to find treason on his flanks.

When the smoke blew away he stood there with General Huang Kecheng almost alone, though Chu De favoured him, as I heard. Liu Shaoqi, to my sorrow, was mute and wavering, or that was how it came to me. Peng was right at the wrong time. He was dismissed as Minister of Defence and replaced by Lin Biao. That, at least, was announced as a fact and little else.

We in Beijing, microscopically examining entrails and blade-bones, found a rich seam of nervous bluff and barely-concealed threats in the communiqué issued after the Lushan meeting. It was a classic of its kind.

Urging everyone to 'carry forward the great socialist cause of our country steadily but also by leaps and bounds,' it pointed out 'that the principal danger now facing the achievement of a continued leap forward this year is the emergence of Right opportunist ideas among some cadres ...

'They slander as "petty-bourgeois fanaticism" the great leap forward and the people's commune movements in which hundreds of millions of people have been vigorously engaged under the leadership of the party.'

What was needed was 'firmly (to) put politics in command, fully mobilise the masses, go all out and strive to fulfil and overfulfil this year's leap forward plan'.

But the key was in the last lines wherein the whole population was urged 'to forge ahead valiantly to carry out this year's national economic plan and fulfil ahead of schedule within this year the principal targets of the Second Five Year Plan'.

The Great Leap Forward was dead.

It was a resolution suited to the gullible, the cowed and the hypocrites. Supporting this strange document, which seemed akin to the Sichuan hybrid cow-pig, Zhou Enlai, that Vicar of Bray of the Chinese Revolution, wagged a threatening finger: 'We would ask those who say that the people's communes are in an awful mess ... "are you not afraid of being thrown over the borderline of the bourgeois Rightists?" '

Marshal Peng Dehuai was one of the greatest military figures in the history of the Chinese Communist revolution. He was born a peasant in the same county as Mao and told me once that his life had been transformed by reading *The Communist Manifesto*. He was one history's tragic figures. Both he and C-in-C Chu De were greater soldiers than Mao and the Lushan incident demonstrated that in the post-revolutionary period in China Peng Dehuai saw clearly how urgent it was to modernise and develop their armies alongside the Soviet Union. It was never done.

History will probably confirm my own view that Peng's generalship prevented the outbreak of nuclear war in Korea when he outmatched his American and other opponents in the first full-scale positional war waged by the Chinese People's Liberation Army.

Liu Shaoqi even more than others because of his enormous influence, by failing to support Peng at Lushan, helped to make inevitable the terrible events of the next two decades, including his wife's sufferings and his own ignominious death in gaol.

If the Marshal had not been shocked and blinded by the failure to support him of those who had certainly known of his intentions and thus lent him tacit support; if he had fought to the end for his convictions; he would certainly have realised then that the meeting had in fact endorsed his policies. He was politically destroyed to save Mao's face.

And so he wrote a crawling self-criticism begging the pardon of Mao and the party. It seemed that the major part of the CPC leaders were not willing to go to the limit against Peng and he remained a silent – or silenced – member of the Political Bureau at least until 1965.

The Lushan story – the background of the sudden sacking of the Defence Minister and his replacement by Lin Biao – plus what I surmised from the Khrushchev visit, was a journalist's scoop but I could not write it.

Such a sensational report would have jeopardised not merely the friends who had told me about Lushan but also quite innocent people who came to some much frowned-on parties held at my house, which was pretty well the only place in Beijing where Chinese and foreigners could mix, ambassadors mingled with *hoi polloi* and everyone brought their own liquor.

There was also the danger, amounting almost to certainty, of getting thrown out of China passportless with the probability that my wife and children – technically Chinese – could be forced to remain.

High risk for low gain. It was after all only a journalistic scoop and scoops, purely as such, were never my purpose. In mentally killing the story I realised that my career as a journalist in China had folded up in the same way and for the same reasons as my career as adviser to the Xinhua News Agency.

Generally a foreign correspondent – if not flung into gaol on a spying charge – can leave where he is and go home. Being passportless and threatened with execution at home restricts manoeuvre if one wishes to leave a country. And leaving China now began to occupy my thoughts.

Governments prefer people with passports; indeed people

without – like the captain of *Koepenick* – are invisible to officials and have found themselves on boats shunting to and fro for ever. It is useless to say you are not stateless, that you could return to Britain at any moment but you prefer not since the British authorities have some absurd notion that you are good gallows material.

My wife was technically Chinese, though she spoke a mixture of Cockney and Black Country English except for announcing on Radio Peking when it was more or less BBC. I made another attempt to get a British passport which was refused – no reasons given.

The price of remaining in China, in my special passportless state, would be to accept and further Maoism, which was impossible even before Mao's anti-Sovietism was confirmed. It would be cheating the readers of my paper.

My wife and I talked it over and agreed that we must now take the questions of leaving the Central Kingdom seriously and keep a low profile till that time came.

On the eve of departure, I was 'invited' to 'exchange opinions'. It turned out to be my second 'kangaroo trial', this time at the office of the *People's Daily*, confronting about twenty CPC ideologues round a very large table. They all knew that I was leaving China and had long departed from Mao's way of thinking, so the purpose of the meeting was obscure. They also knew that the Great Leap was a historic bungle but had to pretend the opposite.

It was a struggle meeting but it lacked the element that makes a struggle meeting terrifying – the victim's inability to survive without self-degradation and acquiescence. At this stage a foreign Communist would not be sent to forced labour or solitary confinement on Number One diet or worse. That came later.

Such a meeting always began with a weighed-out portion of praise for the victim, to demonstrate that the business in hand is for his own good. No less embarrassing for that, though they kept the adulation brief to show displeasure. It seemed that I had been worthy of the highest praise until 1957 and then I had become a right-opportunist. I refrained from countering this with the view that I could say the same for the CPC except that it had fallen victim to left-wing infantilism. It then became a free-for-all. I made some notes after the meeting.

> *People's Daily*: Comrade Ah Lan has some differences of opinion with the Communist Party of China?
> Alan Winnington: I fully agree with the policies of the Eighth Party Congress four years ago.
> PD: A congress is not binding for ever.
> AW: That is up to the CPC.
> PD: Comrade Ah Lan appears to believe that the CPC want war? Is that so?
> AW: I judge that the CPC is opposed to policies based on peaceful coexistence between states of differing social systems, regards war as inevitable and considers that nuclear war would advance the cause of socialism.
> PD: Are you afraid of nuclear war?
> AW: No. I have often enough demonstrated that I am not afraid to die. This is not a personal matter. The CPC pretends to compare the nuclear bomb with bows and arrows – as a paper tiger. It says that a nuclear war would bring world socialism quicker. It links these ideas with a policy of relying on the industrially backward nations – continents – as the vanguard of world socialism. These are Chairman Mao's ideas.
> PD: Which you challenge. Do you dispute that if a nuclear war began – say the imperialists began one – it would result in a victory of the peoples over the imperialists?
> AW: It would be lost by all peoples beginning with the British people.
> PD: So out of loyalty to the British you disagree with the CPC and Chairman Mao.
> AW: No. This is another distortion of my views. Why the CPC and Chairman Mao? Is he not a member of the CPC?
> PD: Do you agree that revolutionaries should sacrifice partial interests to a greater common cause?
> AW: If you mean: to sacrifice the British people to the CPC's mistaken policies – no. Absolutely not. As usual in the recent past, this hypothesis too is based on fallacies as were the killing of the sparrows and the amateur smelting of steel. Moreover in essence it is an argument to involve the

Soviet Union in nuclear war with the USA.
PD: That is not the policy of the CPC.
AW: Not the stated policy. But it comes to that since these are the only nuclear powers. It is based on another CPC fallacy.
PD: Which is that?
AW: That nuclear bombs – these modern bows and arrows – would kill proportionally fewer Asians, Africans and Latin Americans than people in other more advanced countries. In fact they could make the whole world uninhabitable by human beings.
PD: Why should the Chinese desire to see a nuclear war?
AW: Not the Chinese, but the CPC leaders. Maybe because of what some CPC members have evidently described as 'petty bourgeois fanaticism'. It is attempting to go faster than objective reality permits. This is a trend in the CPC which the recent congress condemned.
PD: The Great Leap was a spontaneous mass movement.
AW: I know that that is untrue. But even if so, the CPC should have opposed it. The Great Leap, not being based in reality, turned into its opposite. As Marx said: It is not consciousness that decides our existence but social being that determines our consciousness. All Marxists operate from this position. Lenin said that an abstract concept can turn into a fantasy because the material world goes on independently of the human mind.
PD: You are denying that ideas have an impact on the material conditions that called them into being.
AW: No. But the Great Leap was not based on a study of objective conditions and so it has failed.
PD: That is only what some bourgeois rightists say.
AW: It is true. The CPC has landed to the left of Marxism. Relatively, Marxists have become rightists.
PD: What do you think of Lenin's *State and Revolution*?
AW: A most important work. But more pertinent would be for the CPC to study *'Left-Wing' Communism – An Infantile Disorder*.
PD: Comrade Ah Lan is from a capitalist society and needs to be on guard against bourgeois rightist ideology.
AW: Coming from feudal society, Chinese Communists

have to guard against even more backward ideas. The Great Leap, people's communes, household steel furnaces and paternalism are symptoms.
PD: Socialism is historically inevitable and it is clear that a nuclear war would bring it more quickly.
AW: Marxism does not say that socialism is inevitable. In its first paragraph, *The Communist Manifesto* of Marx and Engels point out that class struggle can end in the common ruin of the contending classes. Today mankind can destroy itself.

No discussion was possible during this arid exchange. Following Peng Dehuai's downfall they were all walking very lightfooted, though there was, as yet, no sign of Mao's coming offensive against most of the best known CPC leaders and against almost all Communist parties in the world.

My own opinions of the implications of Mao's thinking – which fell so far short of future events – were too far-fetched in those days to be listened to, and I kept to the established ground of the Eighth Congress. They kept to the safe ground of published opinion. I think they were glad to get it over and be on the record for 'correct' views.

Like all revolutions, the Chinese revolution was unique within the general principles of the historic era in which it occurred. What would otherwise have been a national armed struggle against feudalism and imperialism developed into a socialist revolution under the late – very late – influence of Marxism flowing from the Russian upheavals of 1917. Mao's *melange* of nationalism and socialism was reflected at every point of life in post-1949 China.

Enormous Soviet aid helped to bring about those golden years in the fifties and national pride which so contrasted with the exclusion of China from international affairs by the USA. National pride produced resentment; Stalin's death produced confusion in which some tactlessness was at bottom Mao's personal dislike of Khrushchev was well known, and the ebullient Soviet leader was not of a type to appeal to reserved Chinese cadres.

Stalin's death, I felt sure, had catalyzed an explosive mixture which had been long building up. Mao had not disputed

Stalin's leadership of the world Communist movement. He had differed sharply with Nikita Khrushchev's condemnation of the dead Soviet leader and – out of step with the other Communist parties – insisted that there must be a world Communist leader. So who would be the next world helmsman? Hardly Krushchev.

There was really only one candidate – Mao – who had led a vast Asian revolution to victory. Today China, tomorrow the whole world of the poor which was crying aloud for a new saviours. Whose name had such allure among the spreading liberation movements? At his age Mao had no patience or ability for the banalities of industrialisation. What was needed was a genius to lead the world's poor to a life of regimented frugality.

One purpose of the Great Leap, apart from disrupting the Soviet-pattern Second Five Year Plan in China, must have been to test and demonstrate an alternative, non-Marxian, road to a chicken in every pot for the wretched billions of Asia, Africa and Latin America. The new conflagration, fanned by the Chinese east wind, led by the rising sun of Mao, would dispense with the need to go through an industrial era.

Those backward continents would push beyond the whole historic epoch of capital by sheer weight of numbers, overtake the industrialised countries including the now burned-out Soviet Union and bring to the backward countries, instead of useless space satellites, the all-embracing people's communes, the first of which Mao named – by no accident – *Sputnik*. Nuclear detonations might wipe out industrialised states but would be absorbed by numbers and dispersion on his chosen three continents.

It was a fantasy world created by a man who spent his time brooding on his place in history; on what would be said of him after he had gone, as he said, 'to meet Marx'; a man who basked in and encouraged adoration. Engels summed up Dühring in the classic sentence where he traces to personal causes 'otherwise incomprehensible scientific errors and conceits ...' in the words: 'mental incompetence due to megalomania.' It was the stage reached by Mao in the early fifties.

Harry Pollitt, when in Beijing, had agreed that I should leave China, but he was convinced that I should not return to

Britain until I had a passport. So were the lawyers advising me over the years, D.N. Pritt, QC, and Jack Gaster, though we all agreed that I had not broken any British law.

But since Washington was behind Whitehall's action against me, the British would be very embarrassed if I turned up and might decide to solve the problem by means of some fudged up treason or spying charge held in camera. It made sense. I asked Pollitt to put the question to the British Communist Party and I would of course respect their decision.

It was simple – no return to London.

Harry Pollitt kept his promise. Three months before, the *Daily Worker* had informed the CPC that I had been appointed to work in the German Democratic Republic and wanted to take my family. This was not opposed, relations between the two parties being still correct, but they haggled over fares, hotels, food on the journey via Moscow and Prague, changing my remaining Chinese money and other petty issues in order to demonstrate disapproval. I ironically suggested that I would take my Chinese army mug on which was enamelled *Cui Qlng Ai De Ren* ('Most Beloved Person') and go begging in the main street. The joke was not appreciated.

A few moments before the Moscow plane left the Beijing airport a car came over the apron to the ramp from which I was waving goodbye to friends. It scattered them and stopped. A solitary Chinese blue-clad cadre stepped out into the hot June sunshine – a minor official of the Foreign Ministry Press Department. There was nobody from the Chinese Communist Party. Twelve years before, at Harbin, all the top brass had gathered to welcome me. The cadre waved. It was too late to shake my hand. Comrade Ah Lan had become a non-person.

At breakfast on my first day in Moscow the news of Harry Pollitt's death was brought to me by weeping staff of the Communist Party guest house who had known him. He remains the greatest Englishman I have known.

Soon after, my wife, now with a British passport as my spouse, went to Britain and decided to stay there with our two boys.

It was personally, too, the end of an era.

Name Index

Acheson, Dean, 126
Allison, George, 43
Attlee, Clement, 116, 126

Baldwin, Hanson, 150
Ball, John, 44
Barnard, Bill, 141
Barrett, George, 137, 141-2
Barrett, Ruth, 141-2
Beerbohm, Max, 193
Belhomme, Albert, 212
Bell, Tom, 38
Benes, E., 64-5
Beria, L., 65
Bernal, J.D., 194
Bethune, Dr Norman, 80
Bevin, Ernest, 116
Birch, Nigel, 167
Bley, Roy H., 156-7
Bonavia, David, 231-2
Bradley, Ben, 43, 49
Bradley, General, 132
Bramley, Ted, 43
Browne, Frederick, 25
Brownlow, Cecil, 135
Burchett, Wilfred, 128-31, 140, 154
Burgess, Guy, 78, 128
Burns, Emile, 43, 53

Campbell, J.R., 35, 43, 47, 60, 116, 160, 166
Chamberlain, N., 45-6, 49-50, 179
Chang Guohua, 229
Chen Long, 188-9, 193, 214
Chen Pota, 188
Chen Yi, 72, 230

Chen Yun, 83, 96, 105, 203, 208
Cheo Ying, Esther, 179, 217
Chiang Kaishek, 62-3, 72-3, 101, 105, 124, 162; and the civil war, 74, 76, 78, 81, 83-4, 88, 96; and US plans for his restoration, 165, 174
Chingling, 212
Choi Tai Ryong, 112-3, 115, 118
Chu De: during the civil war, 61, 74, 81-2, 84, 88, 94, 96-9, 102, 108, during the People's Republic, 124, 209, 243-4
Chu Xuefan, 62
Churchill, Winston, 48-52, 54
Citrine, Walter, 51
Ci Xi, 88
Clark, Mark, 166
Cockburn, Claud, 57-9
Cohen, Morris, 215-6
Condron, Andrew, 196-8, 212

Daladier, Edouard, 179
Dalai Lama, 226, 229, 232, 237
Davidson, Michael, 125
Dawson, Geoffrey, 58
Dean, General, 113, 139
Deane, Philip, 36
Deng Xiaoping, 185, 195-6, 198, 204, 236
Deng Yingchao, 94
Dimitrov, Georgi, 50
Dodd, Brigadier General, 160
Donnelly, Desmond, 168
Dutt, R. Palme, 39, 43, 50, 88, 99

Index

Ede, J. Chuter, 116
Eden, Anthony, 157, 166, 168, 177, 179
Eisenhower, Dwight D., 52
Emi Xiao, 219
Engels, Frederick, 32, 39, 44, 186, 207, 225-6, 249-50
Eunson, Bob, 138

Fan Changjiang, 175-6
Fleming, Peter, 124
Fox, Ralph, 53
Franco, General Francisco, 45
Freeman, John, 23
Freund, Ludwig, 64-5
Fu Cuoyi, 84-5, 88, 90-4, 96, 100-1, 104

Gallacher, William, 39, 43
Gao Gang, 98-9
Gaster, Jack, 178, 251
Gaulle, General Charles de, 59
Gottwald, Klement, 65
Greene, Graham, 25
Gruening, Peter, 139

Hanley, Colonel, 138
Hannington, W., 43, 49
Han Suyin, 237-9
Hatem, Dr George (Ma Haide), 101, 104
Hess, R., 48
Hirohito, Emperor, 52
Hitler, Adolf, 39-40, 45, 47-8, 51-2
Ho Chi Minh, 127, 217
Holmes, Walter, 57
Hong Xiuchuan, 75
Horner, A., 43
Ho Zizheng, 78
Huang Hua, 137
Huang Kecheng, 87-8, 242-3
Hu Congnam, 74
Hutt, Allen, 57-60

Jang Pihua, 175
Jensen, Fritz, 177
Jiang Qing, 78, 237
Jia Yulin, 80, 89, 93, 104

Jodl, General, 52
John, Augustus, 36
Joy, Charles Turner, 129, 134-5, 142
Ju Jiping, 131

Kang Keqing, 94
Kang Xi, 88-9
Kang Yong Dong, 133
Kerrigan, P., 43
Khrushchev, N., 179, 185, 222, 224, 226, 245, 249-50
Kinney, Andrew, 130-1
Kirkhead, Eugene, 170-1
Kuang Kung, 76

Lang Darma, 228
Lan Ping, 78
Lemay, General, 127
Lenin, V.I., 34, 38-9, 47, 53, 88, 186, 207-8, 225-6, 248
Lin Biao, 61, 74, 79-84, 87-9, 92, 99, 243-5
Li Pinghong, 175, 177
Liu Chengzheng, 103
Liu Ningyi, 62, 67-8, 74, 207-8
Liu Pang, 76
Liu Shaoqi, 108, 179, 185, 198, 226, 231, 236-7, 243-4; during the civil war, 96-8, 102; at the 1956 Congress, 195-6; and the Great Leap Forward, 202-4, 206, 208
Liu Sun, 78-80
Lo Runghuan, 79, 87
Low, David, 29
Lu Dingyi, 200

MacArthur, General, 108-9, 115, 118-9, 120-3, 125-7, 174
Macauley, Lord, 105
MacDonald, Ramsay, 22
Maclean, Fitzroy, 140
McCannar, Colonel, 167
McFie, Major General J.M., 167
McGovern, John, 167
Mann, Tom, 43
Mao Zedong, 108, 184, 236, 241-7, 249-50; and the civil war, 61, 72-3, 78, 83, 88, 93, 95-8, 102;

and the One Hundred Flowers Campaign, 185-7, 189, 193-6, 198-9, 201; and the Great Leap Forward, 205-11, 217; and nuclear policy, 219-24, 226
Marshall, General George C., 72, 177
Martin, Dwight, 140
Marx, Karl, 32-3, 39, 44, 186, 207-8, 219, 225-6, 243, 248-50
Moore-Brabazon, Colonel, 51
Morrison, Herbert, 54-5, 126
Mosley, Oswald, 39-40, 42
Mussolini, Benito, 58-9

Nam Il, 129, 134, 142
Needham, Joseph, 153-4
Nehru, Jawaharlal, 220-1
Nevins, Edward, 153
Nie Rongzhen, 87-8
Noel, Frank 'Pappy', 138-9, 142, 146
Nuckols, William P., 129-31, 135-7, 140, 142, 146, 152, 154-5
Nutting, Anthony, 168

O'Donnell, General, 130

Pak Bong Min, 112-5
Panton, Selkirk, 125
Peng Dehuai, 72, 196, 241-5, 249; and the Korean War, 124, 127-8, 135, 142
Peng Zhen, 92-3, 102
Peter, Prince of Greece and Denmark, 234-5
Pollitt, Harry, 31-61 *passim*, 88, 96, 98-9, 177-9, 185-6, 207, 226, 250-1
Pritt, D.N., 178, 251
Pu Yi, 181

Qian Long, 88
Qiao Guanhua, 137-8
Quai Chengwen, 143

Reston, James, 138, 142
Ridgway, General Matthew B., 109, 130-2, 138, 140, 156, 166

Rittenberg, Sydney, 94, 194
Rosenfeld, Dr Jack, 79-81, 87, 104
Rotha, Paul, 36-7
Rust, William, 43, 56-61, 160

Schutz, Bob, 138
Schwable, Frank H., 156-8
Service, John S., 72
Shawcross, Sir Hartley, 115-6
Shen Jiantu, 131, 177
Shen Liantang, 184
Sinfield, George, 57
Slansky, R., 65
Smedley, Agnes, 208
Snow, Edgar, 208
Springhall, D.F., 41-3, 46, 49
Stalin, J., 45-6, 49-51, 54, 72, 88, 99, 179-80, 185-6, 195, 207, 219, 225-6, 242, 249
Stilwell, General J., 84, 184
Strong, Anna Louise, 208-10
Stuart, Leighton, 175
Sun Tianying, 88
Sun Zi, 89, 104-5
Syngman Rhee, 109, 114, 122, 165

Thaelmann, Ernst, 34
Truman, President H., 118, 122-3, 126-7
Tuckman, Bob, 138, 146
Tyler, Wat, 44

Vandenberg, Hoyt S., 151
Van Fleet, General, 132, 150

Wang Chingwei, 175
Wang Guangmei, 179
Wei Ling, 94
Wellington, Duke of, 34
Winnington, Richard, 21-4, 26-7, 29, 31, 33-9, 177
Wu Lengxi, 188, 194

Xiang Yi, 139
Xiao Ximin, 214, 223

Yeh Chou Pei, 210-11
Ye Jianying, 90, 92-3, 101-2, 104

Index

Ye Zhou, 175
Younghusband, Colonel, 227
Yü Zhiying, 62, 74, 86-7, 90

Zhang Jingwu, General, 233, 237
Zhdanov, Andrei, 45
Zhou Enlai: during the civil war, 61, 72-3, 94-6, 98, 102; during the People's Republic, 108, 137, 209-11, 231, 244
Zhou Sufei, 101
Zhu Muzhi, 177
Zorin, V.A., 65, 69